To: Bev Waldorf
on the investiture of Billy Christ
into Canada's Sports Hall of Fame
From: Gerry Christman
June 17, 2015

Also by Gerry Christmas:

Reports of My Death:
Beyond-the-Grave Confessions of
North American Writers
(2010)
The Orawan Poems
(2011)

Breathing the Same Air
A Peace Corps Romance

Gerry Christmas

Copyright © 2015 Girard Richard Christmas.

Interior Graphics/Art Credit:
Orawan Erichsen and Gerry Christmas

All rights reserved. No part of this book may be reproduced, stored, or transmitted by any means—whether auditory, graphic, mechanical, or electronic—without written permission of both publisher and author, except in the case of brief excerpts used in critical articles and reviews. Unauthorized reproduction of any part of this work is illegal and is punishable by law.

ISBN: 978-1-4834-2921-2 (sc)
ISBN: 978-1-4834-2920-5 (e)

Library of Congress Control Number: 2015905295

Unless otherwise noted, all images are from the personal collection of Gerry Christmas.

Lulu Publishing Services rev. date: 4/9/2015

To the Conceivers:
Representative Henry S. Reuss
Senator Hubert H. Humphrey
President John F. Kennedy

For the Believers:
Current, Future, and Returned
Peace Corps Volunteers

"So, let us not be blind to our differences—but let us also direct attention to our common interests and the means by which those differences can be resolved. And if we cannot end now our differences, at least we can help make the world safe for diversity. For, in the final analysis, our most basic common link is that we all inhabit this small planet. We all breathe the same air. We all cherish our children's futures. And we are all mortal."
—John F. Kennedy
"A Strategy for Peace"
American University
June 10, 1963

"If the life will not be easy, it will be rich and satisfying. For every young American who participates in the Peace Corps—who works in a foreign land—will know that he or she is sharing in the great common task of bringing to man that decent way of life which is the foundation of freedom and a condition of peace."
—John F. Kennedy
"Executive Order 10924"
March 1, 1961

"First Charley got a fit, a real one, and Joe threw a terrible one. I don't mind fits in the Home with everybody around. But out in the woods on a dark night is different. You listen to me, and never go hunting gold mines with epilecs, even if they are high-grade …"
—Jack London
"Told in a Drooling Ward"

Preface

The people are real, and the events in this book are true. With some people and events, however, I felt compelled to use fictitious names and locales. This was only done in the most sensitive cases and situations where protecting reputations and privacy rights were tantamount. My purpose is to celebrate the human spirit in both good times and bad, not to denigrate those who are near and dear to me.

Gerry Christmas
Bangkok, Thailand
December 1, 2014

Acknowledgments

My deepest thanks to Orawan Erichsen for not only allowing me to use her mother's picture but also the letter that ends this memoir

Taken on the balcony of her house in Samut Prakarn in 1979, this photograph best captures Aied's "windows to the soul."

Peace Corps Termination Report

Name: Girard R. Christmas   April 10, 1976
Sex: Male   Degree: BA, English
Group 43   Experience: 3 years

Going from Bangkok to Penang by train is a strange trip. The cars are filled with merriment, laughter, and "rat-a-tat" Thai from the moment you leave until the moment you near the Malay border. Then a peculiar thing happens. All talk ceases. The train assumes a kind of pall as it crawls across the line. And one becomes acutely aware of the limits of the Thai language and of the terrible fear that comes the moment those limits have been surpassed.

1

Bangkok is a whir and a blur. Founded on subjective chaos rather than objective reason, it swerves, veers, bumps, and collides with anything solidly rooted, from Pat Pong pussy to plutonian logic.

My three years in Bangkok have made me what I call a "cultural realist." And since the rules of the game demand that I define my terms, I'd better define just what a cultural realist is. A cultural realist believes that cultures have various strengths and weaknesses and that these strengths and weaknesses are best shown in what each culture has contributed to the human race. A cultural realist does not say that one culture is better than another. Once a Westerner subjugates his false guilt for the creation of the modern world, much of the "inscrutability" of the East vanishes. He sees Western technology not as an evil to the East but as a tremendous humbling factor—something so superior to what preceded it that it can only be denied through vigorous emotionalism.

But denied it is. There are various forms in which this denial is expressed, but the most obvious is the constant twaddle about "culture." As more and more technology is laid at the Thais' feet, the number of hands attempting to grab it are matched only by the number of tongues wishing to dismiss it. That the hands and tongues are attached to the same bodies has no relevance whatsoever. Last year, an incident occurred that validates this point.

A large number of irate students stormed the American Embassy, demanding that the US military withdraw from Thailand. What with the rhetoric, insanity, and defamation that followed, few people noticed the obvious: the students wore Levi's and T-shirts, and some even packed transistor radios. Spotting the photos in the newspapers the next day, I realized the validity of Christmas's First Law: *The importance of a people's culture is inversely proportional to the amount of talk expended on said culture.*

During my first year as a volunteer, I must admit I fell for the glitter. Thailand is a land of extremes. It is only human to see the extreme good before the extreme bad, especially when the bad is veiled beneath subtle charms and dazzling smiles. But if one stays in Siam long enough, it becomes clear that most Thais are extremely unhappy. The oppressive poverty, the sweltering heat, and the linear social scene ultimately drain the body and snap the soul. Youth and beauty are the sole treasures here. Once beauty and youth fade, most Thais accept their miserable existence with a fatalism that approaches masochism. This is particularly true of Thai mothers. Locked in a biological, social, and economic prison, they have seen not only their own dreams shattered but the dreams of their daughters as well—for love, in Thailand, is usually equated with beauty and sex. And a man's sexual prowess is gauged more by frequency than by intimacy. This, a Thai girl learns early. Recently, a former student said to me, "Ajaan Gerry, I don't expect to find happiness when I marry. Marriage is the wheel of life, the wheel of life, the wheel of life ..."

But it has become too much the habit to praise Thai women at the expense of Thai men. If most Thai men behave like rabbits, it doesn't necessarily follow that it's their "nature." I've interacted with numerous Thai families, and the most interesting aspect has not been the husband/wife relationship but rather, the mother/son relationship. The mother rarely, if ever, reins in her son. Should he strut about and act smartass, he's spirited and cute—a "real boy." But let the daughter display similar traits, and God help her. She's impolite, unladylike, and un-Thai. As a fellow Peace Corps volunteer once said, "Remember, Gerry, it takes a Thai woman to make a Thai man."

This mother/son relationship is key to understanding the "chico"—that gyrating piece of male garbage that incessantly tools about the streets of Bangkok on a Honda 170. As he was born in the midst of emotional nothingness and nurtured on the teat of narcissism, his brain has, by degrees, atrophied, wizened, and finally disappeared. I know firsthand. Once, as one sped by, nearly flattening me to the pavement, I had a glimpse into his ear. It was like looking through a keyhole: open air all the way.

Seeing me off at the airport, my father said, "Son, I wouldn't be surprised if you came home a Buddhist." Now, I doubt it. Buddhism—specifically, Thai Buddhism—offers the rank-and-file little, except a transitory safety valve in this life, a fleeting expiation to mortal suffering. Buddhism is a thinking man's religion, perfectly suited for philosophers and pedants. But what does it offer the average Thai? A place to sit before a gold-plated idol and burn joss sticks? A place to hide when a wife's wrinkled skin and wasted body are no longer alluring? A place to go and get a saffron-colored robe in order to roam among the people and take what little food they have? A place to parade false respect and false pride for what one is and what one failed to be? All this and more can be found in the *wats* of Thailand——those shrines of makeshift welfare and escapism where the faithful attempt to achieve a perfect zero.

I use the phrase "perfect zero" since that was the one used by my friend Somsak. Our conversation went as follows:

"Somsak, if the purpose of Buddhism is to negate yourself, then I must assume that the ultimate state is nothingness, that you don't worship God."

"That's right," said Somsak. "The Lord Buddha always referred to himself as a man. He never said he was God. Nor did he acknowledge the existence of God. Instead, he stressed good conduct and right action, with the goal being Nirvana——a state of nothingness, a perfect zero."

"Then how can you possibly worship?"

"I'm afraid I don't understand."

"Well," I said, "if your goal is nothingness, you must believe that your ultimate objective is nothing; hence, you worship nothing."

"Hmm ... that's interesting," he said. "I've never thought about it that way."

"Or do your worship the *act* of achieving nothing rather than the nothing as a separate entity?"

"Yes, that would be more correct; that would be more accurate."

"This is heady stuff," I said. "In some ways, it is more philosophic than religious."

"The two are one," said Somsak.

"What do you mean?"

"Well, to understand Buddhism, a person must understand the Buddha's first sermon, the one about the Four Noble Truths and the Eight-fold Path."

"Which are?"

"I'll try to make it as simple as possible," he said. "Forgive me if I make a mistake with my English. This isn't easy to explain in a foreign language."

"I understand," I said.

"The Four Noble Truths spell out the problem all humans face in life," he said. "First, suffering exists. Second, the cause of suffering is desire. Third, with great effort, desire can be destroyed. And fourth, the tool to destroy desire is the Eight-fold Path."

"So Buddhism is a step-by-step process."

"Yes," he said. "The Four Noble Truths state the problem; the Eight-fold Path tells how to solve the problem. But here's the rub. The Eight-fold Path is difficult, most difficult. The first two have to do with *wisdom*. The next three have to do with *ethical conduct*. And the last three have to do with *concentration*.

"Under 'wisdom,' the Buddha said we must have the *right view* of reality and the *right intention* toward reality. Under 'ethical conduct,' we must use *right speech*, *right action*, and *right work*. And under 'concentration,' we must have *right effort*, *right mindfulness*, and *right concentration*. Now, the Buddha did not expect all human beings to be successful, except in a relative sense. In a word, Buddhism is a practical view of life, one that anyone can try."

"I see," I said.

Or did I? For, at that moment, I spotted an ant crawling across the surface of the yellow table where we were sitting. I immediately squashed the ant with the flat of my hand. Somsak winced. I was shocked, since Somsak was far from being a sissy. He was not only smart but athletic as well.

"I'm sorry," I said.

"Mai pen lai," he said.

"But I do mind," I said. "My action hurt you. I can see that."

"Yes, it did. Do you want to know why?"

"Of course I do."

"Okay, let me put it this way. When you saw that ant, you had three choices. You could have ignored the ant, brushed it aside, or killed it. As a Buddhist, I've two choices, not three: I can ignore or brush it aside, but I cannot kill it. That would be bad action."

"'Thou shall not kill.'"

"Exactly," he said. "Killing is a double-edged sword. It hurts both the killed and the killer. It produces bad karma all the way around."

I frowned. Ah, there was the magic word: *karma*. The Thais use it over and over and over to explain everything.

"What's wrong?" said Somsak.

"Well, sometimes I get tired of hearing about karma this and karma that," I said. "All conversations in Thailand seem to end with, 'It's my karma' or 'It's your karma.' Or, in the case of romantic entanglements, 'It's *our* karma.' Buddhism comes across as too fatalistic at times."

Somsak laughed. "I've heard that before," he said. "But perhaps your American thinking is clouding your mind."

"How so? Yes, I know most things in life can be attached to good or bad action. Still, I don't think cause and effect answers everything."

"Can I answer your question with a question?"

"Sure. Go ahead."

"Why is the United States losing the Vietnam War?"

I looked at him, thunderstruck.

"There ... there are lots of reasons," I said.

"Not in my mind," he said. "On the surface, the Vietnam War should be no contest. On one side, we have the United States, the most powerful and advanced country in the world. On the other side, we have North Vietnam––a poor, backward country that can barely feed and clothe its people. Yet, the North Vietnamese are winning the war. How can that be?"

"I don't know," I said.

"The answer is as plain as the rainy season, Gerry. The North Vietnamese are Buddhist. Yes, it's that simple. All their lives, they're taught that the world is a place of great suffering and pain. Every time the American planes bomb their villages, every time the Americans soldiers go into their villages and kill innocent men, women, and children, Ho Chi Minh tells his people to be patient, to accept the pain and carry on."

"But Ho Chi Minh's a communist," I said.

"Politically, yes, but spiritually, no. Spiritually, Ho Chi Minh is a Buddhist. You can see that by his actions, by the way he teaches. He has taught the Vietnamese people to do tiny right actions each and every day. He has them eating little or nothing. He has them living underground in caves. He has them hiding out in the jungle. This is positive karma on a national scale, Buddhism in its purest sense."

"So, are you saying Ho Chi Minh is invincible?"

"Not at all," said Somsak. "What did one of your generals say he wanted to do? 'Bomb the North Vietnamese back to the Stone Age.'"

It was my turn to wince.

"That was General Curtis LeMay," I said.

"What an animal, what a sick human being. But he's right: the United States *could* bomb the Vietnamese back to the Stone Age. What then? The world would hate the United States. Even Nixon knows that. And if Nixon knows that, you'd better believe Ho Chi Minh does too."

"We've much to learn from Asian cultures," I said. "The United States is a young country."

"Still, it's a great country. It'll learn from its bad karma."

"I sure hope so," I said.

Somsak smiled broadly.

"Now look who's being fatalistic," he said.

2

My school was Thonburi Teachers College––a small, intimate place that accepted my own brand of insanity with alacrity. During my first year, Ajaan Sugitra, the head of the English department, left me to my own devices. Whether this decision was based on trust or whimsy, I'll never know. But I do know this: I'll forever be grateful that she did.

My Peace Corps TEFL training had given me about as much firepower as a kid with his first Mattel burp gun. Fortunately, I had an extraordinary group of Thai students who not only supplied me with ammunition but also gave me a new weapon at the end of the year.

I walked into my second year fully armed but unable to shoot. Marilyn, the Welsh VSO (Voluntary Service Overseas) at the school, had somehow concocted the odd notion that popularity and effective teaching were one and the same. Since Marilyn and I had always gotten along, I was a bit taken aback when she began to storm into my labs, corral my students, and make a general nuisance of herself. One day, after she had physically wrenched a female student away, I got the message. From that day forward, our relationship had about as much warmth as a block of dry ice. Superficially, we were still friends. Neither she nor I, however, had any misconceptions. And it was with relief that I saw her leave for England at the end of the school year.

Since that time, I have developed a more compassionate understanding for Marilyn. As with many female volunteers, the frustrations of living in a male-oriented society scarred her deeply. Being a moral and decent woman, she could not escape into sexual escapades. She therefore turned toward the students for love and affection. To Marilyn's credit, she never sacrificed decency for desire. Nor did she become embittered toward men. I can only hope she has now found the happiness that eluded her in Thailand.

My second year was therefore spent teaching as much as the situation allowed while vigorously preparing for the following year. At the beginning of my third year, Ajaan Sugitra left to study for her master's degree at the University of Missouri. Before departing, she appointed Ajaan Sudaporn to serve as acting head of the English department. I felt as if good fortune had favored me twice. Sudaporn was not only a good friend;

she was also extremely able. She approached her work with a sensitivity and organizational mindset that made working for her a real joy. If I had a valid idea, she'd refine it, distill it, and purify it like some wondrous machine processing Oklahoma crude. If I had an invalid idea, she'd masticate it, swallow it, and regurgitate it with the placidity of a Guernsey cow.

I also had the good fortune of working with an extremely bright counterpart, Ajaan Soawapa. Since most of the work demanded a contemplative rather than an intuitive interpretation of literature, Saowapa was a real find. In the past, she'd worked with other PCVs, and the only ones she didn't like were those who approached her country like a biologist dissecting a frog. Like many sensitive Thais, she didn't like volunteers who dissected her culture, her language, and her people and then walked away, leaving the guts to rot in the sun.

The basic idea of a counterpart is good if neither personality assumes dominance—if there is a free flow of ideas that are mutually discussed and analyzed. This was the situation with Saowapa and me. We used each other to arrive at a more precise interpretation, and we presented that interpretation jointly to the students.

We began with Ernest Hemingway's *The Nick Adams Stories* and concluded with James A. Michener's *Sayonara*. This gave the students exposure to both intensive reading (*The Nick Adams Stories*) and extensive reading (*Sayonara*). With intensive reading, our objective was to get the students to think. With extensive reading, our objective was to get the students to read more.

Thinking is a pill that is swallowed with great reluctance, thus *The Nick Adams Stories* had to be explained in such a way that the students could see the similarities between themselves and Nick. This was accomplished more readily than I expected, due to the brevity of the stories. In other words, each tale made a distinct point, with its plot being of secondary importance.

Sayonara, on the other hand, intimidated the students. The psychology involved in teaching this book was fascinating. First, the students had been indoctrinated with Longman simplified readers for so long that they could not imagine reading anything else. Lest you think I exaggerate, I cite the following exchange I had with a student:

"Ratana, do you have a favorite book?"

"Yes, Ajaan Gerry, I do."

"What is it?"

"*David Copperfield*."

"Oh, that is an excellent book. Do you remember who wrote it?"

"Yes, my favorite writer, Mr. Longman."

My mouth flopped open, but Ratana kept right on talking.

"Tell me, teacher," she said. "How can one man write so many good books?"

Second, the students had never been asked to read more than one hundred pages, and here I was, asking them to double that. Handing out the books the first day, I felt about as much animation as a ranger does in the middle of the Petrified Forest.

As if these two hurdles were not enough, I faced a third: vocabulary. Here I was, with fourth-year English majors who had never been told about contextual reading. They had also never been taught the relative importance of words, that some words were more vital than others. Whenever the meaning of a word proved elusive, they would scurry to their dictionaries, unearth the variant meanings, and then spend an hour choosing the wrong one.

I never had so much fun. Every day was like jamming a pair of chopsticks into the students' ears, spinning the noodles about, then hoping someone would eat alone. The ones who worked did. Toward the end of the term, Nuanjan came up to me and said, "Ajaan Gerry, I couldn't stop reading last night. I read forty pages and finished the book!"

It was a pleasure teaching at Thonburi TTC. But the school is not for everyone. Thonburi lies in the shadow of Bansomdej TTC, which tends to attract more of the brighter students. Historically, Bansomdej is one of the most famous teacher colleges in the nation. And though its recent academic achievements have been negligible, the name endures. Bansomdej also benefits from an unusual hook-up with the Ministry of Education: namely, for a larger piece of the budgetary pie, the school allows a number of people from the ministry to teach twilight. This system has worked favorably for both parties for a number of years. Last year, however, five twilight teachers received promotions at twice the rate of the regular teachers. A small scandal ensued, but I didn't hold my breath. "Man," my father once told me, "will not alter his habits for your want of air."

3

As a Bangkok volunteer, nothing pleased me more than the prattle about "the real Thailand." Thailand, as you know, is not one country but two: Bangkok and the upcountry. Just how Bangkok came into being, no one is quite sure. One popular theory avers that the city exists exclusively for the West. In a word, the Thais are not responsible for the city at all, just as Americans are not responsible for the city of New York. That both countries find both cities a necessity is an embarrassment, a downright abomination.

A Bangkok volunteer is an abomination, too. He doesn't really know Thailand since he doesn't live there. The closed, compartmentalized shops that line the streets house Bangkokians, not Thais. And although they may look Thai, act Thai, and speak Thai, don't let that fool you. They're different. Ask any upcountry volunteer; ask any PC staff member.

Unfortunately, most Bangkok volunteers consider themselves real volunteers. This is truly amazing when one thinks of the time and expense the Peace Corps spends telling them otherwise. You would think the constant rhetoric before training, during training, and after training would have some effect. But it doesn't. Maybe the Bangkok volunteers are a little dense. Or maybe the din of the city has affected their hearing and their ability to think straight. I really don't know.

I only know what has happened to me. And I only know that when I look at Thailand, it is like looking at an old, but elegant vase, one full of cracks and splits and cuts. And yet, somehow, it is still intact, still in one piece. I can see the cracks in its religion, the splits in its culture, the cuts in its soul. But it still has a cohesive integrity, an intangible unity and sense of being. It has touched me as few places ever have. I have memories, long and varied, of infinite and tender warmth the likes of which I am incapable of articulating. I can remember slight gestures of good faith that required the utmost courage, for they sprang from the deepest wells of the human heart. I can remember the blind pain on the peoples' faces, pain that spoke of a life worse than death but still spoke of a life that had to be lived. I can remember the momentary joy in the fleeting realization of what life can be rather than what life is. But most of all, I can remember *her*.

I can remember her doing many things, but those things are for me and not for you. This only will I tell you: one night, during Loy Krathong, we went to Lumpini Park to float our candles upon the pond. Lumpini Park was a mud-splattering, body-squashing mess that night. There was no tranquility anywhere. The air held nothing but the sharp crack of fireworks and the grating noise of loudspeakers.

As we neared the pond, I glanced at her face, expecting to see the same annoyance I felt. I was wrong. Somehow, she had left me. Mentally. A soft serenity had descended upon her, producing an inward glow. It was as if I were walking with an ethereal being, a spiritual wraith. A number of screaming urchins surrounded us. They wanted to float our *krathongs* for fifty satang each. She quietly dismissed them. It seemed almost mechanical. Then she knelt, lit her candle, and laid the little boat upon the surface of the water.

I waited for her to leave, but she didn't. Bowing her head in the most exquisite *wai* I have ever seen, she drew into herself even more. I had no idea what she was thinking. Nor did I care. I was only aware that I was experiencing true beauty, and by experiencing this beauty, I was made part of it. It was then that I knew that no man could ever hate a country that had given him one of its women to love.

Epistle One

June 24, 1976

Dear Ajaan Sudaporn:

I've finally arrived home after a very enjoyable trip. The rigors of travel—from jet lag to dehydration—have subsided, and I'm trying to collect my thoughts and plot a new course for the future. My heart is still in Thailand, but that's as it should be. Three years in one's life is rarely snipped off and forgotten, especially when those years stand up favorably in comparison to the preceding ones.

My initial reaction to the United States has not been good. It's not the same country. Nor am I the same man. Enormous evils are at work eroding the moral fiber of the nation. And, while cognizant of these evils, I'm awestruck at the speed with which they are undermining the entire society. Basically, I'm an optimist. Still, the insane self-seeking that abounds is not conducive to a worldview where birds forever chirp and stars forever shine.

My parents are fine. Preferring a subdued and relaxed lifestyle, they have retired to the tiny town of Underhill Center, Vermont, where they garden during the short growing season and socialize with their friends during the winter. Both appear content, totally at peace with life. Indeed, a soft serenity seems to have descended upon them. And although this serenity has come at a considerable cost, it is nonetheless the only reasonable down payment for the House of Life.

Sadly, not all people grow old gracefully. But the ones that do are very lucky. As the flesh wrinkles and sags, as the teeth rot and lose their chomping power, as the hair fades and falls away, a final clarity reveals itself. Then they are taken from us, whisked away to the Great Perhaps. All that remains is the memory of their love and their teachings, which is more than we deserve.

I received a letter from Ajaan Saowapa. She told me that she had entered the hospital for an operation on her leg. With you about to deliver and with her out for a term, the English department must be in a shambles. But life was never meant to be easy. Just remember: the good Lord gave us more to do than we can ever accomplish. So don't try to take up the slack. Of course, I am courting laziness and incompetence with such a lame philosophy, but so be it. "The Middle-Road Path" is far preferable to overextension and exhaustion.

I could babble on, but this letter is two-pronged: first, to tell you how I am, and second, to fulfill a promise I made to Saowapa. When I left Thailand, she asked me to visit Takarazuka, Japan, the setting for James A. Michener's *Sayonara*. Why? To send back a report on how accurately Michener had portrayed the famous song-and-dance troupe. Since Saowapa is unable to teach the book this term, I'd like you to give the enclosed letter to Ajaan Sirima. I believe she's the one teaching the novel now, and my little adventure might add some spice to the course. It might also help Sirima to win over that small but omnipresent group of cynics that populate every teacher's class, the ones that make us earn our bread.

Dreams can come true. A person just has to define what his dreams are, then pursue them with zeal and a lust for living. That many of my dreams have come true only makes me wish for more. I can only hope that you and those I love will join me in the fulfillment of these dreams.

Epistle Two

June 25, 1976

Dear Students:

You can live a book. If you believe in your dreams and trust yourself, it can be done. I know, for I did it when I went to Takarazuka to see the show.

The train from Osaka to Takarazuka takes about forty minutes. It's clean and fast, and one can usually get a seat. I first took the train on a Wednesday, and as we pulled into the station, I was surprised that there were only a handful of people on board. I soon discovered why: it was the showgirls' day off. I wasn't angry. I just stood before the iron bars of the gate in front of the theater and made like a volcano. I then walked about the town. It was a good chance to familiarize myself with the place.

The theater, from the outside, did not look spacious. Still, there were huge placards of the dancers on a billboard next to the main entrance. If advertisements were any indication, this was a large and stupendous revue, just as Michener said it was.

Surrounding the theater were a number of carnival rides for Japanese children and their parents. The rides looked neat and clean, but, having experienced the thrills of Disneyland, I couldn't be bothered. Instead, I walked along the delightful path where Gruver first spots Hana-ogi. The cement has been dyed red, and trees have been carefully selected and planted along the sides in order to render a cathedral effect. I tried to imagine what it would look like at twilight with the beautiful showgirls shuffling on home with gobs of people milling about. But it wasn't easy. At noontide, the place was deserted, and my

American-Thai belly demanded food, not dreams. So I bought a ticket, boarded the train, and went to Kyoto, where I spent two delightful days.

I returned to Takarazuka on Friday. The place was jumping with people, especially young little Katsumis with their buckteeth, plain-Jane looks, and autograph books. I went up the ticket counter and asked the man for a seat in the balcony, since I'd been told by a woman in Kyoto that that was where I could best see the entire spectacle. As the man handed me my ticket, I noticed a large, glamorous poster of a Takarazuka showgirl on the wall behind him.

"Excuse me," I said. "Could I buy one of those?"

"I'm sorry, sir," he said. "Those are not for sale."

I was a bit embarrassed and didn't know what to say. I only knew that I wanted the poster and that I was willing to embarrass myself to get it.

"I'm a teacher," I said lamely.

It didn't make any sense, not to me anyway. But it did something to the man.

"Wait here for a moment," he said, shuffling off with a smirk as big as a clam.

The man returned inside of five minutes with a poster that was the same as the one hanging on the wall. Up close, it was even more striking. The showgirl's hair was cropped short, but her face was perfect. She wore a long, shimmering, gold-sequined gown that contrasted wonderfully with the soft-pink background. I stood, transfixed, my lower jaw agape like an open trapdoor.

"How much?" I said meekly.

"For you, nothing," the man said. "I hope you enjoy the show and like my country."

I thanked him profusely and walked away. *This must have been what Michener meant*, I thought. *By God, Gruver lives!*

My seat was in the first row with an unobstructed view of the stage. Looking down, I could see both the orchestra pit and the entire stage. There was a short strip that ran in front of the orchestra. The showgirls, I later discovered, used this strip for intimate scenes with the audience. Otherwise, most of the action occurred on stage.

And what action! The showgirls exploded onto the stage—dancing, singing, shaking, and shouting to the beat of the music. Lights flashed and faded and a kaleidoscope of colors came and went, but it was mostly showgirls, showgirls, and more showgirls—showgirls coming in from the wings, showgirls coming down on platforms from the ceiling, showgirls coming up magically from trapdoors at the rear of the stage. The eye-sockets become strained trying to keep up with it all.

I soon found that straight concentration was the worst way to view a Takarazuka show. Too much was happening. It was like taking on the Pacific Ocean. The more one fought, the more futile it became. Best to sit back and relax. Let the colors and the music and the costumes and the showgirls surround you and bathe you and pervade you. Let the force come to you, for surely, it was a superior force.

Still, when something caught my eye, I concentrated on it and cut the rest out. That worked well. It gave me a view of the individual performers while, at the same time, enabling me to lapse back into the overview at will.

The show has not changed drastically since Michener wrote *Sayonara*. The only major change is the omission of the classical Japanese dance. That is now separated from the show. If a person wants to see it, he must go at night.

The afternoon show is in two parts. First, you have the wild, splashy affair with all the showgirls jumping and gamboling about the stage. This is perhaps the most spectacular part of the show. I seriously doubt if there is another revue to match it in the world. What with the lavish sets, the meticulous choreography, and the talented dancers, I can't imagine another show to equal it for flamboyance and flair.

Second, you have the story. Here, the Japanese take some melodrama or fairy tale and revamp it. The story is irrelevant. I saw *Puss 'n' Boots* but didn't pay much heed to the plot. The show is pure escape. Yes, in a Takarazuka show, evil characters exist. Still, they're never triumphant. Evil is vanquished, and virtue is rewarded. Poverty is eliminated, and everyone lives happily ever after. It's not the world as we know it. It's the world as we would wish it. And for three hours, this wondrous world becomes real and tangible.

After the show, I decided to investigate the fan phenomenon that Michener talks about in the book. I found some schoolgirls near the dancers' dormitory and sat down with them. They were somewhat shocked, but not annoyed, that a foreigner would wait there. I joked with them and took their picture. They were extremely shy. All had a bad case of the giggles, but I liked them very much.

Finally, some of the stars emerged. They looked quite different than they had on stage. They wore shirts and slacks, and their wigs were off. They had Hana-ogi's manly feminine beauty. They were extremely lean from thousands of hours of strenuous workouts, and their eyes flashed with nervous electricity. Fans were not what these performers wanted. Still, they were gracious and kind, signing autographs and thanking the young girls for their patience.

My group of schoolgirls had a long wait—too long a wait. After the other performers had come and gone, their star refused to show. Finally, one of the schoolgirls asked a florist—a fellow who had just delivered a trunkful of flowers—where their star was.

"She will not come out for another three or four hours," he said. "She has to perform the classical dance."

I thought the girls would be upset, but they weren't. Classical dancing is still the most respected form of dance in Japan; hence, the girls were proud that their particular star had been selected to perform it.

Suddenly, a Takarazuka showgirl sped by me. I knew immediately she was a dancer, since her hair was not only short but also auburn. Impulsively, I called to her, and to my surprise, she stopped dead in her tracks and swung around. I pointed to my camera and then pointed to her. I was sure she'd be annoyed since she was obviously in a hurry. How wrong I was! As I raised my camera and sighted her face in the viewfinder, she flashed an incredibly theatrical smile—a smile full of joy and beauty and youth and understanding. I clicked the shutter and thanked her. She nodded and then turned and disappeared. I never thought I'd see her again. I tried to tell myself that beauty was transitory and best left alone. But this time it didn't work.

I turned back to the students and, seeing they were about to depart, I asked if I could go with them. They said I could, and we walked down the path that runs toward the front of the theater. I was thinking what a pleasant day I'd had, and my mind was all geared for a nice, relaxed train trip back when a young Japanese woman came scurrying up to the main gate next to us. She looked very distraught, and quite rightly so.

She was not only late for the classical dance show, but the management also refused to refund one of the two tickets in her possession. The young woman could not speak English, but I got the gist of her plight from the schoolgirls. In no time, my tongue was wagging away again, seemingly against my will and better judgment.

"How much does she want for the ticket?" I asked one of the schoolgirls.

A slew of rat-a-tat Japanese ensued. For a moment, I regretted my inquisitiveness.

"The ticket cost her 2,500 yen," the schoolgirl said. "The show is expensive since it's performed by our best dancers."

"But we're thirty minutes late for the show now," I protested. "That's a lot of money when you figure I've missed the entire beginning. Tell her I'll buy the ticket for 1,250 yen."

There was another barrage of Japanese. Momentarily, I felt guilty for being so cheap. But the guilt didn't last long. The schoolgirl spun around and said, "It's a deal." She seemed happier about the transaction than I was. I paid for the ticket, said good-bye to my new friends, and turned to go in.

Suddenly, the schoolgirl who'd done all the bargaining stopped me and said, "I hope you enjoy the show. You're about to see what we Japanese really love. You're about to see Japan as we see it."

Our eyes met, and the twisted little juvenile face was suddenly transformed into a face of mature clarity. I didn't know what to say. I'd the same feeling that I used to have in grade school when one of my teachers was trying to explain a concept that was entirely new to me. I stared at her blankly and said nothing.

"Thank you," she said. "Thank you very much."

Then she turned and walked away with her friends. I stood there, confused. But my confusion lasted for only a second or two before I realized why she'd thanked me instead of me thanking her.

I was prepared to enter the theater alone but was greatly mistaken. The woman from whom I'd purchased the ticket not only ushered me to my seat but also tried to explain what was happening. Though we shared no common language, I got the general idea from her paralinguistics and her reference to the pictures in the Japanese program.

Unlike the Takarazuka revue, which emphasized gorgeous showgirls and flashy sets, the classical dance was simplicity itself. The sets were plain, almost stark. There were only two dancers for each set, and each act told a story. It's not easy to describe classical Japanese dancing. It is highly stylized, and the movements of the dancers are agonizingly slow. Each motion, every movement carries a grace and fluidity that even a foreigner can understand.

At the end of the show, I went into the lobby and sat down. I'd decided to let the crowd thin out before I made my way back to Osaka, so I made myself at home. A number of people had the same idea. I therefore allowed my eyes to take in the scene. It was a pleasant way to waste time, until my eyes fell upon a familiar face: the Takarazuka showgirl who'd allowed me to take her picture. I was a bit surprised to see her, since I'd assumed she was tired and had returned home in order to rest. Then a thought hit me. This was her enjoyment. The revue dancing that brought so much pleasure to others was for her a labor. Classical dancing, on the other hand, eased and soothed her. It gave her needed relaxation after such a strenuous workout.

Continuing to look at her, I suddenly realized she resembled one of the showgirls in the revue program. I couldn't be sure she and the girl in the program were one and the same since the girl in the picture wore a flamboyant wig, whereas this woman had a mannish, short-cropped hairdo.

Throwing caution to the wind, I walked up to her and pointed to the picture in the program. She seemed taken aback, so I unclipped my pen and asked her to sign it. She tossed her head to one side and shook it. Then she grabbed my program and pen and ran away. At first, I didn't quite know what was going on. Then I noticed that she'd run over to another dancer. By sheer coincidence, the showgirl I'd mistaken for her was her good friend.

The friend didn't seem too pleased when my pen and my program were thrust into her hands, but she signed it, and the other Takarazuka girl—the nice one—came back and handed it to me. She was about to leave when I gave her my pen and motioned that she sign my program too. Gesticulating madly, she made me realize that she was not a member of Moon Troupe; hence, her picture was not in the program. Somehow, I made her understand that I didn't care. I just wanted something with which to remember her, even if it was a series of scrawls in a language I didn't know over a picture that wasn't her. Finally, she signed the program—first in Japanese and then, to my surprise, in English. The plain, blocked letters *MEGU* jumped out at me.

"Thank you, Megu," I said.

Megu nodded. Then she flashed the identical smile I'd seen her give me through the viewfinder a few hours before.

"Thank you," I repeated. "And *sayonara*."

As she spun away and left me, I'd no way of knowing who Megu was exactly. I'd thought she was just another dancer. It wasn't till I'd returned to Osaka that I learned that Megu was one of the most famous dancers in all of Japan.

This picture of Aied's mother was taken in the mid-1930s.
A classic Thai beauty, Khun Boontan
would lead a long and troubled life.
Honest, warm, and giving, she was
truly a noble human being.

Courtesy of Orawan Erichsen

Revolution from 1966 to 1976. The Chinese like to talk about life's contradictions. Here, indeed, is a prime example of that.

From Taiwan, I went to South Korea. What a grand country! The people are energetic and happy and bright. My inability to speak Korean didn't bother the people in the least. Everywhere I went, people would stop me, invite me to dinner, even ask me to go sightseeing. For the most part, I refused. On one occasion, however, I accepted and went with a journalist to a quiet, intimate restaurant for dinner.

"This is very gracious and kind of you," I said, sitting down in the booth. "Truly, I'm unworthy of such hospitality."

"Not at all," the journalist said in near-perfect English. "I was not always emotionally and economically as secure as I am now. Indeed, as a boy, my parents not only lost their home but were nearly killed."

"What saved them?"

"Not *what* but *who*," he said. "We owe our lives to the bravery of a group of American soldiers. After finishing my education and getting a job with the newspaper, I felt compelled to show my gratitude to these wonderful men, but how? Then it struck me to do so indirectly, by taking American tourists out for dinner. It's my humble way of saying 'thank you.'"

My most delightful time in Korea, however, was with a group of high school girls who I met accidentally in a city park. They'd come to the park to paint pictures but, seeing me, they put their palettes and easels aside and grabbed me by both arms.

I was shocked. In Thailand, such an act never happens. Not so in Korea. I tried not to show my surprise and began to laugh as one of the girls took out her camera and snapped my picture. I then took their picture and tried to leave. But they wouldn't let me. Using what little English they had, two of the girls wanted to know who I was and where I was going. I told them. And before I knew it, I was exchanging addresses and writing questions and answers on little bits of paper.

The whole scene was crazy. But we were having so much fun that nobody cared. A friend with whom I had entered the park later said that I looked like the Pied Piper of Hamelin about to lead the children away into the mountains. And I guess he was right, for a number of people stopped to watch the students and me insanely trying to communicate with one another. Finally, I took their picture with my camera and promised not only to send each a copy but to be their pen pal as well.

After South Korea, I went to Japan. Though not as friendly as the Koreans, the Japanese make up for it with their singularly strange culture. Magnificent gardens, palaces, temples, and art centers are commonplace. Since my time was limited, I concentrated on the culturally rich city of Kyoto.

Besides Kyoto, I visited Takarazuka, a small Japanese town famous for its Siegfeld-Folly-like song-and-dance revues. I watched, enthralled, as the Japanese showgirls did their spectacular version of *Puss 'n' Boots*. Indeed, I was honestly sad when the show ended, for I had to return to the real world of misery and hate.

The Takarazuka show is many things, but real and sad it is not. True, the revue is not free of evil and malice. But, in the end, goodness and benevolence prevail. The show is, therefore, not a reflection of the world as we know it but as we would wish it. For three hours, one is transported into a dream state, a place of everlasting peace and happiness. Oh, if life were only that way!

Before closing this letter, I'd like to thank you for the doll. Yes, I immediately saw that it was Aied. How could I miss the resemblance to the woman who captivated my heart and mind? Oh, Khun Boontan, how I love your daughter! I love her purely and simply and without shame. Thinking of her swells my heart and fills me with a vast emptiness.

But why am I telling you all this? You know how I feel or you wouldn't have given me the doll. I'd like to think that you'd have given me the real Aied, had I been worthy of her love and had she chosen to love me in return. Now that our paths have parted, now that we've gone our separate ways, I can only pray that she finds the happiness she deserves and that from time to time, she tells me how she's doing. Love does not hurt when the one you love is happy. Love only hurts when the one you love is unhappy and silent.

I don't think you'll ever know how much I appreciate the way you accepted me, even when you knew I loved Aied. I was a stranger in a strange land, and you accepted me without fear or apprehension. And for this, I can only say that you have my deepest respect, admiration, and affection. If there is anything I can do for you or your family, please don't hesitate to ask.

Add atop a water cistern at the family home in 1979
Like Aied, she was bright, optimistic, and gregarious.

Epistle Four

September 10, 1976

Dear Add:

Since returning to the United States, I've had time to think about the changes that have occurred while I was away. Living in a foreign country gives a person a different perspective about his country. He sees strengths and weaknesses that before eluded him. Because you are both my friend and a political science major at Ramkhamhaeng University, I thought you might be interested in my political musings. I don't expect you to agree with me, since my ideas are on the strange side and not what you would find in most political science textbooks.

Still, I do expect you to keep an open mind. Politics can easily damage the best of friendships, since a person's political philosophy is based on the way an individual would like the human race to act, not the way the human race is. This makes political science a sensitive subject at best and a volatile subject at worst. As a result, only sensible and rational people can discuss it with any degree of maturity and objectivity.

The United States is not what it was two hundred years ago. It's not the same geographically, spiritually, economically, or politically. Two hundred years ago, the country was crammed against the Eastern seaboard. The vast frontier to the west lay in the hands of Spain and France. There were few major cities, and most people were farmers. In many ways, these early Americans were not as wonderful as the history books would have us believe. Sure, they were hearty and courageous and industrious. But they were also harsh and bigoted and overly God-fearing. Most had been expelled from Europe for their religious beliefs. Indeed, many came from England, whose political system was the most tolerant in Europe.

How could that be? Why did these early Americans risk their lives to escape what, by most accounts, was a tolerant country? The answer is easy: *these people asked—nay, begged—to be persecuted.* Now, this sounds nonsensical, but it isn't. The average human being is a complicated creature—not particularly blessed with reason and commonsense, particularly regarding religion. A man with firm religious beliefs will openly court disaster, even death, to prove to himself and others the power of his faith. Not believing in death affirms his belief in God. And since he believes his concept of God is superior to that of other people, he's not above serious mischief—mischief that may include not only his demise but also the demise of others.

This is what essentially happened in England. Small religious sects, instead of worshipping quietly and humbly, began to make waves in what was normally a placid social sea. Predictably, the reaction of the majority was not nice. It never is. People react in violent ways whenever their institutions are threatened. And, in this particular case, the institution was the Church of England.

That England, with its long tradition of British Common Law, was unable to bring peace to warring religious sects is not surprising. Man's religious beliefs have always trumped his political beliefs. As a result, the flight of religious minorities from England to the New World was a dead certainty. Indeed, these religious minorities were damn lucky to have the New World to flee to. Without such a safety valve, they would've met a similar fate to that of the early Christians.

The American colonists were, therefore, a motley crew of various protestant faiths, long on tenacity and short on tolerance. Still, they oddly adhered to English Common Law, not the law of Jehovah. This can be seen in the two pillars of American political thought: The Declaration of Independence and The Constitution of the United States. Both documents were based on a mixture of English jurisprudence and ideas from the Enlightenment. Indeed, the Founding Fathers looked to England for intellectual guidance even as they were girding themselves for war against the mother country.

This fact alone made the American Revolution a difficult sell to the English people. Americans were fighting not only for civil liberties but, more importantly, for monetary freedom—*the right to print their own money without the shackles of a central bank.* As a result, the British Parliament was severely divided: one faction backed the status quo, while the other faction sided with the revolutionists.

This division was not confined to England. The American colonies were also divided. On the one hand, we had the Patriots, those who wanted to govern themselves. On the other hand, we had the Loyalists, so called for being "loyal" to England and the Crown. Generally speaking, the Patriots were commoners, whereas the Loyalists were people of wealth. Both during and after the war, most Loyalists fled to Canada, where they became known as United Empire Loyalists. Many took their slaves with them.

The American Revolution is peculiar in that it was a revolution of the top-down, not the bottom-up. Spearheaded by rich, educated landowners, the War of Independence was not so much about personal freedom as it was about economic freedom, about keeping a comfortable lifestyle. Even George Washington, the "father of our country," found his way of life threatened. A man of incredible honor and courage, he was not about to give up his plantation at Mount Vernon without a fight. Had the British prevailed, Washington would've been publicly hanged. And yet, till the day he died in 1799, Washington considered himself "an English gentleman." Life is indeed strange.

British political, religious, and economic thought therefore brought about the birth of the United States. It was not an easy delivery. The American Revolution nearly died in its infancy, and for many years, it was doubtful if the fledging nation would reach adolescence, much less adulthood. Eventually, it did. In doing so, however, demographics and social upheavals altered the original intentions of the Founding Fathers.

First came wave upon wave of immigrants. These immigrants, though diligent and industrious, were not as well educated as the New England and Virginia colonists. These immigrants had fled Europe not because of religious persecution but because they were poor and wanted a better life.

Initially, these new immigrants made out all right. The United States was opening up, and there was plenty of free land. Toward the end of the nineteenth century, with the Industrial Revolution in full swing, these immigrants were slaves in everything but name only. Many came from non-English-speaking nations and lacked the education to get good jobs. They therefore fell prey to the capitalists, who in turned exploited them without mercy. Men and women died or were seriously injured in so-called "sweatshops." And it was not uncommon for children to suffer a similar fate.

As horrible as this might sound, the strength of today's United States is due in large part to the exploitation of immigrants during the late nineteenth and early twentieth centuries. Still, that does not justify this cruel and inhumane slaughter of decent human beings. Historians and political scientists, however, have not looked beyond it. And they should, since beyond it lays more than suffering and death. Beyond it lays the survivors.

These survivors huddled together in American cities, often in gangs based on cultural, ethnic, and religious ties. These gangs eventually evolved into political power centers. Now, this is truly significant, for with the formation of these gangs, with the coalescing of these power centers, came a weakening of the democratic process as envisaged by the Founding Fathers.

But what other result was possible? These immigrants didn't come from countries like England, where democracy flourished. They came from countries were despotism ruled, where power had been placed in the hands of a dictator or monarch. Mutual participation for the common good was therefore an alien concept, something outside their sphere of reference. Misused and abused, forced to work long hours for barely enough money to stay alive, these immigrants did the only thing they could do: they banded together and sought political clout. Thus was born the political machines and party bosses that plague us today.

The Industrial Revolution rapidly changed the United States from an agrarian society into a modern industrial state. The political ramifications of this are immense. Before the Industrial Revolution, most Americans bought land and worked it. Sure, a farmer suffered from severe hardships due to flood, pests, and drought. Nonetheless, he was his own boss. Not so the factory worker. He was nothing but a cog in a huge machine—a slave to the wheeling and dealing of the first great American capitalists, the Robber Barons.

The Robber Barons were a cruel, ruthless, murderous, and money-grubbing lot. They lusted after money, not for wealth, but for power. They had no desire to use their huge profits for the betterment of their workers, for the good of mankind. Instead, they bought politicians and judges, legislatures and heads of state. They created all-powerful monopolies, consolidated vast sums of money, manipulated the nation's money supply, and brutally killed anyone who stood in their way.

Not surprisingly, the greed of the Robber Barons gave birth to the American labor movement. At first, labor unions were a positive force headed by dedicated men such as Samuel Gompers and Eugene Debs. Labor unions were a means by which workers could be protected from the cruel, selfish, and corrupt practices of the capitalists. Whenever a capitalist abused his workers, whenever working conditions at a particular factory became unbearable, the workers could now vent their grievances through a union.

With the passage of time, however, both the size and power of labor unions created terrible problems. Labor, once looked upon as weak and noble, became a potent political force. Politicians, promising everything in order to get elected, brazenly courted the labor vote. This was a marked deviation from the early union leaders, who were unselfish and honest and who fought heroically against the evils of capitalism.

Sadly, today's labor unions are riddled with corruption and incompetence. Many union heads of the larger unions get paid as much as business executives. The labor movement has lost the noble ideas and ideals that once made it good and fine. Now it acts in a self-seeking manner with little or no thought of the public good, what we call "the commonwealth." This, of course, is disastrous in a political democracy. A political democracy demands some sacrifice from its citizens. Otherwise, it will perish.

Following on the heels of labor unions came the formation of the federal bureaucracy—what is commonly called "big government." Big government not only destroyed the concept of laissez-faire capitalism, but also ushered in as many evils as it dispatched. Many family-owned enterprises, such as small farms and mom-and-pop stores, were snuffed out. Government contracts and government funding went only to those businesses that could produce on a large scale.

And with these contracts and funding came under-the-table deals and downright rip-offs. One particular scam was frightfully easy and effective. An unscrupulous businessman would underbid a contract, sometimes even going below the actual cost of production. Then, once the funds ran out, the businessman would go, hat in hand, to the government and ask for more money with which to complete the project. The government would have to supply the money or forfeit the initial investment.

Then there were the traditional crooked payoffs between various corporations and politicians. As a result, the federal government, instead of regulating corporate greed and corruption, became an active sponsor to corporate waste and inefficiency. An example of this is the recent case with Penn Central, one of the largest railroads in the country. Penn Central went bankrupt due to poor management. If the United States truly practiced laissez-faire capitalism, Penn Central would've folded, and a newer and more efficient railroad line would've taken its place. But, no, the federal government suddenly stepped in, and the railroad was saved.

In any society it pays to be big, Add. That is especially true in business. A big business has people in big places that can secure big money whenever a big crisis arises. Had Penn Central been a small firm, had it been a railroad with limited assets, do you believe the federal government would have lifted a finger? Not on your life. The federal government only has ears for the largest predators, the beasts with the loudest roar and the sharpest fangs.

One of the cardinal rights enshrined in the Constitution is freedom of speech. Freedom of speech, however, is a toothless tiger without the vigilance and support of the federal government. And, sadly, this lack of vigilance, this dearth of support, is becoming more and more the norm with the increased centralization of power in Washington, DC. The federal bureaucracy is now so fat and inept and arrogant that even the president and the Congress are hesitant to move against it. Within the last twenty years, bureaucrats have received enormous benefits: steady pay increases, extended paid vacation time, cushy retirement plans, and, best of all, automatic job security. What does this mean? Well, simply put, we now have a government composed of a workforce that is not only incompetent but lacking incentives as well.

This is insane. Yet, it carries much humor, especially with the Bicentennial going on. Ah, the Bicentennial, our two-hundredth birthday. People talk about the Federalist Papers, the Declaration of Independence, and the Constitution as if they had been penned last week. Don't they know, Add? Don't they know the farther one gets away from the revolution, the more difficult it becomes to sustain the principles of freedom and justice? And don't they know that once those precious principles begin to ebb away, no amount of pride and nationalism can bring them back? No, they don't. For man is habitually selfish. Sure, he's capable of nobility and grandeur, but only for sporadic moments, only when striving for the good of others.

These four factors: the steady stream of immigrants, which created cheap labor; the Industrial Revolution, which created the first modern American capitalists; the labor unions, which created an incredibly potent political force; and the centralization of power in the federal government, which created an unwieldy and corrupt bureaucracy indifferent to the will of the people, could not have been foreseen by the Founding Fathers. The documents they wrote were for a simpler world, a world in which the government was subservient to people and the people were subservient to God.

The world is much-changed now. The complexities of modern life have left individuals confused, especially in developing countries needing to catch up with the West. In these developing countries, people are looking for the quick fix, the fast answer to transform their societies into modern industrial states. Such quick fixes, however, often lead to bad answers, such as demagoguery, oligarchy, military rule, or a combination thereof.

Sadly, many developing nations are shying away from democracy. Instead, they are embracing communism, fascism, or a military dictatorship. They feel democracy is too slow, too tedious, and, most of all, too egalitarian. Being impoverished and frequently facing starvation, they're fixated more on a full belly than on the vaunted, abstract principles of democracy. As a result, they move from one type of bondage to the next, from serfs of the land to serfs of the machine.

Thus, the dominant question becomes not what is best for our people, but how can we catch up with industrialized nations? Unfortunately, to answer this question, developing countries have had to forego their liberties and turn to Communism. Communism has brought two colossal countries, Russia and China, from abject squalor to relative affluence in a very limited time. And whether or not one likes Communism, one must admit that this was quite a feat.

Still, Communism, by nature, is corrupting. This can be seen when one analyzes the Russian and Chinese revolutions. The Russian Revolution came first. Both Lenin and Trotsky showed great dedication to Marxist thought and were able to form a government vastly superior to that of the czar. But time passed. The founders of the revolution grew old and died. And in their place came a new breed of men and women who, though raised under Communism, didn't have a clue how much their ancestors had suffered under the czar. Yes, they were told about it in school. But being told about how painful a stab in the gut is versus actually being stabbed in the gut are two different things.

These Russian men and women gradually took control of the bureaucracy and exploited it. Today, Russian leaders ride around in luxury cars and live in posh villas that would make many capitalists blush. Oh, they talk a good line about how dedicated they are to the proletariat and how opposed they are to the capitalist pigs. But they eat from the same trough. Their bellies are fat, while the peasants in the Ukraine struggle to feed the nation. It's a sterling example of human nature. And, what's more, it illustrates just how limited political systems are in their ability to advance the human race.

The rapid corruption of the Communist Party in Russia sent a chill up Mao Zedong's spine. Fearing that China would revert back to capitalism at the time of his death, Mao unleashed the Cultural Revolution (1966–1977). Mao didn't want the same thing to happen to China that happened to Russia. He therefore forced young university students and Communist party members to work in the fields with the peasants. He didn't have to worry about men like Zhou Enlai, who had also struggled and fought in the revolution. Zhou had even accompanied Mao on the Long March in 1935. Zhou was completely dedicated to the principles of the revolution and the advancement of the Chinese people.

But with Zhou Enlai's death, Mao was bereft his right-hand man. To compound matters, the country went into a state of mourning that approached frightening proportions. It was almost as if the Chinese had lost their collective father. This alarmed Mao, for what would happen when he died? That question is about to be answered, and the answer is quite predictable. What happened in the United States and Russia will also happen in China, namely, the special interests will seize the reins of power and chart a new course.

With Mao's demise yesterday came the death of the last great political mind of this century. Sure, mass movements will continue to flare up in a number of countries. But these mass movements will be on a far smaller scale, at best atavistic and primitive in nature.

The mass movements in the United States, the Soviet Union, and the People's Republic of China are finished. The oligarchies are now in charge of the human race, and mankind will have to evolve into a higher form of political and social thinking before universal liberty and brotherly love are attained. This will take time. I'll not see it in my lifetime, not by a long shot. Nonetheless, I'm optimistic. Though the prevailing trend is toward dictatorships, I still believe man will one day create a peaceful world—one free of poverty, pestilence, pettiness, and piggishness.

Much blood has been spilled to advance mankind. Most of this blood has been senselessly spilled, and even more will be senselessly spilled in the future. The rich and the powerful will not relinquish the reins of power without a fight. Consequently, if we wish man to live in an atmosphere of freedom and equality, we must continually struggle against not only our own selfish interests but the selfish interests of others as well.

No individual or group of individuals can ever liberate man from the will to power, from his monstrous ego to dominate and control. That liberation must come from within. It must come from the knowledge that true happiness and contentment comes only from acts of charity, from acts of love. This cannot be learned inside the mass of humanity, from inside the herd. It must be learned in isolation, all alone.

Each person's world is different. Each person has his own particular and peculiar ideas as to how to live. Certain individuals are blessed with enormous talents and abilities and are able to impose their ideas on large masses of people. Some do wondrous, altruistic work, such as Christ, Buddha, Mohammed, Lincoln, and Gandhi, while others, such as Alexander, Tamerlane, Genghis Khan, Napoleon, and Hitler, totally muck up the world. But these individuals are the exception, not the rule. Most people never become famous in the accepted sense. Most people enter life quietly and exit life quietly. Their names are not written in any history books, and poets and writers rarely stoop to immortalize them.

And yet, they, too, are immortal. For every person—no matter how obscure—has a life that touches the lives of others. Every person's acts and deeds, every person's loves and hates, affect those around him, even after he's gone. That you and your family continue to affect me, that you and your family continue to bring me great joy and happiness, makes you immortal. And if my memory still lives favorably in the hearts and minds of you and your family, then I've received all the immortality that I could ever wish for.

Dang on the banks of the Chao Phraya River in 1973
A nurse's aide at the time, Dang would
become a registered nurse.
Due to her tree-climbing ability, she often
joked, "I'm a *ling* (monkey)."

Epistle Five

September 11, 1976

Dear Dang:

Happy Birthday! I've enclosed a check for twenty dollars as a birthday present. I want you to buy something for yourself or for your mother. I should tell you that the check is worth about four hundred baht. The bankers in Samut Prakarn should be able to cash it without any trouble. If they can't, however, take it to Chase Manhattan Bank in Bangkok.

You must cash the check yourself. It is a special check, and you will have to show some sort of identification before you can receive the money. The check does not need my signature. Remember that, and don't let any banker tell you otherwise.

You will notice the red letters "Treasurer's Check" in the left-hand corner. This makes it cash for you and you alone. My signature is not needed, as I've already paid for it. So have fun. I only wish I could be with you.

I sent you a parcel last month, but it came back to me inside a week. Fearful of theft, I had it insured. The parcel went as far as California before someone realized insured mail can only be sent to Bangkok, not upcountry. As Samuth Prakarn is considered upcountry, the parcel bounced back to me.

I've decided to take my chances and mail it again—this time uninsured. You should get the parcel toward the end of October or early November, since it must go by ship. From now on, I'll send you money instead of gifts. Though not as much fun, it's safer, and you can buy what you need. Sometimes romanticism must be sacrificed for practicality.

The cold weather came two weeks ago. My father and I finished our work in the garden and began to prepare the house for winter. We bought a cord of wood to burn in the fireplace. I've been spending the last week cutting this wood into kindling. It's good exercise. My body is a series of aches and pains because I'm out of shape. A few more weeks of physical work, however, should make me fit again.

I've been having intermittent headaches since coming home. At first, I didn't pay any attention to them, since I was tired and tense from the long flight home. But the headaches wouldn't go away. I thought perhaps my teeth or my glasses could be causing the pain, so I went to the doctor. My glasses did need to be changed, and one of my wisdom teeth was bad. But neither was the cause of my headaches.

Next week, I have an appointment with a neurologist. I hope he can tell me what's wrong. I don't believe it is anything serious but want to make sure. Daily headaches make life vexing.

Peace Corps Washington told me last week that I'll be going to Western Samoa in November if I pass the physical examination. This made me very happy, since I've been having trouble with Dottie Rayburn, the Western Samoa Desk Officer. She has continually lied to me. I've only been able to secure the assignment by working around her and pulling in other people to help me.

Before leaving Thailand, I'd received oral clearance from Peace Corps Thailand, Peace Corps Western Samoa, and Peace Corps Washington. I even flew to Washington to confirm my assignment. That's when Dottie Rayburn began to give me trouble.

"I'm sorry," she said to me at her desk. "I cannot confirm right now that you can go."

"What do you mean?" I said. "I've been cleared in Thailand, Samoa, and here in Washington. What gives?"

"Do you have written permission?"

"No, no one told me I had to have that. I took the word of two country directors. They're both honest men."

"I'm sure they are," she said. "But I still cannot confirm your assignment at this time. Stay in touch, and I'll see what I can do."

I didn't know it at the time, but that was the start of a two-month battle with Rayburn. Returning to Vermont, I began telephoning her on a daily basis. After being put off a number of times, I began to take notes. I soon came to the conclusion that Rayburn was stonewalling. She was trying to put me off until it was too late, until the trainees left for staging in San Francisco.

That's when I decided to fight back. I first called a Peace Corps recruiter in Boston and asked for advice. The recruiter was nice but not reassuring.

"You're in for the fight of your life," the recruiter said. "I've seen this happen before, and the desk officer always wins. Your only chance is to take off the gloves and fight dirty. Good luck. You're going to need it."

Sure enough, Dottie Rayburn continued to handle me as if I were a leper. Finally, with only a week to go before staging, I let her have it.

"Enough's enough," I said to her over the phone. "If you cannot give me a straight answer, I'll have to take this up with a lawyer from the American Civil Liberties Union. I've been taking notes on our conversations. They make for interesting reading."

There was a momentary silence on the other end of the line.

"Let's not muddy the waters," she said.

"What do you mean by that? As an American citizen, I can seek out legal assistance whenever I want."

"Well, I hope it doesn't come to that. Give me a couple of hours, and I'll see what I can do."

The telephone rang two hours later.

"I've got good news for you, Gerry. We might be able to squeeze you into the program. But you'll have to work at a government junior high school. I cannot give you a teaching assignment at a prestigious missionary school."

"That's all right with me," I said. "Do we have a deal?"

"Yes," she said. "We have a deal. You'll receive your airplane tickets in the mail within a few days."

"Thank you, Dottie."

"Don't mention it, Gerry."

Situations like this sadden me. I don't like to send nasty letters or have to fight for a cause that is rightfully mine. But, unfortunately, not everyone is good. So, sometimes, one has to stand up and fight. This is a terrible waste of precious time and energy, time and energy that could normally be used for the betterment of the human race rather than the petty self-interests of a few.

But all is well now. Even if the job in Samoa doesn't pan out, I still have a number of options: an excellent ESL master's program at the School for International Training in Brattleboro, Vermont; a number of English teaching positions in Japan; and the need for Peace Corps recruiters in upstate New York, just to name a few.

I still fret about when I'll be able to get back to Thailand. I not only need more stability in my life but in the Thai political scene as well. I can do something about my own situation, but I can't do much about Thai politics. You and I need to be vigilant regarding the growing social and economic tensions in Southeast Asia. We might not be able to alter events, but we can protect ourselves. I therefore want you to be careful, Dang. Some Thais don't like Americans, and you must be careful not to talk about me too much.

Right now, you're all right, but we don't know what the future holds. You said in your last letter that Thailand is now awash with crazy people, real troublemakers. Stay away from these people, and, for God's sake, don't argue with them. They think dirty thoughts, and, what's more, they think other people think the same as they do. You're a good woman, but goodness doesn't always protect a person from evil. So stay close to your friends and family. That's where you'll be safe to do good work and help other people.

You probably think I'm overreacting, that I'm fretting unnecessarily. But I'm not. I don't think you understand the risks you took by being seen with me. Most people don't take kindly to interracial romances. Most cannot see beyond their culture, beyond the narrow alleyway of personal bias and prejudice. They therefore become confused when they see a man and a woman from two different races walking together in public. You'll never know how proud I was to be with you, and you'll never know how much respect and love I felt for the way you conducted yourself. You never made me feel uncomfortable, and you never made me think that you were ashamed to be with me.

This took real courage on your part, and I love you for it. The way you feel toward me, however, has altered the way you feel toward Americans. You look upon us the same way you look upon your own people: as human beings. This is wonderful. This is the way all peoples should look upon themselves and others. Unfortunately, they don't. And because they don't, many innocent people get hurt.

I don't want you to be hurt because of me, Dang. I'm as responsible for the way you feel about me as I am for the way I feel about you. So, again, I'm asking you to be careful, to use caution. Keep your feelings for me to yourself. Don't bring confusion and worry into the lives of your family and friends. Everything will work out for the best if we use our heads and proceed slowly. People, even loved ones, never eagerly embrace change. And there's a reason for this. With change comes pain. It's an ordeal that often brings great sorrow. Let us hope that you and I can dodge this sorrow, that we are two of the lucky ones.

Epistle Six

October 5, 1976

Dear Tocher:

I got Samoa. I appreciate your suggestions, but, as Old Blue Eyes crooned, "I Did It My Way." My letters found their mark. After I threatened to bring in the ACLU, Dottie Rayburn backed down. I'm grateful to Mick Zenick, Peace Corps Thailand's new country director, and Ruth Ellerbee, the educational placement officer. Both supported me to the hilt.

On November 16, I leave for a three-day staging session in San Francisco. Then, on the nineteenth, I fly to Western Samoa for a six-week in-country training program. The training group in Samoa will be about the same size as Group 43 was in Thailand. But I don't expect the diverse insanity to repeat itself, not unless Bruce Shingledecker and Mark Kaminski decide to reenroll. In a way, I wish they would. They would supply the much needed levity to counterbalance the rigor-mortis lectures on TEFL and cross-culture.

I've been able to do some reading on Samoa, and what I've read sounds good. In some ways, Samoans are similar to Thais: both are proud of their cultural heritage; both stress family cohesion; and both clearly delineate the sex roles at the adolescent and adult levels.

Unfortunately, the Samoan sex scene is not as romantic and free as the novelists would have us believe. True, most girls have liaisons before marriage, but these liaisons are often fleeting and superficial, more casual than personal. As a result, sex plays a minor role in the selection of a spouse. I don't know whether this is good or bad. Sex varies from person to person; hence, it is impossible to predict certain outcomes for individual people, be they Samoan or otherwise.

A Samoan woman's adolescence does not appear to be as long and as strong as that of her American counterpart. This is probably due to openness rather than attitude. Samoans live in thatched-roof dwellings called *fales*, which are wall-less and devoid of privacy. Children therefore see sex all their lives; hence, few taboos surround the act of reproduction. Only the girls from more prominent families are expected to be *taupous* when they marry. Still, I wouldn't be surprised if they "rode horses" the week before they tied the knot.

Speaking of tying the knot, what am I going to do about Dang? She wrote me a letter the other day. I couldn't believe her passion and her vehemence. We had one of those quiet romances, no flamboyant fireworks or electric sparks. Just quiet walks in the parks, an occasional movie, and hands entwined in the dark—that sort of thing.

But underneath her calm exterior, Dang burns like a smoldering ember. I honestly don't deserve her. No one has tried to understand me and to become part of my life as Dang has. Indeed, what the hell does she see in me? Is she's stark-staring mad, lost in some romantic fantasy? Damned if I know. I only know that I'm up against something that is far beyond my comprehension.

What frightens me most is Dang's high moral fiber, her stratospheric standards. I respect and love these standards, but can I live up to them? Not on your life. Why doesn't Dang get herself a guy like our mutual friend Ajaan Somsak, someone who can make her safe and secure?

Yeah, I can hear you. You're telling me that she loves me, but it's a lie. It's a lie because I made it a lie. I gave her an image of someone I'm not: the true-blue *jai dee* man. Then I didn't have the guts to strip the façade away and expose the real me. In doing so, I used the age-old rationalization: never hurt a woman's feelings.

Another lie. Still, is she that stupid? Women have never impressed me with their judgment. Sometimes they feel things, sense things, beyond my comprehension, beyond my male logic. Ergo, does Dang love something I can't see, some abstraction similar to Plato's Theory of Forms? What an ego-trip that question is! And what a stupid assumption it presupposes!

Nevertheless, I trust Dang's instincts far more than I trust mine. There's only one thing to do now, namely: *let the future unfurl and hope for the best.* The future may bring us closer together or pull us apart. But I'll always have my memories: the train in which I first saw her, the waterfall we both climbed and swam in, the restaurant in which I asked her to marry me, the way we held hands.

It seems so long ago. I was much younger then. I didn't think Dang was too important. I was new to Thailand and had much to do. There was also plenty of time. I was breaking in *pakamas* faster than I could count. And, what's more, they didn't seem nearly as hard against my butt as they are now.

Epistle Seven

January 3, 1977

Dear Mom and Dad:

Well, I'm here. Paradise Lost and all that jive. Never mind that it was never found to be lost in the first place, especially by those globetrotting writers of yore. If anyone came close, Maugham did. Samoa is teeming with worn-out boozers and flipped-out world travelers who shirk the chainsaw of the modern world. So they squat here, and the sun fries their minds like fish in a skillet. It's the story of the remittance man all over again. Only this time, there's less shame but more to be ashamed about.

As for the Samoans, they're great. The spaced-out whites stumble across this worldly stage like vaudeville teams before a jaded audience. For life, to the natives, is a pleasurable thing: a stroll on the beach at sunset, a bit of nooky beneath the palms, begetting another mouth nine months hence, should nature so deem.

Time is much more elastic here, with stress and strain stretched to such an extent as to be nonexistent. Still, all is not heaven. God was never so simple, for boredom is part and parcel of Samoa. It comes with the balmy weather, the abundance of food, and the sainted proximity to the sea. Nor is this boredom to be sneered at, to be taken lightly. Either a person adjusts or packs up and goes home.

Some of the trainees in my Peace Corps group have already returned stateside for any number of reasons: loneliness, homesickness, culture shock, or downright ennui. Still, most of us will stay. Training is over, and the more ominous problems have been resolved. I didn't mind training nearly so much this time. Language still left me like a babbling baboon. Nonetheless, I was a social smash. Rowena Fraser, a buxom and brilliant Harvard gal, even lambasted me for being too popular. "Listen to me, Gerry Christmas," she said, wagging her index finger in my face. "You're so good-natured, I could puke."

At the end of training, a vote was taken to elect two representatives for the volunteer council. Each of us had to write two names on a piece of scrap paper. One of the trainers turned to me and whispered, "It didn't take higher math skills to figure out who one of the reps would be. Your name was on nearly every single ballot." Now, that's what I call ironic. If there was anything I detested as a PCV in Thailand, it was the pompous fools on the volunteer council. I therefore endeavored to abdicate, but to no avail. Hell, these guys don't even have ears.

My three weeks in the village were delightful. I lived in a fale with a Samoan family consisting of a mother, a father, and their fourteen children. The first day, one of the sons took me out into the lagoon in an outrigger. It was somewhat hairy trying to balance the hollowed-out log, but I managed. The water inside the reef rarely gets over one's head, thus the emerald-green effect stretches out for a good half mile. The marine life is spectacular and, happily, sharks seldom venture inside the reef.

Still, a man-eater did kill a volunteer three years ago. The young man, however, was diving in an area outside the reef where sharks abound. There are conflicting stories to what exactly happened. The most commonly heard account is the one where he literally had his head torn off. His girlfriend was swimming with him and the only thing that saved her was the rest of his body, which served to satisfy the other sharks until she clambered into the boat. The incident left the poor woman temporarily insane. Nonetheless, she bravely returned five months later to finish her tour of service.

Is there a moral to this sordid tale? For me, there is: swim as little as possible, and, if one must go swimming, stay inside the reef. Better to be a "chicken on the land" than a "chicken of the sea."

Village life waned after two weeks. The silhouettes against the sunsets, the wide and languorous palms, the swish-sway of the native girls fades quickly. I soon discovered that village life is one of repetition and monotony: it's a good place to visit and mellow out on taro and mangoes and breadfruit for one or two days. But that was about all. So I opted for a school near Apia. I was assigned to Viamauga Junior High School, located beyond the town and on high ground just below Samoa College. Oddly enough, there's a tiny village adjacent to the school; hence, I'm blessed with the best of both worlds.

Right now, I'm staying at my headmistress's house. Her name is Aliatasi Tauaa, and she is the proud owner of a color TV. Aliatasi loves American wrestlin'. One night, she asked me if the fighters really hit each other that hard.

"No," I said. "It's all fake but makes for good entertainment."

I could see that she was disappointed, but what else could I say? Had I said it was real and she'd found out later I'd lied, where would I be then?

As a result, I watch *NBC Nightly News* a week after you see it. I don't suffer from culture shock very easily. Still, the first time Aliatasi turned on the tube and up popped Chet Huntley and David Brinkley, I was stunned.

But such luxury is ephemeral at best, especially in Samoa. My small, one-room abode is now being built on the school compound. For the first month, I'll have no running water and will have to cook my meals on a two-burner kerosene stove. Also, the *faleuila* is not part of the house. I will therefore have a nice little walk into the bush before going to bed. Makes me appreciate home, the true paradise I left behind.

Epistle Eight

January 5, 1977

Dear Tocher and Brenda:

I'm glad to see that someone is doing something sensible on the twenty-ninth of this month. Sadly, I can't make it. Our training program will be in full swing during your nuptials, even though I'm now a volunteer. Please don't ask me to explain that. The whole Peace Corps program is so screwed up here that I've contemplated cracking some balls with a pair of coconuts. Alas, there's nothing to crack.

The country is delightful. Yes, it's a paradise of sorts. Yet, every paradise suffers from the same malady: ennui. There are huge, enormous lapses of time that must be filled each day. Otherwise, the high-charged, incentive-driven Western mind percolates and pops. Samoa is the land of the sodden white man. This sub-specie is especially ubiquitous in and around Apia—his great potbelly thrust forward, his face red and bloated, his great ass waddling on spindly legs.

Apia is also a mecca for the world travelers (WTs). After gorging on mushroom omelets in Bali, WTs plop down here. I saw two beauts yesterday. Blank-eyed, scantily clad, and culturally crude, they sauntered into a Chinese shop and "did their thing." My humanitarianism must be on the wane, for I fled the scene as soon as I saw the shock and stupefaction on the shopkeeper's face. Leaving, I was left with a single, solitary image: a huge tattoo of Jesus Christ. It had been chiseled on the back of one of the WT's.

The Samoans are good people. It's incredible how much water runs off their backs. Sure, they can be volatile at times, but all is forgiven the next day. I wouldn't call them a physically beautiful people. The great writers have created that myth. The women reach the peak of their beauty in their late teens and early twenties. With no thought to diet, no wonder they go to fat, especially after popping out four or five kids in four or five years. Sitting and weaving mats by the hour doesn't help, either. Naturally, the various parts of the anatomy react accordingly. The power of gravity never ceases to amaze me.

Still, there remains the good humor. That seems to last till death. For Samoans like a good time more than any people I've come across. In the village, the *fiafia* is their answer to our bash. A fiafia can take on numerous forms, depending on the age and sex of the participants. My favorite is the one put on by the young women of the village. The guests sit at one end of the *fono,* while the girls sit at the other. *Kava,* the ceremonial drink of the land, is presented to the more important guests along with some gifts, usually homemade mats and necklaces.

Then the entertainment commences. It's not one-sided. Each group is expected to entertain the other. The activities can become downright lewd if the more prominent villagers let their hair down. But this usually doesn't happen with the young women present. I've seen older men and women hump the poles of the fono. But the young women have their reputations to lose, so they tend to err on the side of caution. The segregation continues throughout the entire fiafia. The only mixing comes with the dancing. Of course, I've formulated a law regarding this behavior, namely: *sexual taboos are inversely proportional to the self-control of a people.* Accurate, if not profound!

Despite Samoa's warmth and charm, I can't get Thailand out of my head. That place captured my heart. I listen to the news over the radio with one selfish, never-ending prayer:

please, God, don't let the damned Commies close it down. As a result, my inner self has become quite lonely. I'd pack my bags tomorrow if Dang told me to come back and marry her. I, too, am selfish. Any thought to the contrary is silly and self-defeating. Even Ben Rode's ironclad resolve has softened and eroded. During his visit here, all we did was drink scotch and swap stories about his sweetie and my sweetie back in Siam.

Epistle Nine

January 13, 1977

Dear Mom and Dad:

It's difficult to describe this place. Actually, it's not a place but a state of mind. *Palagis* have numerous adjustments to make when they come to these sandy shores. Any idea of strict order and regular routine must be discarded. Indeed, any thought of time itself must be jettisoned. This has a queer effect on the mind, as the human brain exists and thrives only when put to work. In the short time I've been here, I've noticed marked changes in my mental state. Like everyone else, I've more free time than ever before. My brain has therefore attempted to stay active even when there's no substantial mental stimulus.

And therein lies the trap—for most people eventually give up thinking. No, I'm not exaggerating. That's what Samoa can do to you. The brain seeks out work, and for the first few weeks, there is a soft easing of tension and a sense of "being in paradise." Then one day, you wake up, and presto—*no thought*.

Take today, for instance. I set out for Apia with the thought of going to the Peace Corps office to check an advertisement on a bed sale. Walking into town, I met lackadaisical Dan Minor, a fellow volunteer who teaches physics and math at St. Joseph's High School. Dan conned me into going to two nondescript restaurants, the Horatio Nelson Public Library, and a number of small shops. Dan and I didn't do any serious eating, nor did we do any serious reading, nor did we do any serious shopping. We just farted around.

Late in the afternoon, we meandered down to the Peace Corps office, located at the far fringe of the harbor, just outside of town. There, after checking our mail and bullshitting with other PCVs, we left. Not till halfway home did I realize my mental blunder: I'd failed to check the ad. But that wasn't what scared me. It was the way Dan reacted. As soon as I turned to tell him, he beat me to the punch. My facial expression must've flicked a switch upstairs, since he immediately said, "We blew it, didn't we?" I knew then that I wasn't alone. Both of us had become twits in a remote and distant island where thought and thinking, mind and meaning are irrelevant and senseless.

Ah, but all is not bleak. There's a silver lining to all this, namely: *the mental erosion does not seem to be permanent.* In other words, with those volunteers who stay for the requisite two years, little or no mental erosion is apparent. There are enough books to read and places to see and students to assist to ward off being brain-dead.

Not so with the volunteers who stay for three or more years. Indeed, they mutate into odd and fanciful creatures. It would be both inaccurate and unkind to say that they become more Samoan. The Samoans are real people, and any volunteer working three or more years doesn't rate such an elevated classification. Such a creature invariably has a vacant, vacuous expression that resembles a frog blinded by a southern redneck with a gig in one hand and a flashlight in the other. Asked the most common and mundane question, he will invariably take a good two to three minutes to open his mouth. And even then, any meaningful utterance is, at best, problematic.

Samoa doesn't captivate volunteers like Thailand did. Most of my PC friends in Thailand left with good experience and a desire to return. Few Samoan volunteers feel that way. It's not that they hate the country or the people. On the contrary, many have deep and profound respect for both. It seems to be something subtler, less easily pinned down. The volunteers, though emotionally attached and fascinated by the island and the people, seem wary of being assimilated into the *fa'a Samoa*, into the all-absorbing *aiga*, into the carefree and thoughtless life that is uniquely Samoan. For these people, if they take a shine to you, want you to become a family member in all respects: socially, economically, spiritually, and, yes, physically. Consequently, the pressures toward assimilation increase as time passes.

This is in contrast to the acceptance I felt in Thailand. The Thais love you and accept you; they don't love you and absorb you. You can, therefore, keep your identity and yet feel a part of the people and their way of life. Not so here. Samoans are like dry sponges with volunteers being nothing but idle puddles of water about to be sopped up. And once sopped up, one stays sopped up. No one will come along and wring out the sponge. That would take too much energy.

In the last two or three days, I've formed a plan. This plan is counter to PC policy, PC philosophy, and PC propaganda. But I don't give a damn. Essentially, my plan is this: *remain emotionally free during the next two years.* To this end, I'll have to minimize my cultural involvement and maximize my teaching involvement. Moreover, instead of being an active participant, I'll have to become a detached observer—a reversal of my role in Thailand.

I'm doing this for self-preservation. I've left pieces of my heart scattered in Siam, and I want them to stay put. Once a man overextends himself, once he tries to plant too much acreage with too little seed, he comes up with a bad harvest. Instead, he should stick with what he knows can be done and with what he knows he can do well. I've left the land of my heart—the promise of my dreams—back in Thailand. Someday, a whole man should return to reap the golden harvest. And I intend to do just that. But until that day comes, until the reality of now turns into the reality of tomorrow, I must sharpen my scythe.

Epistle Ten

January 17, 1977

Dear Mom and Dad:

The impossible has happened. Life has downshifted from second into first gear. For three consecutive weeks, I've done nothing but eat and sleep. Spotting a spare tire around my midriff, I decided to fast. I cut taro, bananas, and breadfruit from my diet. That did the trick. My weight plummeted back to normal. Still, I'd learned my lesson: *eating in Samoa is not like eating in Thailand.* The starches and carbohydrates here make that prohibitive.

One can see that everywhere, especially with Samoan women. By her late teens, a Samoan woman is a jaw-dropping, physical marvel: incredibly strong, striking, and statuesque—a rival to the best viragoes that Scandinavia and Ethiopia have to offer. Then, in a matter of ten years or so, she undergoes a tragic transformation, ballooning into an enormous mass of fat and flesh, of brawn and blubber—what one merciless PCV has dubbed a "Taro Queen."

I'm still living at my headmistress's house. Not exactly a hardship situation. Indeed, all modern conveniences are at my fingertips. Next door, however, is another world. Aliatasi's great-uncle lives there. People say he's eighty-seven years old, but I don't believe it. He couldn't be that young. He's tall and thin, with virtually no fat to his brittle bones. The skin about his torso is dry and wrinkled and hangs flaccid in long, irregular folds. His head is tight and small, resembling an onion just plucked from the ground. Not surprisingly, he spends the majority of his time in bed since it's most painful for him to move about. Still, boredom must be his sidekick, since he periodically ambles over to see me. Of course, I cannot understand a word he says. Even if I could speak Samoan fluently, I doubt if we could communicate. His hearing is about gone, and his speech is slurred. Nonetheless, I like him. His warm and radiant smile is a constant wonder to me.

The first time I met the old man was strange. I was watching TV alone when he came up behind me. I never heard a footfall, just a slow, slide-tap of wood upon the linoleum floor. I turned and there he stood, naked, save for a tattered *lavalava* about his bony hips. He held a long bamboo pole in his right hand that served as a staff. As he moved toward me, I was sure he would fall since the floor was slick and his staff slid whenever he leaned against it. But at his age, a person is always about to fall. It's a liability that comes with the accumulation of too much time.

Finally, the old man made it to the chair beside me. It took him five minutes to sit down. I could see his brain ordering his extremities, but his extremities were adamant and refused to take said orders. The next fifteen minutes were full of smiles and laughter and inarticulate babblings. The only thing I understood was the saga of his tattoo. Like most old Samoan men, he had a huge, elaborate tattoo that extended from above his hips down to his knees. If a Samoan man is nude and viewed from afar, this tattoo looks like a pair of skin-tight, navy-blue short pants with an outrigger across the lower back.

A Samoan tattoo is more than a tattoo. It's a coming-of-age testimonial. Both an art form and a badge of honor, it's visual proof that a man can withstand pain, that he's now a complete man, a man ready to assume his rightful place in society. Traditional Samoan tattooing is a primitive procedure:

a shark tooth dipped in navy-blue dye is driven into the skin with a small hammer. Since blood oozes from the skin for the first day or so, most men sit for hours in the lagoon, thereby allowing the saltwater to placate the pain and diminish the chance of infection.

The old man related in detail how he came by his tattoo. I didn't understand everything he said, but I did comprehend that the procedure was extremely painful, especially the part in and around the naval. As the old man prepared to leave, I had the strange, sick feeling that getting his tattoo was the highlight of his life. It seemed preposterous, absurd. *Death is sometimes absentminded*, I thought. Later, after dinner, I talked with Anita, the maid. She didn't have much to say about the old man. He lived alone and was very old. And, oh, yes, he'd never married. The girls had never thought much of him. I couldn't help but wonder where those girls were now.

I met another old man yesterday. I went into a furniture store to buy a table and chairs for my house. A small, wiry American in his early sixties called me into the office of the Samoan who owned the store. The two were playing the national sport, beer-swilling and bullshitting, when I entered the room. It didn't take me long to get the old man's history. He gladly vouchsafed it inside of five minutes. The parts he wanted me to know, anyway.

The old man was an ex-PCV, an ex-CEO, and an ex-lost soul who had at last found "tranquility" in the South Pacific. His cloudy past was nothing but misery in preparation for the wonders of Samoa. Though he never said it, I got the distinct feeling that he'd abandoned whatever family he once had and initiated a new one here—replete with wife, kids, and title. His notoriety among PCVs hinged on a single incident. Seeing a group of volunteers board an airplane bound for the United States, he bellowed, "Suckers!"

I listened to the old man talk on and on and on. I listened to him tell me about the heart and soul of the Peace Corps. I listened to him tell me about the mindless materialism of America. I listened to him tell me what a fool Margaret Mead was, how her book *Coming of Age in Samoa* was complete bunk.

Here's the Sage of Samoa, I thought. *A man with all the answers.*

Overall, the old man came across as cantankerous and irksome. He'd used the tools from a preconceived hell—Western know-how, Western technology, Western wealth, and Western creative juices—to fabricate his Kurtz-like heaven on earth. Talk about a walking, talking contradiction: he hated his roots, yet he used said roots to grow a new tree.

I looked at the old man closely as he continued his chatter. Finally, my patience grew thin, and I asked him a few pointed questions. Instantly, he became ill at ease, almost offended.

"Why don't you come back next year and tell me what you think then?" he said curtly. "You'll be in a better position to understand my views at that time."

I looked at him again. I could see him clearly now. Steeped in his outward trappings, feeling content with the primitiveness of his surroundings, he'd wrapped gauze about his past and shut it out. He was lost in the here and now. A big fish in a little pond did not quite describe him. A minnow out of water was more like it.

Epistle Eleven

January 23, 1977

Dear Mom and Dad:

I've been put through a cement mixer that has sputtered, stalled, and solidified. By now, I'd hoped to move into my house at Viamauga, but the screening and the electricity have yet to be completed. Tomorrow, I leave for nine days of in-service language training at the other end of Upolu. With day one of school only two weeks away, you can readily ascertain the brilliance and the farsightedness of the Peace Corps staff. It wouldn't have been so bad if I'd settled in or if most of the other volunteers had settled in. But we haven't. One would think that the PC staff would take that into account and make the necessary adjustments. Think again. Instead, the staff floats on like a huge, inexorable cloud—unseeing, unknowing, unthinking, incognizant of the rain it brings into our lives.

A number of volunteers went out of their way to inform the Peace Corps that the extra language training was a bad idea and they didn't want to go. The staff acted predictably by first lending a sympathetic ear and then abruptly making attendance mandatory. Nonetheless, the senior volunteers did win a victory of sorts. Since village life is particularly tough on them, their aching bones will be spared and they'll get their training in Apia. One of my friends will join them. He received special dispensation (from the Peace Corps Pope?) because he can be downright obnoxious when he vents his super-size spleen. Leo the Lip had it right: nice guys finish last.

Samoa is gearing up for Queen Elizabeth's visit next month, on February 10, to be exact. My school is one of four government schools that have been chosen to greet and entertain her. I will therefore be present when she sets her regal toe upon Samoan soil.

The queen will only be here for one day; hence, everyone is praying for fair weather. I seriously doubt if the queen has any idea what a big deal this is for the average Samoan. With the *matai* system being a fundamental part of the social structure here, Samoans have a deep and abiding affinity for anything hierarchical. And one cannot get much more hierarchical than Her Majesty, the Queen of England. The Samoans are therefore planning a massive fiafia. The mind reels at the thought of the fine mats and the fat pigs that will be lavished upon her.

After the fiafia, however, Tusitala will strike from beyond the grave. The queen has been scheduled to walk up Mt. Vaea and pay her respects at the hallowed tomb of Robert Louis Stevenson. It will not be an easy climb this time of year. The heavy rains have made the narrow path nearly impassable. I'd planned to walk up there a number of weeks back, but some Samoan friends dissuaded me from doing so. Topography, like everything else, changes with one's position on the social ladder.

Since the past week has been uneventful and since my neglect in describing Apia is long overdue, I had best do it in the limited space that's left. Apia can best be visualized as one enormous *Y*, with the harbor being the open, bowl-like space at the top of the letter. The letter itself contains the two principal streets on and beside which everything oozes. I use the word *ooze* because this is a place of "ebb and flow" rather than "stop and go." In recent years, the car has become ubiquitous. This, however, has not altered the Samoan stride, which is somewhere between slow and stationary. With my

American stride, I can walk from one end of town to the other in twenty minutes flat as long as I don't meet someone along the way. Of course, I always do. It is, therefore, impossible to go into town and return inside an hour. I've endeavored to do so many times without success. Instead, I usually take a good two hours, arriving home just in time for supper.

Oddly, I can get a greater variety of consumer goods in Apia than I could in Bangkok. As impossible as this might seem, it is nonetheless the truth. Despite its size, Bangkok has little variety in the way of shopping. Most shops are mom-and-pop affairs; thus, the inventory is limited. Not so here. The big stores in Apia are Morris Hedstrom, Burns Philip, and Mackenzie. All three have large stocks from different parts of the world. Moreover, there's an enormous People's Republic store that specializes in Red Chinese products.

These four establishments satisfy about 90 percent of my wants and needs. The small specialty stores dotted throughout the town take care of the rest. My only real gripe is with books. The Wesley Bookstore has a monopoly, and a poor monopoly at that. Its religious books equal or exceed the amount of fiction, and said fiction is predictably British. Of course, this is to be expected. Still, it rankles me. I've never understood, nor will I ever understand people who limit themselves to religious texts. The real hereafter will come soon enough, so why waste one's time reading what are, at best, speculative accounts?

Apia's hotels, on the other hand, are a study in contrast. Ranging from the opulent to the oily, they offer an odd selection of creature comforts. The Tusitala, named in honor of Robert Louis Stevenson, is a giant among pygmies. Designed and built along the lines of a Samoan fale, the Tusitala is a prime example of great architecture and poor planning—for tourists have yet to come here in droves. And those that do tend to be world travelers—young people whose limited budgets force them to seek cheaper and seedier accommodations.

To make matters worse, the tourists with means gravitate to Aggie Grey's. It's not as posh as the Tusitala, but, thanks to James A. Michener, everyone wants to meet the redoubtable Aggie Grey, supposedly the model for Bloody Mary in *Tales of the South Pacific*. Michener, himself, has neither confirmed nor denied that Aggie Grey was his muse. But that has not stopped Aggie from staking her claim. This has incensed her younger sister, the proprietress of the more modest but brilliantly dubbed Apian Way. Just after training, I spent a few nights there and really got an earful.

"How dare my sister steal my thunder?" she shrieked. "She knows that Mr. Michener had me in mind when he created Bloody Mary."

Considering the character of Bloody Mary, one has to conclude that the Grey sisters are more at home with notoriety than respectability.

The most amazing eatery in town is the Faleburger, an American-styled greasy spoon that could give Burger King a run for its money. No, I haven't lost my taste buds. The owner of the Faleburger is a genial Samoan who has recently returned from the United States, where he ran a Big Boy Burgers for five years. He has only been in business for four months, but people are already standing in line for his grub—myself included. His most popular dish is the fish burger. He uses fresh fish straight off the boat, and is it ever toothsome!

Epistle Twelve

February 13, 1977

Dear Mom and Dad:

Queen Elizabeth II and her consort, Prince Philip, sailed in, sailed by, and sailed out. The convulsion that had gripped Samoa for more than a month has passed. The biggest matai of them all has left her frozen fantasy behind. Still, her hallowed voice lingers, thanks to a taped speech that's played hourly over the radio. Perhaps it's all for the best. Streets lined with schoolchildren programmed to do all the right things at all the right times. Gantries decorated with intricate flower arrangements and bizarre word greetings. Voluptuous festivities and succulent feasts every time she turned her regal head. Fine mats—the finest to be had on the island—lavishly bestowed upon her. She appreciated it. But appreciation is a limited concept. It's a moment of thanks for many moments of pain.

I got a good look at the old gal. Since our students had to perform a Samoan dance, I had to stand out in the open field with the kids. The sun was unmerciful. I could've easily fried an egg on the top of my head. Predictably, Viamuga was scheduled at the end of the program. It didn't matter. Some bureaucrat had come to the happy conclusion that it was more aesthetic to keep the children out in the open rather than in the shade. Though unacquainted with the flunky, I'm sure he had the benefit of the canopy that covered the queen, the prince, and other dignitaries. Hierarchy is the same everywhere; it only changes clothes.

Our students performed admirably. The precision was crisp, the volume was deafening, and the execution was spot-on. The only glitch came at the very end. But that was to be expected, for the finale was extremely complex, with all the children twirling a paper Union Jack while singing "Long Live the Queen." Still, everyone was pleased with the performance. Even Aliatasi, my moody headmistress, cracked a smile as the students came off the field.

For my part, it was a great opportunity to meet the students before teaching them. Samoan children can be boisterous and unruly, so I welcomed the chance to observe and understand them. I even met a boy who didn't conform to the usual behavioral pattern of teasingly slugging another student whenever there's nothing better to do. The boy and I were having a nice conversation, when one of the female students hauled off and hit him. I'd seen this happen before and expected the usual Samoan answer: a slug in return. But this boy was different. He simply turned and gave her a look that a spider monkey would understand. Then, he turned back to me, shook his head, and said, "Sometimes I don't understand God. He left something out when it came to girls." I laughed outright. But that didn't faze the girl in the least. She turned and slugged the girl next to her.

After Queen Elizabeth and Prince Philip left, I met Tapuono, one of my Samoan language teachers. Tapuono is not merely a teacher; she's a living legend. She must tip the scales at a good 250-plus. Yet, she is one of the finest dancers on the island. I've seen her dance a number of times and never tire watching her perform. Her fluidity, her grace, and her artistry are something to behold.

Indeed, Tapuono has to be one of the most suggestive pieces of flesh in the world. Once, at a fiafia, with Tapuono dancing seductively before a group of matais, I heard a fellow volunteer mutter, "She's just made five offers in the last five seconds."

"Not only that," I said. "She's told each and everyone of them what she's going to do!"

That says more about Tapuono than anything else. Much of her magic comes from the flirtatiousness of the eyes and radiates down to the nether zones. But the eyes are not all. Her fingers do the talking too—up and down, over and about, in a symphony of graceful lasciviousness.

Without a doubt, Tapuono is the finest natural performer I've seen in a Samoan. And she's a damn good teacher to boot. But most of all, she's a friend. She could go anywhere in the world and be loved, for she is an emotional beast without bestial emotions. Luckily for us, she is perfectly happy living in Samoa. Sure, she toured New Zealand with a dance troupe and was a smashing success. Nonetheless, she was eager to return home to her husband and her children, which speaks volumes for both her good sense and her great heart.

My house is nearly ready for me to move into. The plumber finally installed the sink, and the carpenter did a swell job with the cupboard. The carpenter is now making a closet that we designed together. He's an interesting guy. Unable to attend school as a child, he learned English from the GIs who were stationed here during World War II. Carpentry was always his love, so he decided at an early age to spend his life with wood. It was a good decision. He now does what he loves and gets paid handsomely for it.

The carpenter and I took an instant liking to each other. Since he lives in close proximity to the school, I expect our friendship to grow and flourish. As you have probably deduced, I'm forming those necessary emotional links that make a volunteer's life bearable and worthwhile. Whether I fit into this way of life well enough to stay for two years remains to be seen.

Certainly, the islands do not fascinate me the same way Thailand did. But that's to be expected. One can hardly expect a scattered number of dots in the Pacific Ocean to match the allure of a large, exotic landmass the size of France. Fascination and mystery are fellow travelers. But there's not much fascination and mystery to a small group of islands where a private pee is impossible. Still, I should be able to learn something about life and living here. Samoans may have many faults, but at least they're open, honest, and genuine. That's plenty for any man.

Epistle Thirteen

March 14, 1977

Dear Mom and Dad:

Last week, Mike Bowker and Bruce McKenzie invited me to Palauli, a district on the southern edge of Savai'i. The invitation was an informal one, so I asked my friend Conrad Wesselhoeft, a volunteer from Seattle, to join me. That was the easiest way to balance the equation.

Not that Bruce and Mike are bad guys. Quite the contrary, both are extremely bright, physically fit, and fiercely independent. Though being their friend, I never see them in and around Apia. During training, they decided to be as self-sufficient as possible. When not teaching at Palauli Junior High and Uesiliana Junior High, they immerse themselves in Samoan language and culture, raise their own chickens, go line- or spearfishing in the lagoon, and tend their own vegetable garden. About the only items they buy from the store are salt, pepper, flour, rice, and butter. In words, they are quintessential volunteers, poster boys for Peace Corps, Washington.

Conrad and I caught the morning ferry from Mulifenua on the Upolu side to Salelologa on the Savai'i side. The drive by bus from Salelologa to Palauli was a short one west along the southern coast. There, Bruce and Mike greeted us.

Bruce McKenzie is a powerhouse to be reckoned with. Standing slightly under six feet tall but seemingly a good three inches taller due to his auburn Afro, he has enough physical and mental wattage to run Con Edison. Having quarterbacked a high school football team, Mike is not exactly a slacker either. Still, Mike will be the first to admit that no one in Peace Corps

Samoa can hold a candle to Bruce for sheer stamina and drive. God made him to eat the world.

We went to Bruce's place for dinner. Small and compact, the house has a living room on the right side and a bedroom on the left with a small bathroom in the middle. The kitchen is to the rear. Out back, there's a chicken coop and vegetable garden.

After a quick lunch, Mike laid out the itinerary.

"We've two choices," he said. "Either we screw around here and do nothing, or we take you to see some of the sights. Which is it?"

I looked at Conrad and Conrad looked at me.

"How about we take in the sights?" Conrad said. "Gerry and I aren't tired. What do you propose?"

"Well, Olermoe Waterfall is always a crowd pleaser," said Mike. "It beats the hell out of the dinky waterfalls in Apia. That's for sure. You guys probably didn't bring cutoffs, but we can probably find something for you to wear."

"As a matter of fact, we did," I said.

"Great," said Mike. "Let's get going, then."

Olermoe Waterfall is straight out of Herman Melville's *Typee*. Though not huge, the waterfall is nonetheless incredibly tall and falls like a shot into a crystal-clear emerald pool surrounded by lush vegetation. Symbolically, it mirrors the salient features found in a woman's joy box. As a result, we instantly shed our clothes and dove in.

It soon became apparent that Mike and Bruce had been here often. Conrad and I were perfectly happy to swim about in the pool. Not so our hosts. Somehow, they had learned to clamber up the sides and dive, a la Tarzan. Though a good swimmer, I dared not do the same. To Bruce and Mike's credit, they didn't urge either Conrad or me to be foolhardy. That's not their style.

We spent a good three hours gamboling about the waterfall. Surprisingly, we had the place to ourselves. I guess it's like other wonderful sites the world over: familiarity breeds contempt. I came away in complete agreement with Mike: there's no waterfall to match it in Apia, not even Papaseea, the one immortalized in W. Somerset Maugham's "The Pool." Finally, around sunset, we headed back to Bruce's house.

"Make yourselves at home," Bruce beamed. "I'll go and get some cool ones."

Mike, Conrad, and I sat down on the frumpy, old chairs. They were surprisingly comfortable considering all the wear and tear they'd been through.

Bruce soon returned with the beers. After doling them out, he sunk into a huge, putrid, green chair and held court.

"From the looks of things," I said, "you guys are pretty self-sufficient."

Mike beamed.

"We try to be," he said. "But it's not without its hazards. Is it, Bruce?"

Bruce didn't say a word. He only smiled slyly.

"What do you mean by that?" asked Conrad.

"Well, last week, we were spearfishing out in the lagoon," said Mike. "Bruce was swimming ahead of me by fifteen to twenty yards. Suddenly, a shark slid in between us and started to follow Bruce. I could do nothing but watch it slither behind that great alabaster body and hope for the best. I was absolutely breathless. Then, for no apparent reason, the man-eater turned and swam away to my right."

"Did you warn Bruce?" I asked.

"No need to," said Mike. "Anyway, we had to catch some fish for dinner."

"It's just as well," said Bruce stoically. "Sometimes, ignorance is bliss. Say, since we're talking grizzly stuff, what do you guys think about the murder over in Tonga?"

"You mean the Deb Gardner case?" said Conrad. "Christ, she was from my home state of Washington."

"I hear she was the hottest minx in her group, hands down," said Mike, running his hand through his thick, dark hair. "That's what did her in."

"Didn't another volunteer kill her?" I asked.

"Yup," said Bruce. "Some guy named Dennis Priven. Whereas Gardner was outgoing and free-spirited, Priven was a real slug, totally lost in his petty, geeky little world. One night, Gardner made the mistake of letting another volunteer drive her home on his motorcycle. That flipped Priven out. He went to her house and stabbed her twenty-two times with a six-inch, serrated diving knife. She died on the way to the hospital but not before identifying her killer."

"Shit," I said. "I hear he got away with it, too."

"Appears so," said Bruce. "Tongan law says that murderers should be hanged. But Mary George, the country director, did everything in her power to get him off. The poor Tongans thought they had an open-and-shut case, but George, a born-again Christian, claimed she had a dream—a dream in which a Tongan, not Priven, killed Deb."

"You gotta be kidding," said Conrad.

"I wish I were," said Bruce. "Most of this shit was going down during our Peace Corps training, so we didn't get wind of it here in Samoa. But in the Kingdom of Tonga, it was another story. The Peace Corps went into overdrive and got

Priven the best defense attorney on the island. Still, not even the best attorney could get him out of the country. So, to save his ass, the Peace Corps lied again. This time, it promised he'd be locked away for life. When Priven was found not guilty by reason of insanity, George made her move. She flew him out fast. Damn fast."

"Do you think justice will ever be served?" said Conrad.

"Not likely," said Mike. "What does the life of a PCV, even a hot PCV, mean to the folks back home? Hell, most of them don't even know Tonga exists. Now, had she been murdered stateside, it might be different. Being killed on US soil and being killed on foreign soil are two different things—unless, of course, you're military."

"You've an excellent point there," I said.

"I agree with Mike," said Bruce. "It's an out-of-sight, out-of-mind situation. But just because Priven is free in the United States doesn't mean that we can't make life difficult for him."

"I think I see where you're going with this," said Conrad. "The case has all the hallmarks of a legend. If we keep the story alive by word of mouth, who knows? Perhaps someone may write a book about it."

"Let's hope it's a good book," said Mike. "Say, I've had enough of this depressing stuff. How about some dinner? What do you city slickers want? Fish or chicken?"

"Chicken would be great," said Conrad. "Can we do anything to help?"

"Sure can," said Bruce. "Follow me."

Bruce led the way out the back door to where the chickens were.

"You have to earn your meals around here," Bruce said with a smirk as he took a squawking chicken in one hand and, with a deft whack, knocked it senseless on the chopping block.

"Here, Gerry, you hold its head, and you, Conrad, hold its legs. I like to make this as quick and painless as possible."

Bruce then took a hatchet and neatly severed the head from the body. Blood squirted profusely from the trunk, so Conrad and I released the bird. It walked about, headless, two or three times before dropping dead beside the vegetable garden.

Bruce took the poor creature in his hands reverently, almost religiously.

"Life feeds off life," he said, solemnly draining the blood from the body. "It's a cruel world sometimes. Okay, let's go back in and have another brewskie before the women get here."

"The women?" I said incredulously. "What women?"

"Oh, I forgot to tell you. Mike and I have been dating two Samoan teachers over at the school. They're coming over tonight to cook up a real feast. You know, *palusami, alaisa fa'apopo, keke pua'a, oka l'a,* and *paifala*. I've no idea what they're going to do with this chicken, but they'll figure something out."

"Are you guys serious?" asked Conrad.

Bruce smiled.

"I'm dead-ass serious. Don't let this out, but Ruta and I are going to be married in September. Yes, both of you are invited. Mike is dating a gal named Sete. What an eyeful she is! They really love each other, but it hasn't registered yet. It will in another few months."

Conrad and I stood there, stunned.

"Come on, you guys," said Bruce. "I hope that chicken isn't weighing too heavily on your conscience."

"No," I said. "It's just that you are still young. Why do you want to get married?"

"Don't talk nonsense, Gerry. Ruta will stand by me through thick and thin. I don't have to be old to know that. Now, come inside. The beer is getting warm."

Epistle Fourteen

April 4, 1977

Dear Mom and Dad:

Since space on an aerogram borders on the sacred, I must conjure up visions to save paper.

Vision one: asleep on the tiny island of Monono, I awake to find the cloth partition ablaze in saffron flames. I beat the fire to the lava floor while three Samoan men scurry to help me. The flames miss the thatched roof by less than a foot, and a black hole, the size of a small manhole, is left in my mattress. I go back to sleep with the three Samoans chanting: *"O luki, o luki, luki ..."*

Vision two: I go to school one day only to find one teacher has left for New Zealand without even notifying his parents, let alone the headmistress. His girlfriend was killed last year, and the nightmare still lingers. I feel sorry for the guy, but the rest of us have to absorb his students. Not an easy task, since all classes are "standing room only."

Vision three: while having a "discussion" with his wife, another teacher puts his hand through the jalousie windows. He severs the muscles and tendons in his right forearm and has to be hospitalized for a fortnight. More students to absorb.

Vision four: yet another teacher exploits the situation by cracking a deal with Aliatasi. He'll be allowed to teach all subjects in one classroom to one group of students instead of specializing. To sweeten the deal, the teacher's wife has been thrown into the mix. I come to school one morning and am blithely told that I'm not only teaching English, but math and social studies as well. I bite the bullet, but not too gracefully. My teeth aren't what they once were.

Vision five: for a few weeks, a Samoan colleague and I teach three classes at the same time. If this is paradise, we need to redefine the word. To compound matters, I don't know from one hour to the next what subject to teach. During this time, I'm obsessed with a recurrent daydream: sitting atop a coconut tree and playing bombardier on my headmistress's head below. It gives me great solace and helps to maintain my sanity.

In the midst of this chaos, Tocher Mitchell arrives in Samoa with his wife, Brenda. Tocher and Brenda want me to take a week off to go sightseeing. Fat chance. My students, though bright and good-natured, are not exactly disciplined. Like young lions, they cannot be left in their cages alone.

Tocher and Brenda are not exactly impressed with Samoa. Brenda, especially, has a tough time. Being from Hong Kong, she can't come to grips with a freewheeling culture. The disorder and the casualness in particular drive her bonkers. I can sympathize. Samoa is not a place for a person who has been indoctrinated with time management and the Asian work ethic. This is not to say that Samoans are wrong, that their live-and-let-live attitude is bogus. Far from it. All I'm saying is that some personalities demand structure and order, two traits not particularly valued in the South Pacific.

To solve the Tocher/Brenda dilemma, I ship them to my Samoan family in Manono for a few days. That kills two birds with one stone. First, it puts Tocher and Brenda into a more peaceful and serene setting, and second, it frees me to teach. Talk about thinking like a Samoan: I'm already starting to unload my problems onto the broad shoulders of the aiga.

Gerry Christmas

Soon after Tocher and Brenda depart, the Samoan teachers begin to trickle back. Since my students are the slowest and since they need a person who can speak Samoan, one of the returning teachers is assigned to my class. I return to what was essentially my original schedule, which stressed English and straddled me with fewer hours.

This new routine, however, is ephemeral. One of the Samoan teachers gets into a drunken brawl and has to be hospitalized due to stab wounds. I'm asked to cover for him. I almost say no. Sick of the constant upheaval, I think seriously of terminating, of boarding the next 707 out of Apia.

But the silly bastards need me. Not like Thailand needed me—not to teach English and to build a bridge of understanding between people. No, that's too radical an idea, a mite too esoteric for this place. For, don't you see? Teachers here are vehicles of discipline first and dispensers of knowledge second. Samoans, being a passion-driven lot, have little or no control over what they do or what they say. If a student feels compelled to slug another student, he hauls off and slugs. It's that simple. It's a reflex action without thought, without any rhyme or reason.

I spend half of my time yelling at my students. You'd think that would make me unpopular. Well, guess again. Most students like me. Why? Because, contrary to my Peace Corps cross-cultural training, I refuse to hit them. Initially, my students had a hard time understanding this. They're hit so often at home that they expect to get slapped around at school. Not being a violent man, I avoid hitting them at all costs. This is not easy. Today, for instance, a student made a fan while I was teaching writing. I took the fan away and told him in no uncertain terms to pay attention. Five minutes later, there was another fan in his hand. This student has been giving me trouble all term, and I have had a number of talks with him. After each talk, he'd swear to mend his ways and promise to improve his conduct.

But he never has. The fan was the straw that broke my back. I grabbed the student by the scruff of the neck and pulled him out of his chair. Despite being angry, I was in complete control of my emotions. I pulled the kid across the floor and pushed him out the door. I then shoved him down the hall and pushed him into the headmistress's office. Aliatasi was a bit shocked until I explained the situation. I then left, knowing full well the kid would get the crap beaten out of him. I didn't have any more trouble with that student or the rest of the class.

Now, don't get me wrong. I do not enjoy acting like this. Indeed, I've promised myself that if I can't teach without corporal punishment, I'll leave Samoa. It isn't worth it. No Peace Corps assignment is worth a negative change in one's personality.

For the most part, I've made a separate peace with Samoa. Indeed, there are times when I truly love this place. Samoans are an enormously generous and guileless people whose islands, though small, are incredibly beautiful and enchanting. But I'm not a tourist on holiday. I've a job to do, and that job demands understanding, controlling, and educating Samoan students. I haven't mastered that yet. But I should in the near future. For I've a goal two years hence: I want to leave Samoa with my head held high, with fond memories in my brain, and with love in my heart.

Epistle Fifteen

April 14, 1977

Dear Mom and Dad:

This week, I finally stopped babysitting and began to teach. Our last love-nest casualty has returned from the Battle of Hassling, and we are back to full-force once more. Perhaps I should elaborate on that last sentence. Lokeni, our social studies teacher, went on a mammoth bender. My friend Malua took him home and put him to bed. Or so Malua thought. Lokeni rolled out of bed and crawled from the house. His goal? His girlfriend's abode down the road.

Somehow, Lokeni made it. Stomping on hens, tripping over pigs, kicking every dog, he made it. His girlfriend must possess a wide and forgiving spirit, for she took him in and gave him comfort beneath her mosquito net. Everything would've been fine if the girl's brothers hadn't returned and caught them in the middle of the good old "in and out."

As one of my friends has aptly noted, Samoa is a shame culture, not a guilt culture. You can do anything here, as long as you aren't caught. But caught, Lokeni was. And though the girl's brothers like him, they did what Samoan culture demands and took him to the brink of death. Out came the machetes and the stones. The job was quick and fast and brutal. The brothers placed most of their effort on the face. Less than an hour later, an oozing mass of pulp—a visceral piece of humanity—staggered into the hospital.

An emergency operation was immediately performed. Lokeni received glucose and blood transfusions. He'll live to drink another day. God is not necessarily on the side of the biggest intellects. He's on the side of the most active glands.

You'd guffaw if you could see me now. Domestically, I'm a mess. I do my own cooking, wash my own clothes, clean my own house, and dream of the days of yesteryear, of paying peanuts to a Thai servant to cook my food and clean my house and wash my clothes. After three months of menial chores, my face is starting to resemble a Samoan who's stood under the wrong coconut tree at the wrong time.

Sometimes, while scrubbing the socks and the shorts and the shirts, I hearken back to an argument I had with two female teachers in Thailand. They argued that the Thais would never adopt the washing machine, that the thought of mixing clothes together was unthinkable, a barbarism of the West. I argued that man is fundamentally lazy, that Maytag would eventually rule the world. I don't pretend to be a futurist, but I did take Nostradamus 101.

One year on, here I am in Samoa, isolated and alone on a chunk of volcanic rock with no dials to turn and no buttons to push. I swear, there's no justice in the world. Each night, I've the same recurrent dream: a foxy Thai chick is washing my clothes. A dream like that makes it damn hard to get up in the morning.

As for the cooking, I didn't get much in the way of your French genes, Mom. Unfortunately, Dad's English genes reign supreme, much to the distress of my gastrointestinal tract. Had the Almighty not blessed me with a cast-iron stomach, the curtain to this particular Peace Corps show would've come down long ago.

As I formulated my Laws for Thailand, I'm now beginning to formulate my Laws for Samoa.

Law 1: *What's yours is theirs, never the other way around.* Being a palagi makes me rich. But being an American palagi makes me superrich. The aiga makes for some interesting excuses to "borrow" whatever I have, from my saw to my ice water. There's no thought that I'm a greenhorn to the country and to the culture. There's no thought that I'm a single Peace Corps volunteer living on a limited salary. Indeed, there's no thought at all. I wouldn't mind if the Samoans were a responsible lot and took care of things. Then I'd lend things out and get them back on a regular basis. Unfortunately, this is not the case.

Which leads us to Law 2: *Once things go out, they're gone.* That enormous, nebulous entity known as the aiga sucks in all objects, large and small. The aiga is in constant flux, an unending flow of life upon life upon life. When I say Samoans can number twenty and eat two portions one day then number two and eat twenty portions the next, I'm not exaggerating. Don't ask me where the food goes. Not even the Samoans know. The best guess is that it goes down the food chain: from the parents to the children to the dogs to the pigs. Should the food run out somewhere along the chain, well, tough luck.

Which brings us to Law 3: *Adults eat, children work, dogs bite, and pigs die.* A simple cycle as long as you're not a child, a dog, or a pig.

Still, Samoa is an interesting place in which to live and to learn. Some of the remittance men have taken exception with the work of prominent anthropologists, especially Margaret Mead. Nonetheless, after being here for six months, I hold that her basic points are valid, particularly those dealing with children-to-children and adult-to-children relationships. Most island critics nail Mead for not stressing the matai system, of not honing in on the Samoan power structure. But that was not the thrust of *Coming of Age in Samoa*. Mead was concerned with Samoan women, not Samoan men. One is therefore left with the question: Did her critics ever bother to read her book? I seriously doubt it.

It was a true joy talking with you over the phone. Your thoughts about moving to Rochester to be near Bill and Maribeth are fascinating. I hesitate to venture an opinion, since I'm too far removed from the situation. That being said, I feel certain that your decision will reflect what's best for you. That you've not lost the spirit of adventure, that you still believe that life can be a continuous series of positive images and experiences, that you're not afraid to take chances when most of your contemporaries are wrapped up in their cocoons, gives me great pride and happiness and hope. Pride in that you're my parents; happiness in that you're still finding life a joy; and hope that I might be able to tread in your footsteps so that we all might meet in eternity.

My Form 5 students at Faleata Junior High School (1977)
First Row: Lauese, Petelo, Losi, Fonofili
(head down), Malo Uale
Second Row: Malo Mataia, Oliana, Simanono, Aa
Third Row: Maulato, Johnny, Saisirita,
Fia, Joyce, Marie, Nonu, Ioana
Fourth Row: Unknown, Ioane, Iosefa Oti, Lami,
Uahota, Ie, Lei, Asafa, Iosefa Kalone, Poutoa

Epistle Sixteen

May 18, 1977

Dear Mom and Dad:

Two weeks ago, on a bright and sunny Wednesday morning, something snapped.

I was cannonballing toward exams, a mite overcharged with three days to go, but in control. I had to give a make-up exam and a writing assignment to three separate classes, but my headmistress, Aliatasi, had refused to copy the stencils the day before. She'd been giving me trouble all term. When I first told her how I taught, black clouds coalesced in those big, brown eyes.

Aliatasi is a huge, towering woman who uses her immense mass to intimidate and browbeat the staff. Fed up to the teeth, I decided to fight back. She respected me for it. That, I could feel. I could also feel that behind that huge mountain of flesh lurked a frightened and insecure soul, a spirit entangled in the dark and dreadful web of control and caprice. Still, I thought I understood her, that I could handle her. That was my mistake.

Aliatasi's office is divided in two. The first is where the staff gathers for conferences, and the second is where Aliatasi works. Stepping through the door, I could see that she was collecting money from negligent students. I decided to wait until she was finished, as she's not what one would call a "dormant volcano."

I sat down at the far end of the room and watched her. *Damn it,* I thought. *This is one of her black mornings. She's sitting there like a lump of lard. Look at that crude and flabby scowl. And that voice. She sounds more like a hyena than a headmistress. Now, now, Christmas—take it easy. Aliatasi did put you up in her house while you were waiting for a place on campus. And she's no fool. Moody, yes, but fool, no. Still, hell to work for. You personally supplied the paper, stencils, and ink for the copying machine, and she still doesn't want you to use it.*

After the students had left, Aliatasi went back to work. She could see me but refused to acknowledge my presence. I waited ten minutes. Then I got up and sat in the chair next to her desk. She didn't say a word. The Great Samoan Sphinx. I waited and waited and waited. I couldn't have been more than a foot from her dark, leathery face. Suddenly, an elderly matai entered and walked over to the chair directly opposite Aliatasi and me. She instantaneously put down her pen and raised her head. I looked at her face in astonishment. Hallelujah! It was the dawn of a new day: eyes dancing, teeth sparkling, a smile of sun and fun. Then came the voice—all sugary and soft, like cotton candy at a county fair.

It made me want to puke. I rose from my chair, swung past the old man, grabbed my valise, and plunged out the door. My house was only a few hundred feet away, and I made for it. Once inside, I tried to cool off. It took me a good ten minutes.

I'll give her another shot, I thought. *Then I don't care. Then she can take this job and stuff it. She can sit back and stuff her fat face with taro and breadfruit till hell freezes over. But I won't be here.*

I found Aliatasi standing alone in her office. I asked her if she'd please run off the stencils for me. Please. The answer was predictable: "After school." My reply was mechanical: "Okay." I walked out of her office and told one of my colleagues that I'd not be teaching. He said that he'd cover for me. I then went to my house, took off my lavalava, got into my blue jeans, and walked down the road to the Peace Corps office. Aliatasi saw me go. Entering the Peace Corps office, I went directly to the country director's office. Luckily, Dick Cahoon was there.

"I just got a phone call from your headmistress," he said. "Did you know that you are officially fired?"

"Correction," I said. "I quit."

"Was it that bad?"

"Yes, Dick. It was that bad. I tried my best, but she made teaching there impossible. What do we do now?"

"I don't know. I'll see if another school will pick you up. There're other schools that need volunteers. Lafi Tuitui over at Faleata Junior High comes readily to mind. I will give him a call this afternoon. In the meantime, do your best to placate Mrs. Tauaa."

"No problem," I said.

I was a good soldier and met with Aliatasi the next day. Predictably, the meeting was a chilly one.

"I will gladly give my final exams," I said.

"There will be no need for that, Mr. Christmas. Just leave my school as quickly as you can."

And with that, she left for home in a taxi.

The twig had snapped. It took me five days to tie off my work, pack my belongings, and vacate Viamauga. The next day, Dick Cahoon came through for me.

"I've got good news for you," he said. "Lafi Tuitui has agreed to take you on. Good luck with your new assignment."

"Thanks, Dick. I'll do my best."

Arriving at Faleata with a letter of introduction from the Education Department, I was surprised to learn that everyone called me by name. How could this be? Then one of the Samoan teachers clued me in. Aliatasi had called Lafi and told him about me. A few days later, I asked him what she had said.

"Do you really want to know?" he said.

"If you don't mind telling me."

"Well, she said you were sick in the head."

"Really? Why, then, have you taken me on?"

"Curiosity," he said with a mischievous look in his eyes. "Anyway, I like to evaluate people for myself. Welcome to Faleata Junior High, Gerry. I hope you are happy here."

What a breath of fresh air! Physically, Lafi is massive, even larger than Aliatasi. Furthermore, he views life in a completely different way—with a no-nonsense frankness and honesty that is truly refreshing.

Though still emotionally fragile, I'm coming to grips with my demons. Every man must learn to live with pieces of himself held together by internal guts and external love. Minor miracles follow major disasters. My miracle is this: I'm now living in a ramshackle apartment not far from the hospital with a sixty-six-year-old cowboy named Bill Kirley. Hearing Bill was without a place and having a spare bedroom in the apartment, I asked if he'd like to room with me. He took up my offer without even seeing the place. That's what I call desperation with a capital *D*.

Bill is a remarkable man. As a sixteen-year-old cowboy working as a ranch hand in North Dakota, he was thrown from his horse and broke his neck. He wasn't supposed to live, let alone walk. Defying the odds, he did both but was left with half his body paralyzed. But that did not deter him. Staying as lean as a rail, he learned to walk by thrusting the paralyzed part of his body outward on a cane and then stepping forward with his good leg.

Bill's injury, though horrendous, did have a positive side: it made him into a serious student for the first time in his life. He not only went on to earn a bachelor's degree in special education, but he began to write western fiction as well. He now works at the Western Samoa Association of the Blind, where he teaches braille.

Epistle Seventeen

July 18, 1977

Dear Mom and Dad:

Well, guess what? I've fallen in love. But it isn't the love that can last. Nor is it the love that can damage the way I feel for Dang. It's a love founded on pity and upheld by helplessness. Her end will be tragic. Of that I'm sure. The first night I saw her at the Manuia Club, I was struck so dumb that it took me a good twenty minutes to screw up the courage to ask her for a dance.

There she stood, alone on the dance floor, in that strapless, velvety, hooker-green dress—a dress that accentuated every curve and contour of her exquisite form, from the fullness of her breasts to the tampering V of her waist to the soft sashay of her hips.

"Her name's Samaria Saga," a fellow volunteer said, reading my mind. "And, believe me, you don't want any part of her."

"How come?" I asked.

"Because she's poison. That's why. Anyway, she doesn't like white guys, and she hates Samoan men even more."

"Is she a dyke?"

The volunteer guffawed.

"Hell, no. She's just into Asian men, particularly Japs. You go figure."

Ignoring the warning, I walked onto the dance floor and introduced myself.

"Good evening, Samaria," I said. "May I have this dance?"

She looked at me oddly. I could see that calling her by name had produced the desired effect: there were question marks in those huge, almond-shaped, brown eyes.

"Yes," she said simply.

Placing my right hand on her back, I drew her to me. Her back muscles felt like steel girders wrapped in silk. She danced like an angel—effortlessly, anticipating my every move.

"You dance beautifully," I said.

"I should hope so," she said. "I'm a professional dancer."

"Really?"

"Last year, our troupe toured Japan. We had a wonderful time."

"I bet you were the star of the show."

"How did you know?" she asked innocently.

"Well, to be honest, you're the most gorgeous woman I've ever met."

Her eyes widened.

"Do you know I'm engaged?" she said.

"No, I did not. Had I known, I'd never have asked for a dance."

"Oh, don't worry," she said. "I'm engaged to a Japanese businessman. I'll be going to Japan next year to marry him."

"Congratulations," I said. "I hope you will be very happy."

"Thank you," she said.

After that, I began to meet Samaria every Saturday night at the Manuia Club. We quickly became good friends, and in a matter of weeks, I'd won her trust. Then the big night came. I walked into the club and found Samaria down in the dumps.

"What's the matter?" I asked.

"I received a wire from Japan yesterday," she said. "My boyfriend has had a change of heart. He's decided not to marry me."

For the next two hours, she bared her heart to me. It soon became apparent that here was an adolescent mind encased in a woman's body—and not just any body, either. Samaria was incredibly statuesque and voluptuous, even by Polynesian standards. I'd not lied that night on the dance floor: *she was indeed the most gorgeous woman I'd ever met.*

But Samaria is more than drop-dead gorgeous. She's very intelligent, too. A graduate of the finest girl's school on the island, she speaks English as fluently as she speaks Samoan. But most men never think of her intellect. They're infatuated with her body, with the way she moves, with the sheer femininity she exudes. No wonder she smokes and drinks.

For a month, Samaria has had me in limbo. I've been accepted by her family, especially her older sister Masina. But yesterday, I realized that our friendship was shaky at best. I'm typing this letter not more than fifteen feet from her, and she has no idea how I feel. She seems so complacent, so jaded. What's with her, anyway? Has all the romance been beaten out of her? Damned if I know.

Nonetheless, Samaria still has a chance. But it will have little to do with me. It will have to come from her, from deep down inside. And it will take courage in spades—enough courage to find a new path, to blaze a new trail, to find something to live for. The other night, she mentioned marriage, not to me but to an Australian. I don't think, however, that marriage is the answer right now. Not unless the man is special. And by special, I don't mean a guy with a carton of Marlboros and a case of Vat 69.

Still, I am indebted to Samaria. She has opened the half-caste world of Samoa to me. Indeed, I now understand this world far better than other volunteers. For the half-castes are the elite of this country. Living in close proximity to Apia, they've had better access to the missionary schools. Once in these schools, they were able to assimilated Western thought and Western culture.

Tragically, most half-castes have not been able to use this knowledge. Both Samaria and Masina are prime examples. They openly hate their country. They hate the violence and the pettiness and the corruption. Living in a linear and limited society, they feel hemmed in, trapped. Finally, they know that their biological clocks are ticking. If they're to escape, they'd better do it within the next few years, before their bodies go. For brains do not get a Samoan woman out of this hellhole; looks and natural grace do. The best way for a Samoan woman to escape into the wider world is to marry a white man. Failing this, she has few options outside the confines of Coconut Road.

Think I'm exaggerating? Try these two visions on for size.

Vision one: I'm lying on the floor of Saga fale with Samaria and Masina, not twenty paces from the main house—a pink, concrete fale palagi.

"Why don't you sleep out here at night?" I ask. "Wouldn't it be more natural and better for your health?"

Samaria and Masina look at me in horror.

"No way," Samaria says bluntly.

"Why not?"

"I wouldn't last an hour out here," Samaria says grimly. "I stupidly tried to do it once. I woke up screaming 'Rats! Rats!' But it wasn't rats. It was a man's fingers fondling my *susu*. I was only fourteen years old."

Masina turns and looks at me with her enormous, cobalt eyes. Not blessed with Samaria's superstructure, she's still fetching.

"Sometimes, even the main house is not safe," she says sternly. "I've had men crawl right through my bedroom window to get into bed with me. *Moetotolos*. That's what we call them. Goddamned filthy night crawlers!"

"Aren't there any laws against rape?"

"Not really. Rape is a family affair here. The men of the aiga are expected to protect their women. But some aigas have little or no men. This makes their women vulnerable."

Vision two: Masina, Samaria, and I are walking down the dark road on our way to the Manuia Club. Everyone is happy and upbeat. Suddenly, there's a skid and a thud at the intersection some fifty yards away. We scoot to the scene. It doesn't take us long to figure out what has happened: a drunken Samoan in a pickup has rear-ended the car of two Japanese volunteers. All three men appear to be all right, thank God. But a small group of Samoan men from a nearby village have surrounded both vehicles. One Samoan man utters something indistinct to the Japanese, who are now out of the car. A second Samoan man—a towering figure—doesn't say a word. Instead, he punches the two volunteers in the face. Both go down hard, one with a smashed nose. Samaria and Masina immediately intervene. Samaria is particularly courageous, for she grabs the huge Samoan by the arms and tries to reason with him.

Meanwhile, I keep my distance. The volunteer with the broken nose is bleeding like a stuck pig. I try to get one of the onlookers to hail a taxi in order to take the man to the hospital, but no one will listen to me. Instead, they meander about and fart around. Forced to take matters into my own hands, I run into the street and flag down a pickup truck. Samaria and I throw the poor bastard into the back and then climb in, too. The volunteer is in terrible shape. At first, I question whether he can breathe or not. Luckily, he can. At the hospital, the doctors patch the man up. On the way home, Samaria is incensed.

"While you were getting the truck, not one person tried to help Masina and me," she says.

I turn to Masina. Rarely have I seen such fury.

"Now you know; now you know," she sputters. "Those ... those goddamn Samoans ..."

For a moment, I forget that she is talking about her own people.

Epistle Eighteen

August 8, 1977

Dear Mom and Dad:

The veneer of Samoan culture is very thin. I've scratched through it, and what I've found isn't pretty. Hatred and violence bubble up in myriad places and in multitudinous ways. The warm faces with the soft and open smiles seduce only the wide-eyed tourists and the besotted beachcombers.

The Samoan cuts grass with a bush knife or a machete. Some folks find this quaint and picturesque. With each and every whack, with each and every assault of the great against the small, the sweat pours and gratification is found. For that's the name of the game here: *if it's there, hit it*. Hit it with anything: your hand, your stick, your rock, your bottle, your knife. You're on the right side when you hit. You're on the wrong side if you *are* hit. Paradise isn't a place where you turn the other cheek.

Love is a physical concept in Samoa. The initial meeting is full of banter and banality. And if the right sparks fly, the twosome make for the bush. As a result, the deep searching out of one another's longings and desires is absent. The women marry young and fast, and a baby usually pops out with the passing of each year. The diet is not kind to the body; thus, the fat comes and stays. By the age of forty, many Samoan women are prisoners of their own flesh, often outweighing their husbands. Indeed, there is a Samoan saying that reflects this phenomenon: "For the first twenty years of marriage, the man beats his wife. For the second twenty years, the wife beats her husband."

But it's the beautiful women who break my heart. So many men rush them that they don't have a chance to figure life out. My friend Samaria Saga is a prime example of this.

Samaria is sensitive and warm, kind and beautiful. But deep down inside, something is broken. Right now, she's in the fast lane but doesn't want to be there. She wants to switch lanes and slow down but doesn't know how.

I wish I could save her, but I can't. I'm not strong enough. Samaria needs a man of great strength, someone to love her with all his heart and soul. And that is what hurts me so much. I can see her potential, what she should be. But I can't get her there. I can't get her the things she needs: the home, the devotion, the security, and the love. Sure, I could roll the dice, but I don't have the guts.

Last night, I took Samaria and Masina to dinner at Aggie Grey's. Predictably, a couple of men approached our table without being asked. Knowing the rules, I sat back and watched as Samaria and Masina gave them the bum's rush, Samoan style.

At ten o'clock, some of Samaria's friends came running up to the table. Something "terribly exciting" had happened, and Samaria asked if she could leave. I couldn't have made her stay with a block and tackle. Flashing my widest smile, I leaned back in my chair and told her to scram. Then she came at me—all hair and eyes and mouth and skin. Target? My mouth.

At the last moment, with her lips hovering not two inches from mine, up went my hand to her jaw. The skin felt like fine silk, even better than it looked. But somehow, I didn't want the kiss. Not then. Not that way. I'd be reading things into it that weren't there. A kiss is best given and received on equal terms. And Samaria's and mine, at that point in time, were hardly equitable.

I caught the wry smile on her lips as she whirled and ran away. I could feel at least twenty pair of eyes boring into the back of my skull, and they all said the same thing: *What kind of a nut would refuse a kiss from a piece like that?*

The answer? *I don't know. I don't pretend to be Socrates.*

There's wisdom in knowing you're lucky. You've a set of values down pat, and you won't let anyone mess with them. It makes you believe that good things will happen to you if you only have the patience and the will. Sure, you'll get hurt. But you've got solid stones upon which to rest that bleeding heart. And everyone knows that bleeding hearts heal if left alone. Everyone with solid stones, that is. Poor Samaria will continue to bleed until she reaches down into her heart and pulls out the good stones that lie dormant there. And when she does, all will come right again: the smile, the laugh, the grace, the belief, and, yes, even the love.

There's a bit of Samaria in us all. Not to realize that is dangerous. Our little lives are good or bad depending on the forces within ourselves and the forces of those around us. Moreover, these forces are highly volatile. They've thrown not only individuals but also whole nations into chaos. Therefore, it behooves us to recognize and to cherish our good stones, to make sure that none are misplaced, that none are lost.

My students and I on the playground
of Faleata Junior High (1977)
First Row: Malo Mataia, Ioana, me, Lemisio,
Malo Uale, Simanono, Marie
Second Row: Unidentified students from other classes
Lemisio was part Melanesian, hence
his curly hair and darker skin.
Melanesians were often discriminated
against, but not Lemisio.
His personality, large heart, and intelligence
made him extremely popular.

Epistle Nineteen

August 13, 1977

Dear Mom and Dad:

Death brings life to us all.

She stopped coming to school six weeks back. The headaches were getting bad, and she couldn't study. So she stayed home. I didn't hear anything about her until Wednesday, the day she died.

We had a faculty meeting at the school, and the Samoan teachers decided that the staff and the Form 5 students should go to the girl's aiga to pay our respects. A teacher would give a speech, the students would sing some hymns, and money would pass hands. Money is always passed, be it a time of joy or sorrow. It is the preeminent Samoan gesture.

I didn't have a white shirt at school, so my colleague Lau'ese went to his place and got me this fancy, frilled job with vertical ridges down the front. He also gave me a tie that looked like a licorice noodle a mad dog had gotten hold of.

When we arrived at the girl's house, some of the furniture was in the front yard. The front room had been cleared in order to have space to view the body. I followed the students and staff into the house, first removing my shoes at the door. The room took up the entire front part of the house. Mats had been laid over every inch of the floor. The students took up three-quarters of the room, and the teachers flanked one wall. I was told to sit next to Lafi.

There she was, not ten feet away, lying on a mattress with her body covered with white lace. The lace went up over her mouth, but the nose, eyes, and hair looked very normal, very regular. And yet, there seemed to be hollowness, a deep emptiness about her. The school's wreath—a plastic, pink-and-green affair—stood against the pillow above her head. It went well with the ferns and the flowers, which had been abundantly placed over the lace at her feet. She'd have looked like Sleeping Beauty if it hadn't been for the wads of cotton shoved in her ears.

Her mother knelt beside her. You could tell from her puffy and pink cheeks that she'd been crying for days. The grandmother sat next to the girl's head. She held a fan in her hand, and she slowly moved it up and down to keep the flies away. She had control of herself—the control that comes with the passing of time and the coming of snow to the hair. Below the flowers, at the extreme foot of the mattress, sat three little girls. They had that young, confused look about them. They wore new, white dresses with shiny, white sequins. They seemed more ornamental than human.

The father was off to the other side of the room. I couldn't get a good look at him, but his position seemed to signify something. He was outside our sphere, in a good place to judge our performance. For that's what Samoans demand whenever tragedy strikes: a performance. The grief and the sorrow are an inexplicable blend of banality and bathos. As expected, John—a young teacher known for his laziness, ineptitude, and gift of the gab—spoke for the school.

John's version of John Barrymore was followed by the students' version of Sarah Bernhardt. They did a good job. Samoan children love to sing. Their voices were a welcome opiate, a drug we all needed. As they sang, some of the depression and grief seemed to rise and float away.

I've found their souls at last, I thought.

Then I looked at their faces: seriousness without sadness. Fooled by form again. In the eyes of a few, there was a glimmer of loss, of a candle snuffed out. But only with a few, and only a glimmer.

I turned and looked at Lafi beside me. He was looking at the dead girl, and his gaze was steady and steadfast. A lock of curly hair hung down the middle of his forehead. A slight sweat covered his brow, and his huge shoulders were hunched up at his neck.

I looked at the girl again. *Wouldn't it be nice to will a miracle? Wouldn't it be nice to bring her back, to pull off a resurrection? Stop being delusional, Gerry. Cease being daft.*

The singing stopped, and John started to speak again. Suddenly, the father interrupted him. There was the usual banter about money. Two more *tala* and some choice crap from John placated the old man. All in keeping with the *fa'a Samoa*.

Lafi rose. He walked up to the parents and said something quickly, something from the heart. Then he turned and knelt and kissed the dead girl on the forehead. All sorts of images and visions flooded my mind. I got up without feeling, without thought. I shook hands with the parents. As I turned away, curiosity got the best of me. I went to one knee and kissed the girl. No heat. Like kissing cold stone.

Outside, some students began to laugh and to smile. Not me. Suddenly, I realized I didn't even know her name.

Epistle Twenty

September 22, 1977

Dear Mom and Dad:

The Samaria saga continues to unfold. Three weeks ago, Samaria and I were sitting in the living room of her house, talking. She seemed more at ease than usual, and though the flow of words was inconsequential, the mood set by those words was not. It was about nine o'clock, and the night air wafting through the front and rear doors made everything most pleasant.

Suddenly, a man appeared at the front door. A long, seedy, string-bean fellow, he sported hip-hugging blue jeans, a Day-Glo red T-shirt, and an iridescent-green baseball cap. He strutted across the room and scowled at me. Blue and red tattoos ran up and down both arms. Clearly, he was a sailor who'd been at sea too long.

"You a Yank?" he spat out gruffly in one of those micro-Germanic accents that smacked of Denmark or the Netherlands.

"Yes," I said flatly.

Feigned stupidity is the best way to save a friend's face. And that's exactly what I did now. Samaria started to say something but was stopped when two village girls in extravagant formal gowns swept into the room. A second sailor followed in their wake. This man, unlike his friend, was much more amiable and outgoing.

"Are you here on business?" the second sailor asked.

"No," I said. "I'm just a friend of the family."

That took me out of the equation. I was soon forgotten, and the bargaining began in earnest. The seedy sailor opened the bidding.

"You come with us," he said. "Good time, yes?"

I tried not to look at Samaria, but I could feel the electric current in the air. The pretty girl walked over and sat mutely beside me while her buxom friend did all the talking.

"Where do you want us to go?" she said.

"To the ship," the seedy sailor said. "We go to the big ship."

The buxom girl was unimpressed.

"We like hotels better," she said. "But what's on the ship to drink?"

I could see a medium of exchange was about to be established. How was this business transaction going to turn out? I leaned back on the sofa and watched as the tickertape mouths went on clicking.

"Beer," the seedy sailor said bluntly.

The buxom girl frowned.

"We don't like beer," she said. "We want whiskey."

"That can be arranged. Do you want anything else?"

The answer came as fast as a broker working the Big Board for AT&T.

"Yes, twelve tala."

That was three times the market value, but the two mariners did not bicker. The four quickly left, leaving Samaria and I to clean up the stock exchange. We both knew the script, what we each had to say.

"I don't like men like that," she said, looking away. "They think they can buy those girls, any girls."

I wanted to put my arms about her and hold her tight. I wanted to tell her to forget about it, but that would only freeze the whole episode in her mind.

"They really can't buy them, you know?" she said, biting her lower lip.

There is something magic about that line. It brings back pride and self-esteem while enabling the speaker to look the other person in the eye without fear of being rebuked.

"I know," I said, looking deep into those big, brown, almond eyes. Samaria was clearly hurt, but her gaze remained fixed and tearless.

Her internal plumbing is still strong and tight, I thought. *It might spring a leak later on, but no one will see it.*

For another fifteen minutes, I sat in the living room and listened to her talk. She didn't say anything important, but the mood became more subdued, more settled. I could only hope that after I left, sleep would seize her.

Epistle Twenty-One

September 29, 1977

Dear Mom and Dad:

I received a lovely letter from Dang yesterday. She has graduated from nursing school. But she doesn't seem to have picked up much in the way of common sense: *she still wants to marry me.* In fact, she told me to save my money so we can establish our nest. I've yet to tell her that I plan to fly to Thailand in December. Indeed, I've already reserved my seat. The round-trip fare is one thousand US dollars, but I'll need $1,500 to cover expenses. Could you liquidate my assets and send me the money as soon as possible? If there isn't enough in the bank, I'd appreciate a loan.

Dang wants me to wait till my tour of service is finished here in Samoa, but I disagree. A two-year separation is a long time. Anyway, the tone of her letter seemed to imply that her family's resistance is weakening. Being a "Thai lady" makes it difficult for her to articulate her emotions. That's not in keeping with the role. Of course, she only succeeded in winning over my heart that much more. The depth of her love astounds me. For the first time, a woman has offered me something monumental, something freely given, something that cannot cut or scar me. That's love, I suppose.

My December trip might well end with marriage. But it all depends on Dang and the circumstances with her family. With her father being a monk and her mother relying on her to survive, I can well understand why the family needs a chunk of Dang's income. Economics often trumps love, especially in developing countries.

Dang also enclosed a note of a more mercenary nature. It appears that the cosmetics I gave her made her dark skin even darker (horrors of horrors!). She therefore needs some gunk to make her face "bright and beautiful." Revlon Tawny Bronze was the real culprit. So, Mom, could you do me a big favor and send Dang some face powder (to make her "bright and beautiful" again), two or three white slips size 30 (to keep her happy in the wards), and five plastic change purses (to dole out to her family and friends)?

You can bill me later, much later.

Epistle Twenty-Two

October 5, 1977

Dear Mom and Dad:

A remarkable thing has happened. I've learned the truth about Samaria. You probably don't want to hear about it, but I must get it down before the details get fuzzy.

Samaria, Masina, and I went to the beach last week. Both sisters wore skimpy bikinis. When Samaria unwrapped her lavalava, I was positive her coconuts would roll out. But somehow, the top held. Whoever designed her bikini would've done Frank Lloyd Wright proud.

After a short swim, we sat beneath the palms and drank a bottle of cheap red wine. The wine had a lubricating effect on Samaria's tongue, especially when we started talking about La'ei, their eldest sister, now living in New Zealand. La'ei is their mother's favorite, despite having shamed the family by getting knocked up. Masina and Samaria were then forced to shoulder the family's financial burden while living with the knowledge of their mother's favoritism. I turned to Masina and asked the key question.

"Your mother got pregnant before marriage too, didn't she?"

Masina raised her eyebrows—the nonverbal Samoan affirmative.

"And much more," she said. "Listen, Gerry. I'll tell you something that I haven't told anyone in years. My mother had a lover before my father died, and they continued the affair after his death. She wanted to marry him, but I stopped it. I told her that Samaria and I would leave if she did."

"How old were you?"

"Samaria was eight and I was ten."

"Why did you want to leave? Was he a bad man?"

"No," said Samaria. "I don't think he was bad. He just did something terrible."

Her eyes became vapid and vacant. She seemed to be drifting far, far away—way, way back in time. Still, the words kept coming.

"After my father died, the man slept in our house in my mother's bed. I slept beside them. Masina was in the other bed with our brother. Late one night, it began to rain, and the thunder and lightning woke me up. I could hear him atop my mother, pumping away. She told him to stop. She was afraid that I'd wake up and hear them. But he wouldn't stop. He didn't know how to stop. And then I saw it. *I saw it all.* The lightning lit up the entire room. I began to beat his back with my fists as hard as I could. 'Stop, please stop!' I screamed. 'Leave my mother alone! Leave her alone!' Then I began to cry. I can't remember how long I cried."

Her jaw was now firm and rigid, and there was a hurt-hatred look in her eyes.

"Samaria," I said. "Do you enjoy being in love?"

"No," she said. "The first time was the worst. My boyfriend knew I loved him, and he took advantage of me."

"Is it always that way?"

"Yes, it's always that way."

"Does the touch of a man's hand bother you?"

"What do you mean?"

"When a man holds you, when a man caresses you, do you have a funny feeling? Does your skin begin to crawl and your stomach turn somersaults?"

"Yes, yes, that's exactly how it is." She became excited. "Every time. Every time a man holds me close, I feel that way. How do you know?"

I remained silent for a moment. I couldn't answer her, since I didn't know. She was animated and open, and I wanted her to stay that way for as long as possible.

"Samaria, do you hate men?"

"Yes, I do. I hate them all."

"Do you hate me?"

"No," she said, smiling. "I don't hate you."

I turned to Masina.

"And what about you?" I asked.

"I hate them too. But Samaria and I want to understand men. We know we don't act right with them. Nor do we feel comfortable around them. But we do know how to use them, and that's not good. That's not the proper way to act. We don't want to be this way. But we haven't anyone to talk to. There's never been any man in our family. There's never been anyone to tell us about men. Just our father, and he died a long, long time ago."

"We like talking to you," Samaria said. "We can ask you things we can't ask a Samoan. We can never talk to a Samoan man about these things, can we, Masina?"

"No, that's for sure," said Masina.

"Gerry, what would you do if you were in our place?" asked Samaria.

"You've got to get out," I said. "That's the first thing you must do. But don't expect that to solve your problems. A great amount of damage has been done, so the repair work will not be easy. It will take time and work and love to patch you up. More time and work and love than I can give you. I'm sorry."

I looked squarely at Samaria. Her face was shining like a sun of understanding.

"Don't be sorry," she said gently. "We'll make it. We'll all make it."

I smiled back.

"We might," I said. "We all just might."

Four of my star students at Faleata
Junior High School in 1978
From left to right: Johnny, Malo Uale, Marie, and Joyce
Joyce and Johnny fought for top honors,
with Joyce coming out on top.
The following year, Johnny prevailed.

Epistle Twenty-Three

January 15, 1978

Dear Mom and Dad:

I'm now living on the school compound with a Samoan family. Saolele, my best buddy at school, had an extra room in his house, so he asked me to join his aiga. Returning from Thailand, I knew my living arrangement with Bill Kirley was problematic since he's now married to Ruta, a student from the blind school. Before meeting with Bill, I spent the first night with my good friend Conrad Wesselhoeft. Together, we discussed my predicament.

"Bill's in a real bind," Conrad said seriously. "As you know, it's not easy for him to get around. To my knowledge, he has yet to do any house-hunting. Indeed, I doubt if he will be able to find a new place to live."

"Otherwise, how's he coping?"

"Well, Ruta's blindness complicates matters. As you know, Bill's no youngster and, being partially paralyzed, it's not easy for him to get around. Bill and Ruta are not only in need of new house but are also going through a period of adjustment. I honestly don't see them solving these problems any time soon."

"I thought as much," I said. "Perhaps I'd just better move out. I'll talk to my headmaster and see if there's a place for me to live near the school."

"That'd be damned decent of you, Gerry."

"Not really, Conrad. There're no other options."

The next day, I met with Bill, and we came to an agreement by which he would buy some of my kitchen appliances in exchange for me relocating. Without cheating myself, I gave him a good deal. I could see Bill was hard-pressed to make ends meet, so I went out of my way not to milk him.

I owe Bill a lot. He's taught me a good deal about life, and for that I'm grateful. Their marriage is a noble experiment, since Ruta's only chance to regain her sight lies with Bill taking her back to the United States for surgery. The chances of success are slim, but what a glorious gesture.

Epistle Twenty-Four

February 1, 1978

Dear Mom and Dad:

I'd better bring you up to date with what transpired in Thailand. Truly a kaleidoscope of images. Dang was the same dreamy, ethereal wraith, trapped by her language and her family and her culture. She loves me more than any other woman ever has. Of that, I'm certain. But I saw it wasn't right the first night we were reunited. She asked me to a party at her hospital. All her nurse and doctor friends were there—and she was so proud and happy. Sadly, I wasn't.

Dang couldn't see it. She couldn't see that our chances had diminished, become nearly nonexistent. She couldn't see through the gaiety and the laughter and the pride and the love that it was impossible. I saw it instantaneously. Someone took a picture of us, and the look on my face tells it all—like someone threw a pie in my face. And with it came the brutal realization that she loved me more than I loved her.

I love her more like a sister, I thought. *But how can I tell her that? How can I tell her without breaking the wings of a bird and having it crash to the ground?*

I finally told her a few days later, but she wouldn't accept it. I told her again and again without result. I even made an appointment to meet her at her house. The vultures were there to meet me. Her father and two fellow monks sat in the front room to begin the negotiations. I said hello and walked by them. As religious men, they have no place in family affairs. I wasn't impolite. I was only being correct.

I tried to speak with Dang's mother, but she wouldn't talk to me. So I took Dang upstairs and talked to her alone.

"Gerry," she said. "Please wait for me."

"No," I said. "I can't wait anymore."

"Just a year," she said. "My father said I could marry you next year if you allowed me to return to Thailand every year to help the family."

"Those are impossible conditions," I said. "I can't make promises that I cannot keep."

I took her by the hands.

"Dang," I said gently. "You love me more than I love you."

Her head went down and she began to cry.

"I know," she said.

We saw each other a few more times. I knew her family was not going to yield, so I did everything in my power not to see her. But Dang's father wouldn't keep his mouth shut and openly criticized me. As a result, Dang turned on him.

"Try to forgive him," I said.

"I can't," she said. "I love my mother more than my father. He drank too much and had seven *mia nois*. My mother and I had to throw him out of the house. That's when he became a monk. He doesn't care about my future. He doesn't want me to be happy."

Dang saw me off at the airport. She tried to kiss me goodbye, but I didn't let her. I'll never know if that was the correct thing to do or not.

While this drama with Dang was unfolding, another drama was taking place. Realizing Dang and I were toast, I considered myself free. Another emotion, a long-buried one, quickly came to the fore. This had to do with Aied, the woman whose karma never seemed to match with my karma.

Gerry Christmas

As you know, I fell in love with the Aied the first time I laid eyes on her. But for years, ours was a star-crossed affair, an off-again, on-again relationship. Now, suddenly, I felt a need to see her again, to find out if a spark was still there. Arriving at her mother's house and seeing her standing in the doorway, I suddenly went all mushy and soft inside.

Wow, I thought. *Everything she does and says, even when she's wrong, makes me happy.*

But throughout the years, we've had little chance. What with her working upcountry, what with her father's politics and her mother's poverty, what with my friends saying she's too saucy and sexy for me and that it would never work out, we've had our work cut out for ourselves. All those barriers, all those obstacles, seemed to fall away the moment I saw her again, the instant I looked into those eyes and she looked into mine.

By nature, Aied is suspicious of men. Nonetheless, she cares for me. That much I know. We went out together a number of times with her sister or one of her friends.

One night, however, we went out to dinner alone. First we ate dinner at a restaurant in Siam Square; then we went to a nightclub that was pitch-black and incredibly cold. There, we laughed and shivered together.

Next, Aied and I, along with her brother and sister, attended a New Year's party till four in the morning. We had a great time dancing for a good three hours.

And then came the crisis that prompted me to send for the money. It wasn't easy, but I discovered Aied's teeth were giving her trouble. She'd been taking painkillers because she couldn't afford a dentist. Most of her money was going to her mother; thus, she had nothing left. I finally talked her into letting me pay for her teeth.

But all those things didn't tell me how she felt about me. Something else did. I was over at her house waiting for her to come home from work. I'd gone to the outhouse and was stepping back through the back door when I saw Aied standing alone at the kitchen table. She was dressed in her light-blue uniform and was reading a Christmas card. The card had come late, and it was from someone in Samoa.

There was pride in her eyes. There was pride in the way she stood, neat and erect like a soldier at attention. And that pride came to me and made me proud too. At that moment, I had a glimpse into her heart. At that moment, I sensed that her feelings for me were deeper and truer than I'd ever hoped or dreamed. At that moment, I thought of how wonderful it would be to have her with me forever and ever and ever ...

Aied outside a Buddhist temple in Bangkok, Thailand (1979)
Unlike most young Thai women, Aied bobbed her hair.

Epistle Twenty-Five

March 5, 1978

My dear Aied:

This is the most difficult letter of my life. Everything has to be clear. Everything has to be right. You have to understand me completely. There are many things I must tell you, and you must see them as my eyes see them. Only then can your decision be right. Only then will you do the best for yourself and your family.

I love you, Aied. I've told you that many times, and I've written it in many letters. But you've never really believed me. For a long time, I didn't know why. Now I understand: *you don't trust men.* I believe you love me as I love you. I believe that with all my heart. But you're afraid that my love will be transitory, short-lived. You're afraid that when your beauty fades, when your youth goes, I'll cease to love you. But that's not true. True love is a pure thing. Youth, years, time, do not alter it. It is everlasting.

And yet, how are you to be sure? How are you to know that I'm not lying to you as other men have lied to you? Just let me say this: I see much of your mother in you, Aied. Sure, you're different in many ways. But her goodness and her deep and silent feelings are alive in you, her daughter. If all men loved women for only a short time, why do I see such inner beauty and strength in your mother? What will stop me from seeing the same wonderful things within you as we grow old together?

The real truth is that some men love one woman all their lives. Some men want more out of marriage than beauty and sex. Some men want to grow old with their wives. Some men accept age and what age does to the body. They see beyond the physical and their love gets stronger and richer, not weaker and poorer. I'm one of these men. You've made me one of these men. I can see you and I growing old and loving one another more and more and more.

Life wasn't made to be easy. There's a constant battle against danger and death, of pitting happiness against hardship. United by love, a man and a woman can face anything. That's not a belief but a fact. When a man needs help, he can look to his woman for sympathy and understanding. And when a woman needs help, she can look to her man for strength and security. Together, they fight the twin devils of life: loneliness and death. And if true to one another, they can be victorious.

I want you to be my wife, Aied. That's right. I want you to marry me. Saying "I love you" isn't enough anymore. Any man can tell a woman he loves her. That's simply a personal feeling. It might be a high and fine feeling, but it lacks courage. And love, like anything else, is weak without courage.

You must realize that my love for you is deeper than that of other men. You must realize that I'll go any place, pay any price, and face any obstacle to be your husband. I'm not afraid of barriers. I'm not afraid of the language barrier, the culture barrier, the religious barrier, or the family barrier. Only you can stop me. Only you can say that you don't love me and that you don't want to marry me. Should you express such a sentiment, then, okay, I'll spend the rest of my life *dreaming* of you instead of *living* with you.

But I don't believe you'll say no. I've looked deep in your eyes, and I've seen the love burning there. One thing bothers me, however. You state: "We're from different worlds." And, yet, is that true? Did I live in Thailand for three years without learning to love and respect your people and their beliefs? Of course not. Whenever a person lives in another culture, he adopts certain ideas and manners that he never had before.

When I returned to the United States, for instance, my father turned to me and said, "Gerry, you're now more Thai than American." That cut me to the quick, frightened the bejesus out of me. Had the Peace Corps altered my identity? Had it turned me against my native land? Mulling this over, I realized, yes, I'd changed. Sure, I was still an American, but now I'd acquired a second culture, one that made me a better man. Thai culture, my Thai friends, and especially you opened my heart and broadened my mind. I now try to embrace all people. I try to understand not just their cultural differences but their hopes and dreams as well. That's the ultimate beauty of the world, Aied: wherever one goes, whatever culture one enters, the hopes and dreams of *sane* men and women everywhere are the same.

I've no desire to change you. You must believe that. You and I are the products of our distinct genetic mix and our cultural and educational pasts. I don't want to sever you from your language, your culture, or your religion—for then you would no longer be you, the woman I love.

There's no reason why we can't keep your language, your culture, and your religion in our home, wherever that home may be. Of course, I'd like to speak better Thai and have our children speak it too. That would make you the teacher and me the student, an interesting switch. The same is true of your culture. Our home could be a mixture of Thai and American, and we could celebrate the holidays of both. More excuse for fun! As for religion, I believe that children should be brought up in the faith of the mother. This makes for a happy home.

Buddhism, being one of the world's great religions, has many similarities with Christianity; thus, I'd gladly go to a Buddhist temple with you and the children.

I know you don't want to leave Thailand. Were I Thai, you wouldn't have to. But, my dear, you must understand that most *farangs* have no long-term future there. After leaving Samoa, I hope to become a foreign-service officer. I love Asia and want to spend my life working in Asian countries.

As a foreign-service officer, I might be sent to Thailand. That would enable you to see your family regularly. I cannot promise you anything at the present time, however. I can only promise to reunite you and your family whenever possible. This is especially true with your mother. I cannot forget the woman who gave birth to you. Without her, I wouldn't have you to love.

The same can be said for your father. A father has different worries and concerns about his daughter than he has about his sons. A father wants his daughter to marry a man who will properly take care of her. This is natural, since the father has spent years raising her and he doesn't want some idiot breaking her heart. Therefore, before we marry, I must have a long man-to-man talk with your father. He must know that I'm willing to shoulder any responsibility to ensure your happiness and security. I know that your father has a special place in his heart for you, Aied. What he doesn't know is that you *own* all of mine. Once he does, once he sees how much I've thought and planned for you and your future, he'll accept me. Of this, I'm sure.

So much for your parents; now's the time to talk about mine. You must have all kinds of pictures in your mind of what they look like and how they act. Let's take my mother first.

Marcelle Antoinette Christmas is short and plump. She has gray hair, sparkling, sky-blue eyes, and a warm and generous smile. She likes to cook and sew and read. Everyone—and I mean everyone—loves her. She was very poor when my father married her. But he didn't care. He was looking for a good wife and mother and found one in her.

My father, William Richard Christmas, is tall and thin. He's also extremely intelligent and deep, a true intellectual. When he became engaged to my mother, his friends were concerned. Sure, they liked my mother, but there were obvious differences. My father was Protestant, whereas my mother was Catholic. My father was English-Canadian, whereas my mother was French-Canadian. My father had a college degree in mathematics from McGill, whereas my mother only had an eighth-grade education. "Too different," his friends said. "The marriage would never work." My father thought otherwise. He followed his heart, and he's never been sorry.

My parents' marriage hasn't been perfect. Nothing in life is. But it has been good. It's made my father a better man and my mother a better woman. Love was the building block of their partnership, with commitment being the cement. Some forty years later, their marriage still stands.

My parents would be elated if you were to marry me. They know my mind, and they trust my judgment. So don't fret about them. They'll see the same wonderful traits in you that I do. And, never having a daughter, they'll love you completely and unconditionally.

I'm willing to wait for you, Aied. We face many problems. But we can solve them if we have faith in one another. I don't expect you to trust me. Not yet. You've been hurt too many times. But give me a chance. Give me a chance to solve our problems—a chance to prove myself to you, a chance to be worthy of your heart and your love. That's all I ask.

"My body has many diseases," you once said. Your eyes seemed to say that I should hate you because you have health problems. Don't you know that your weaknesses make me love you more? Indeed, if you had both eyes poked out, if you had both arms chopped off and your legs were on backwards, I'd still want to marry you. Tell me what's wrong with you, but don't expect me to stop loving you.

Aied, please understand this: *I love your spirit, not your body.* When a man thinks of love in a physical way, he misses all that's good and dear in life. He stops being a man and acts like a boy. Well, I've more important things to do with my life. My boyhood is finished, and I know what I want: a loving wife and family, interesting work, and religious faith. The last two I have; the first depends on you.

Dick and Marcelle Christmas shortly after
moving to Scottsdale, Arizona
Mom's breast cancer was in remission at this time.
Sadly, it would resurface and take her life.

Epistle Twenty-Six

March 20, 1978

Dear Mom and Dad:

The news of the surgery to remove Dad's prostate came as a shock. Of course, I could bitch about not having been informed earlier, but that would be disingenuous and belittling what was assuredly a sterling example of "grace under pressure." Bill was particularly reassuring over the phone. Furthermore, his letter was a fine act of thoughtfulness. What a blessing to have a doctor for a brother!

I'm sorry I couldn't talk with the convalescent over the phone. Sometimes, however, it is best to let "sleeping dogs lie." Anyway, mothers have the right to gab with their sons clandestinely once in a while. It's all part of the birth pact.

I'm staring at a measly eight more months. Then the marathon run as a PCV is over. Two friends want me to go with them to the States: the first on the Jules Verne express through Asia and Europe, and the second on the Joseph Conrad freighter through the islands and Southeast Asia. I'll probably say no to both. Time, money, and energy are on the ebb, and I'd like to get home for Christmas and the wassail bowl. Prostate or no prostate, I can count on Dad to mix up one mean, ritualistic concoction of Myers rum and miscellaneous fruit.

Moreover, it's time to reorder my life. My emotional entanglements in Thailand need sorting out, and that can't be done if I'm bouncing around the globe. My immediate problem is Aied. Reason and common sense tell me that I'm wasting my time with her. But damn it, I love her. I knew that the moment she came down the stairs of her house to meet me during the Christmas holidays. By some weird quirk of fate, I'd my glasses off and all I saw was this tiny, erect blur across the room. Still, I knew it was Aied. I fumbled at my glasses, but by the time I had them in place, she'd skirted away.

Aied wasn't gone for long. Reentering the room, she came over and sat down next to me. As expected, her raw beauty—a fascinating mix of the exotic and the sexy—captivated me completely. But even more captivating is her deep, rich, seductive voice that's both bewitching and beguiling.

Aied doesn't have a clue what her voice does to a man. Indeed, it's a bit of a curse since, coupled with her beauty, it can be spellbinding, so spellbinding that the meaning of her words is often lost to the modulation of sound. This is a shame, for her mind is sharp and insightful, full of ideas worthy of thought and consideration. I honestly think this is the reason Aied finds most men boring.

Back in Samoa, I decided to seize the water buffalo by the horns and wrote Aied a letter in which I poured out my heart. I told her everything: my hopes, my fears, my feelings, my plans, and, most importantly, my belief that I could make her happy. The letter took me two hours to write. But anything less would have left her with an incomplete picture.

Aied's a complicated number. She'll do some thinking before she answers me. I expect a polite no, not because I believe she doesn't love me. Beneath those layered Siamese emotions, I honestly think she does. But she is extremely loyal to her mother, and her mother needs her now. And therein lies the great unknown. If her mother believes me, if her mother trusts me, if her mother senses Aied's true feelings, I may be in for surprise. But it's one in a thousand. All I can do now is go about my business and hope for the best. At thirty-four, I've learned that the earth turns at its own speed.

Three excellent Samoan students on the playground
during "morning tea" (1978)
From left to right: Maulalo, Ie, and Lauese

Epistle Twenty-Seven

April 1, 1978

Dear Mom and Dad,

It's been a coon's age since I've written about Samoa, so here are some snapshots to bring you up-to-date.

Snapshot one: Hita is crying right in front of me in the classroom. It takes me a long time to find out why: one of the Samoan teachers has beaten her butt black and blue because she wasn't wearing her uniform correctly. Oddly, that teacher rarely hits boys.

Snapshot two: last week, I went to a *real* Chinese restaurant that served *real* Chinese food. Of course, one of my friends tried to skip out without paying. I surreptitiously slipped the money to the owner. A PCV must cover another PCV's ass, even an ugly PCV's ass.

Snapshot three: recently, a Cessna crashed into a mountain, killing the pilot and all nine passengers. The following day, a rescue helicopter crashed too. Thankfully, the two men in the helicopter survived.

Snapshot three: the other day, I met a wizened, old matai. We really knocked it off. He even wanted to share his title with me. The sauce had clearly loosened his tongue and heightened his generosity. Whether he was drunk or sober, it was still a nice gesture.

Snapshot four: Saolele is now a matai. He didn't seek the title, since he didn't want the added responsibility. But Samoan culture trumps the wants and desires of the individual.

Snapshot five: I made spaghetti for the entire aiga. I worked my butt off; hence, the end product met my high standards.

But only Saolele and I liked it. The others politely spun the spaghetti strands in their plates hoping that an *ietu* would transform it into Franco-American.

Snapshot six: when Bill Kirley married his pretty primitive, PCV Shelby Henderson didn't like it. Senior women volunteers don't smile on old bulls mounting young heifers. Now Shelby is marrying a Samoan buck fifteen years her junior. As Dad always says, "The big *H* stands for hypocrisy, not heroin."

Snapshot seven: while visiting the home of some friends at St. Joseph College, I ran into PCV Terry Berry. His face, normally handsome and animated, was not dissimilar to a pizza plastered on the puss of Boris Karloff. Asked what the hell had happened to him, Terry said blithely, "I crashed my motorcycle." I should've known. Motorcycle accidents kill more PCVs than cobras, crocodiles, scorpions, centipedes, and sharks combined.

Snapshot eight: last week, I blithely strolled into the Peace Corps office to get my mail. The PC nurse—yes, the same sweetie who asked me to buy her a ring in Thailand—said, "Nice shirt, Gerry. Why don't you give it to me?" I would've laughed in her face if she hadn't been dead serious.

Snapshot nine: my students are beginning to return books for more books—contrary to all laws of the fa'a Samoa, but in keeping with Christmas's Law of Universal Greed and Personal Betterment.

Snapshot ten: while walking down Beach Road on the way to Nelson Library, I spot a lambent-eyed, soft-smiling Samoan lovely blessed with Coppertone skin and a spectacular superstructure. She smiles broadly and gives me not one but two come-hither looks. My blood begins to boil, but I keep on moving. I'm no loser, but I know my physical limits.

Epistle Twenty-Eight

May 27, 1978

Dear Mom and Dad:

I've a remarkable tale to tell, a tale that begins in Thailand and ends in Samoa. Two years ago in Bangkok, some friends and I went to a soul-food restaurant owned and operated by two Vietnam War vets who'd opted not to return home. One of the owners came over to our table for a chat and was intrigued by my surname.

"I've only heard that handle one other time," he said. "I was out West, passing through Phoenix or Albuquerque or some such Southwest city. I happened to be there when General Christmas died, alone and penniless, in a cheap hotel room. A reporter dug into his past and unearthed some intriguing stuff. General Christmas had been a soldier of fortune in two or three banana republics. I don't remember exactly which ones. Anyway, there was a huge spread about him in the newspaper, and it made quite a stir. You're not related, are you?"

"No," I said. "I don't think so." And the matter died there.

Last week, I attended an in-service Peace Corps workshop at Samoa College. After one of the lectures, Al Fagot, one of the senior volunteers, came up to me.

"Gerry," he said. "You're not related to anyone in Nicaragua, are you?"

My mouth fell open and my eyes bugged out like a gigged frog.

"Somebody in Thailand asked me the same thing," I said. "This is getting weird, really strange."

"How about having lunch with me?" said Al. "I would like to get to the bottom of this."

"I'd love to," I said.

Al was devouring a hamburger when I met up with him in the college cafeteria. He didn't waste any time.

"My family's from Virginia, but they moved to Nicaragua after the Civil War," he said. "I spent most of my youth there. General Christmas was a close friend of the family. Known for his fearlessness, he used to walk around our house carrying a whip and sporting two pearl-handled pistols. Christmas was a confederate of General Sandino, the famous Nicaraguan revolutionary. Sandino fomented two unsuccessful coups against the corrupt government of General Somoza, one in 1924 and the other in 1928. Somoza was a real bastard. Propped up and protected by United Fruit Company, he was a true enemy of the people.

"Christmas and Sandino fought like hell against him. Christmas was some man. He not only stole machine guns and Springfield rifles from the US Marines but also had a pilot friend named Ludwig pitch mock dogfights in order to arouse local support for the cause. I last saw Christmas after the collapse of the 1928 uprising. The government troops were hot after him. But he managed to escape in a dugout canoe. I can still see the poor bugger paddling to beat hell as the bullets whizzed about his head."

"I'm not sure if I'm related to him or not," I said. "According to my father, the family split into two branches, the first settling in Canada and the second settling in Virginia and North Carolina. I belong to the Canadian branch. A few years ago, something odd happened to me while visiting my cousin Venice in Montreal. She and her French-Canadian boyfriend took me to the racetrack. Bill Christmas, a horse owner from North Carolina, had entered one of his horses into a race. I sent word to Mr. Christmas asking for a chat. He sent a note back stating that he didn't have relatives in Montreal. Later, in the press box, we met over hors d'oeuvres. We were thunderstruck at the similarity in our faces. Indeed, our noses were exactly alike."

Al guffawed.

"You know," he said. "That's what made me ask you about General Christmas. He had the same bulbous nose you have. It must be a family trait."

We talked some more, but the years had clouded Al's memory. For instance, Al could not recall General Christmas's first name.[1] I volunteered the name Bill, as that seems to be the predominant male name in the family.

"That rings a bell," said Al. "But I'm not sure. Anyway, there's one way to find out. I'll write a letter to my aunt. She still lives in Nicaragua, and I'm sure she'll know. Nicaraguans haven't forgotten Christmas and Sandino, you know? They're national heroes."

Late that afternoon, I went to the library. I wasn't very sanguine about my prospects. The Nelson Memorial Library is a far cry from the Library of Congress. It's more like a howl. Furthermore, not many folks out here know about Central America, let alone are interested in it. Still, I decided to give the modest place a try. The librarians were very kind. They roamed and rummaged like a pack of moles. We didn't get anything on General Christmas. But Al's information about General

---

[1] This would turn out to be General Lee Christmas, the color-blind railroad engineer from Louisiana who, after being fired due to his handicap, moved to Central America, where he became a revolutionary in Costa Rica and Nicaragua.

Sandino proved to be accurate. His full name was Augusto Cesar Sandino, and he did lead revolutions in 1924 and 1928. One of the books called it "the Somoza Period." And it would seem that Sandino never gave up in his attempt to liberate his country. He was eventually assassinated.

I cannot extract any more details from this end. I'd like to get the full story on General Christmas, to understand exactly what his actions and motives were. Fate seems to have intervened twice; thus, I feel compelled to dig deeper.

I not only want to flesh out General Christmas's life but also find out where he's planted. If, as Al suspects, he's related to us, we should at least honor the memory of the man. By this, I do not mean to transfer his remains to our family crypt. Our family is too far-flung for that. I only want to see that he's not forgotten. General Christmas appears to be a minor historical figure. And Nicaraguans, not to mention Central American historians, would probably like to know where he's buried.

But for now, I'll leave that up to you. I'm going to send a copy of this letter to brother Bill. Hopefully, he will unearth something regarding this intriguing soldier of fortune. Just remember: follow the Christmas nose!

Oliana with her male classmates at Faleata Junior High (1978)
From left to right: Ioane, Uarota, Lei, Oliana,
Lami, Johnny, Iosefa Kalone

Epistle Twenty-Nine

May 28, 1978

Dear Mrs. Stevens,

I'd like to thank you for offering to send books to my students here in Western Samoa. When I wrote Harriet Van Meter, the illustrious head of the International Book Project (IBP), I'd no idea that she had a network of industrious volunteers throughout the United States. Judging from the tone of your letter, I suspect you are not only a personal friend but also one of Harriet's fiercest allies. I'm therefore honored that you've chosen to assist me.

In the next couple of weeks, you should receive a bunch of letters from my students. I thought you'd like to know my kids personally, so I'm having five of them write you. Don't blame them if they all ask you for books. That was part of the assignment.

My recent trip to Thailand was wonderful but sad. I saw many old friends and further confirmed my conviction to return one day on a permanent basis. I love the United States but seem to work best in Asia; hence, I'm going to apply for the foreign service next year. My chances are not very good. I don't know anyone with pull at the State Department. And that's really how most people secure appointments. Equal opportunity, you know.

As a PCV in Thailand, I fell in love. That's what bothers me now. I'm going crazy trying to devise a scheme to convince Aied to marry me. In her heart of hearts, she loves me but has had a difficult youth and doesn't trust men. Her father left her mother for a younger woman. This is a common occurrence in

Thailand since the laws there make divorce easy with little or no protection for the woman. When a Thai man wants to leave his wife, for instance, he simply packs up and goes. He often sets up house with another woman called a mia noi. Usually, the mia noi is young, pretty, and poor. She normally cohabits for the sake of security, not love.

When I first met Aied, she told me that her father had left her mother. That was four years ago. I tried not to fall for her. But, as you know, the harder one tries, the faster the process is accelerated. Unfortunately, I lost contact with Aied for a year and a half. During that time, she'd left Bangkok to work at an undisclosed place in the rural Northeast. Not until I was about to leave Thailand did we establish contact again.

Returning to Thailand, I found Aied's household a mess. Her father's mia noi had proven to be a handful. He had therefore jettisoned her in favor of another woman. Aied's mother, now in her fifties, seemed old and haggard. And well she should. Having borne seven children in borderline poverty—two children by hubby number one and five children by hubby number two—she was no longer interested in sex. To make matters worse, her oldest daughter had married a slug and now had a child.

"My older sister, Aew, will divorce her husband soon," Aied said. "I'm sure of that."

"Really," I said. "Is it that bad?"

"Yes, it's that bad. Her husband is a terrible man. He never spends any time with Aew and the baby. All he ever does is party with his friends."

"But what about the child? There're no daycare centers in Thailand. How does Aew expect to live?"

Aied raised her eyebrows.

"There's only one way," she said. "My mother's going to take the baby in. Then Aew can go to work. She plans to open a travel agency in Pattaya. I think she'll be good at it. She speaks good English, and everyone says she's the smartest and most beautiful girl in the family."

"I don't agree," I said.

Aied's face went dark.

"Don't *baak wan* me," she said. "I'm not that stupid."

"I'm not saying you are," I said. "But not all men are like your brother-in-law. I don't look upon you as a commodity, as something to buy. Yes, you're young and beautiful, but you're not a new car, something to exchange for a new model once you get old and creaky. Love, like wine, can get deeper and finer with age."

"All of that sounds nice," she said. "But how can I be sure of you? How can I trust you when I see how my mother and my sister have been hurt?"

"I don't have an answer for that," I said.

My problem with Aied doesn't end there. I'm also having trouble with her beauty. Aied is a strikingly beautiful woman, the kind of woman that drives men crazy and makes other women resentful. But her looks belie her true nature, which is incredibly innocent and forthright. This contradiction between her outward appearance and her inward soul is what appeals to me. It's not so much what she is; it's what she can become. I can't imagine ever getting to the bottom of her. And I've told her that.

Beauty in Thailand is different than beauty in the United States. In the States, beauty takes on many forms, and age often enriches our concept and appreciation. Not so in Thailand. Beauty here is confined to youth. It's more physical and transitory.

This is what Aied finds confusing. She wants the long-term concept but has been reared in a culture where the short-term concept is pervasive. Whenever I tell her how I feel, she feels conflicted. She doesn't know whether to believe me or not. She wants to. She wants to with all her heart. But her experience has shown that, with few exceptions, men are liars. Once, right in the middle of a conversation with me, she said, "Can I believe you?" There was so much hope in the way she asked that question. Her eyes were burning into mine—looking, searching, trying to fasten onto something nice for a change. It almost broke my heart.

Then, as in other moments, I felt that I could never love another woman, not ever. That sounds overly romantic. But I'm thirty-four now, and my glands aren't the enemies they once were. My spirit, not my body, needs a companion. And in Aied, my spirit has found its companion, whether I'm near or far away.

But all is not hopeless. Aied's younger sister, Add, believes me and wants Aied to marry me. Indeed, had I fallen in love with Add, I wouldn't have had so much trouble. But we all like challenges. The Almighty has so rigged our natures and our lives that we respond to little else. As a result, I can do nothing but be the steady drop on the implacable stone. It's rather fun. One never knows: the crack may appear at any time.

I hope you and your husband are well. The world needs kind hearts like yours to ease the pain. Please forgive me for babbling about my personal problems. But it does me good to vent. It clears the cobwebs so I can view the room of life in all its majesty and glory.

Someday, I'd like to meet you. Perhaps Aied will be at my side.

Margi Stevens's pen pals at Faleata High School (1978)
Left to right: Saisarita, Rosita, Simanono, Ioana, and Janet

Epistle Thirty

June 23, 1978

Dear Mom and Dad:

I've fallen in love with Samoa. Like most love affairs, I can pinpoint the exact moment it happened. I was walking beside the harbor on Beach Road on the way to the Nelson Library when suddenly, in mid-stride, I just clicked in. Gazing out at the ocean with the breeze in my face and the heat of the sun on my back, I suddenly realized what a wonderful place Samoa is. "Ah," I said to myself. "This is, indeed, paradise."

I'm enjoying my work too. My Form 4 class, the one I teach five hours a day, is especially good. Lafi has given me the smartest kids, so I'm shoveling the information into them like a stoker on a high-baller train. While in Thailand, I bought some simplified readers for my Samoan students. The little devils treat the books like toilet paper. Nonetheless, they are now reading on a regular basis. So who am I to complain? Sure, their book reports are primitive and choppy, but that's to be expected. No one learns how to husk coconuts with a machete on his first try.

I've also started a letter-writing project with the class. Instead of sending a personal thank-you note to Harriet Van Meter, the founder of the International Book Project (IBP) in Lexington, Kentucky, I'm having my students send letters to Harriet's volunteers scattered throughout the United States.

Five of my students are sending letters directly to Margi Stevens, the wife of the famous puppeteer Steve Stevens. Below is a copy of a letter to Margi that will help you to understand my Samoan students. Margi Stevens is one of Harriet Van

Meter's most active book donors. I'm truly blessed that she has shown an interest in the students at Faleata.

Dear Margi,

I'm sorry I haven't written sooner. Rather than write a personal thank-you note, I thought you would like to hear from my class directly. Your first shipment of books benefited the school immensely. However, my headmaster and dear friend, Lafi Tuitui, has decided to keep the books in his office since they are about the only ones we have. Some of my kids wanted to write to you, so I turned that request into a classroom writing assignment.

You will therefore be receiving five letters from Rosita Paterika, Simanono Oge, Saiairita Ropati, Janet Betham, and Ioana Fonoti. Below, you will find a short biographical sketch of each student.

Rosita Paterika

Rosita is a village girl. She has huge, round eyes and a fleshy face. She's very talkative in class. Indeed, I have to tell her to "clam up" a lot. But Rosita is a good girl. Her sense of humor bubbles about the room, and her personality makes her popular with the other students. Coming from the village, Rosita has strong family ties and loves Samoa; hence, I doubt if she will ever study abroad. I've never met her parents but suspect that they are good people since Rosita is such a happy and well-adjusted child.

If you could send Rosita a short letter, she'd get a bang out of it. She's never received a thing from the "outside world."

Simanono Oge

I'm a lucky man. Reading these letters from my students makes me realize that I've one of the best jobs in the world. This is my fifth year as a Peace Corps volunteer. I spent three delightful years in Thailand before I came here. Thailand and Western Samoa are dissimilar. They do have this in common: damn nice people.

Simanono is a case in point. Her sense of right and wrong runs deep and true. I can always rely on her honesty and common sense in any class dispute. She wouldn't say so in her letter, but last year, she was the top student in Form 3, which numbers more than a hundred students. Simanono is a tall girl, even for a Samoan. She's rock-solid intellectually, emotionally, and religiously.

Saisirita Ropati

Saisirita? Perhaps I should use two question marks. Or perhaps three exclamation points are more to the mark. Saisirita is the tiniest kid in the room. But her cranial capacity more than compensates for her diminutive size. Spotting the other students a good year, she's still one of my brightest kids. Her big, brown eyes are incredibly alive and inquisitive. I really enjoy teaching her.

As you can see, Saisirita's first sentence reads: "With great respect, I hereby submit my letter to you." You'll never know how proud Saisirita was of that opening line. I told her that it sounded like it was from a lawyer. But even that did not dissuade her. It's the way she feels, and I can't go against that, even for the sake of style!

Janet Betham

Janet Betham is the funniest girl the class. Her dancing eyes and light banter make for great fun––at times too much fun. I keep Janet on a short rope with a tight knot. But it would be running contrary to the evolutionary process to subdue her at all times. Her mind is extremely active and enquiring. She should become a delightful woman once the pimples have run their course. I should know. I've been there myself.

<u>Ioana Fonoti</u>

Ioana has a soft, seductive, beseeching look that can melt rocks. She came to me the other day and asked to write to you. Having four of my kids already on your back, I wanted to say no. But I couldn't. Big-eyed, big-boned, big-hearted Ioana is not the type of student a teacher says no to.

Judging from your letters, you seem to be an indulgent soul. I'm therefore taking advantage of your good graces. I hope you don't mind. Perhaps it would be easier if you replied to the children as a group—with one letter. They wouldn't mind, and it would save precious time. I've already warned them that they might not receive any reply at all.

The students understood me, but Samoan kids, like children everywhere, are deaf and dumb to pessimism. Saisirita, for instance, came to me personally to ask if I'd mailed the letters to you. Until that moment, I didn't know how important her letter had become.

I never expected that this assignment would generate such an interest, would motivate the students in such a positive way. A commonly held myth is that Samoans, being so isolated, don't care about the outside world. I guess we can scratch that silly notion off the list. Instead, we now can say that Samoans' relaxed manner belies a deep intelligence, a strong inquisitive streak.

Finally, I have a confession to make. Sensing I was doing a lousy job, that I was not giving my students the education they deserved, I turned to you and Harriet out of sheer panic. You probably surmised as much. Children, especially Samoan children, don't possess the greed cynics would have us believe. Greed is an acquired, not an innate, trait. In this case, however, I feel justified. It drives me nuts seeing my students going home without books. "What could they do with the proper tools, with the right books to improve their minds?" was the question that haunted me.

But my students need more than books. They need a voice from across the seas. For five of my girls, Margi, I hope you become that voice.

Not for me.

Not for you.

But for them, my friend.

Epistle Thirty-One

June 23, 1978

Dear Mom and Dad:

My little experiment with the International Book Project is yielding huge educational and personal benefits. Margi Stevens has already replied to five of my girls, and you should have seen the response: their faces lit up like pinball machines.

Margi also wrote a personal note to me suggesting I have my class write to Teensville, a pen-pal organization in New Hampshire. We did that two weeks ago.

Margi then sent copies of the girls' letters to Harriet Van Meter, the founder of IBP. Last week, I received a letter from Harriet asking for pictures of the girls. Harriet was so impressed with the girls' letters that she wants to write an article and circulate it nationally in the IBP bulletin. A friend is coming over to Faleata next week to take the shots.

Though the missives are fun, I'm getting my jollies in another department: history. Toward the end of last term, I discovered that my students knew little or nothing of the outside world. How had I missed this? What had made me so delusional? Well, I'd been suffering under the misconception that they were getting basic history in their social studies class. What a loony assumption that was! Then Margi Stevens sent me some beat-up *Golden Book Encyclopedias,* and a germ of an idea began to take shape. What if I combined reading comprehension with the study of ancient civilizations? Most of the articles on the early civilizations came to a single page when I stenciled them. Moreover, they were clear and concise;

hence I didn't have to simplify the English. Only one question remained: Would the lessons work?

I wasn't so sure after the first one, the one on Ancient Egypt. Sure, the students liked the part about the mummies, especially the rouged cheeks, the artificial eyes, and the saline-solution injections. Still, I could see bewilderment, visible consternation, on the students' faces. Two days later, I hit the Babylonians. I was in the midst of explaining how the Babylonians used base six for their number system and how that still determines our system of time in seconds and minutes along with the number of degrees in a circle when Poutoa, my Gilbert Islander, evinced a quizzical look, an expression of total incredulity.

"What's the matter, Poutoa?" I asked. "What is it that you don't understand?"

He blinked a few times and then stuttered, "Is this ... is this true?"

Suddenly, I realized my folly. I'd neglected to stress that the material was factual; hence, many students had thought the lessons were something I'd dreamt up.

Thanks to Poutoa, the lessons have gone well ever since. Last week, I gave the students a test on the Egyptians and the Babylonians, and Lei, the shyest boy in the room, got a perfect score. This in itself is refreshing since Lei suffers from a severe confidence problem.

Today, I finished the Ancient Greeks. Monday will see my second test, this time on Greece and Persia. Before doing the Roman Republic and the Roman Empire, I'm going to give the students a change of pace and cover Greek and Roman mythology. The Samoans have their own body of myths and legends, thus a comparison should prove interesting.

Then it's on to China, Japan, the Middle Ages, the Renaissance, the Reformation, the Enlightenment, the French Revolution, Napoleon, the British Empire, and, of course, the two World Wars. Sandwiched in along the way will be Christ, Mohammed, Buddha, and Confucius. Somehow, they deserve a nod.

As much as I enjoy my work at Faleata, I will not extend for another year. The lines in my face have deepened, and my hairline continues to recede—telltale signs that it's time to turn in my medical kit and fly home. I've pulled some weird boners in my time, but joining the Peace Corps wasn't one of them. True, I've had my moments of loneliness. Still, the more one is alone, the more company one has.

I may not have dispelled my demons, but I've learned to identify them. I now know that most of life's problems are self-inflicted, that they spring from the inability to harness selfish emotions and petty desires. I also know that I'm not the meek and humble guy most people take me for. Not being able to read themselves, many people are incapable of reading me.

I'm humble before no man. I'm only humble before God. I found that out one starlit night as I was walking home after seeing *Jesus of Nazareth* on the tube. The Milky Way was spread out before me in all its glory. The wonder of life and motion tumbled before my eyes. I stood, transfixed, before the cosmos, my arms dangling at my sides like wet towels. I can't remember if I cried or not. I only know that I couldn't take my eyes off the bright light that dazzled me. At that moment, I was without fear. At that moment, death didn't exist. Only life. And it went on and on forever.

Two delightful students on the playground
during "morning tea" (1978)
Left to right: Nonu and Aa with Oliana
and Simanono in the background

Epistle Thirty-Two

June 24, 1978

Dear Margi:

You're marvelously overwhelming! Janet got her letter first and treasured it so much that she wouldn't let me read it. Sadly, Janet's been demoted this term, so I no longer have her in class. I miss her very much. Still, I agree with Lafi that five promotions and five demotions every term is a viable educational policy. It acts as a spur, an incentive to succeed.

Please do not mention this to Janet. She's a sensitive kid and I don't want to hurt her feelings. If she applies herself, I feel confident she'll be promoted back into the A stream at the end of the year.

I had to wait another two weeks for the other four letters. For a while, I thought they'd jumped the slow boat to Karachi. But, happily, I was wrong. They came the day before Ioana returned to class. Her parents had sent her to American Samoa for her education, and nobody had told me. What prompted her return remains a mystery. I'm just happy to have her back, to have that big, brown, smiling face again in the room.

I got to your Teensville idea last week. I didn't know whether or not the students would go for it. At first, the class reacted like a group of clams. In desperation, I wheeled on Lauese, one of my more outspoken boys.

"Lauese," I said sternly. "Why don't you want to write to someone your age in America?"

His eyes grew wide, and he gulped a few times before answering.

"I'm ... I'm ashamed of my English, Mr. Christmas."

I did a complete spin on my heel and bonked myself on the forehead with my right hand.

"Do all of you feel the same way?" I asked, turning to the others.

Heads began to bob in unison.

"What utter nonsense," I said. "You should be proud of how good you are in English. Believe me, you're much better in English than I am in Samoan or in any other foreign language, for that matter. So straighten up, be proud, and stop thinking so low of yourselves."

I mailed the letters the next day.

Your generosity knows no bounds. But I don't know if I can take advantage of it. The books you describe in your letter sound terrific, and we'd be grateful if you sent them to us. Your "books of master sheets," however, have me flummoxed. We do have an A. B. Dick spirit duplicator and do need the carbons for the stencils. Now we have to place our tests barbarically and painstakingly on the blackboard since we only have one hundred spirit carbons to last the entire school for an entire term.

If your "master sheets" could help us, we'd truly be in your debt. As for the record player and the slide projector, no soap, but thanks just the same. Though lacking a tape recorder, I can get my paws on a cassette player quite easily. Laura Watson, my Peace Corps counterpart at Faleata, has one. Laura would probably benefit from your kindness more than I would since she's extremely innovative, a true joy to have around.

I received gobs of books from you, but the ones you named don't ring a bell. Most of the books have arrived, though. Lafi had me store them in his office, so a nice library is slowly taking shape. Some books have yet to be sorted, and your readers might be among them. I'll check on Monday and give you a definite answer. I've sent all the slips to IBP, so Harriet should know what, if any, books have been waylaid.

Your *Golden Book Encyclopedia* has been a great help to me. Toward the end of last term, I discovered that my students knew little or nothing about ancient civilizations. With Lafi's permission, I took selected articles on the early civilizations and used them for reading comprehension. At first, I wasn't sure if the kids would like them. But now they do. One boy even got a perfect score on the first test.

Harriet Van Meter wrote and asked for pictures of your five Samoan girls. A friend will be coming next week to take their pictures, as I lost my camera between airplane flights two years ago. I'll send Harriet the negatives since the prints developed here are rather shoddy. It appears that Harriet wants to use the pictures in an upcoming IBP newsletter. What a gas that is! You sure know how to turn the right wheels, Margi. I'll send you some prints, but don't expect stateside clarity. When it comes to my puss, that's a blessing.

You asked for an autobiography. Since I'm running out of aerogram blue, this will have to do: thirty-four years of age, male, bespectacled, sky-blue eyes, bulbous nose, controlled epileptic, Canadian by birth, American by luck, Bostonian snob till the age of thirteen, Floridian bumpkin after that, cabinetmaker in Connecticut, VISTA volunteer in Utah, PCV teacher in Thailand and Western Samoa, ready to marry the slant-eyed girl of my dreams.

And, yes, there is a God.

Epistle Thirty-Three

July 16, 1978

Dear Mom and Dad:

I've a little tale to tell, a tale that will help you better understand this fascinating land.

My Samoan family has been under great stress. About five months ago, Saolele became a matai. His mother, a woman of great charm and wit, forced the title upon him in order to chomp a bigger chunk from his paycheck. Possessive and selfish, she regularly comes to the house to borrow money with which to gamble. Indeed, gambling is her passion. I've seen her gamble for more than twenty-four hours at a stretch without being bored. It is truly a great sickness.

Saolele's wife, Alofa, hates her mother-in-law. The old lady has so drained her husband's meager earnings that feeding and clothing the children have become difficult. When Saolele yielded to the will of his mother and became a matai, Alofa was disconsolate since a title shifts a man's primary responsibility from his wife and children to the aiga, or extended family.

But Alofa kept her own counsel and devised a clever plan with which to protect herself and her young. During the term break, she went to visit her mother in Savaii, by far the largest of the four islands that make up Western Samoa. When the second school term began, she did not return home to Faleata. She made Saolele return alone without the children. Saolele said that nothing was wrong, that Alofa just wanted to be with her mother because she was pregnant again. The latter was true; the former was not.

Alofa's absence gradually had its intended effect. Saolele is a family man who needs the banter of his wife and kids. After about five weeks, he started to go squirrelly. It was then that Alofa sent for him. He was gone a good four days. Finally, a deal was struck: Saolele would become a matai in *her* family. This was Alofa's insurance policy, since Saolele would not only have obligations to his parents' people but to his wife's as well. Double slavery.

The night before leaving for Savaii to assume the new title, Saolele asked me to accompany him. Having promised some friends that I would take them to a waterfall on Sunday, I refused. Saolele looked disappointed. Suddenly, a thought hit me.

"What time are you leaving?" I asked.

"Three o'clock tonight," he said. "The service is at eight tomorrow, so I must hurry."

"Could I go and come back the same day? Or would that be impolite?"

"No problem," he said. "When you come to shoot, shoot. Don't talk. Shoot."

I laughed. That was Saolele's favorite line, especially whenever someone vacillated, as I was doing now.

"Why don't you ask your friends Tony and Tom and Terry and Dan to go along?" he said. "It'd be a good cultural experience for them."

I thanked him and hurried off into the night.

Tony wasn't home. He'd gone to the other guys' house. I went there. Barreling through the door, I must've looked like Eliot Ness busting up a speakeasy.

"You're invited to Saolele's matai ceremony tomorrow in Savaii," I said. "Anyone up for a little adventure?"

Only Terry seemed game. Dan was in love with the Sandman; Tony had the hots for a girl in Lafaga; and Tom had a burr up his poop chute.

"I don't have time to stand around and talk," I said. "If you want to go, be at my place at two a.m."

As I bolted out the door, Tom said something about my lousy Samoan. He wasn't telling me anything I didn't already know. I kept on walking.

I wanted to get five hours sleep before I left, so I hastened up the back path to the house. In the front yard I could see the silhouette of Kasa, the family dog, in the pale moonlight. I called him but he didn't move.

That's strange, I thought. *The silly beastie loves me with all his heart.*

Then it hit me. Something was terribly wrong. Kasa's body was twisted, and there was a weird look in his eyes. Then, when I touched him, he moaned. I lifted Kasa off the ground and carried him into the house. He was all banged up, but there was no external bleeding. He hadn't been stoned. A car had hit him.

Telephone calls followed thick and fast: first to Dick Cahoon, then to Shelby Henderson, and then to Seska, the veterinarian. It was like a B movie. Seska was ready to go to a party. I could see that as I neared the clinic. She stood before me in a long, blue evening gown.

"Go to the clinic," she said.

"Is it still open?" I asked.

"It is if I unlock it."

At the clinic, Seska could not find any broken bones or internal bleeding.

"Lucky dog," she said. "Not many survive a hit like this."

I hurried home, dog in arms.

Three hours' sleep instead of five. Not advisable for an epileptic. None of the boys showed, so Saolele and I struck out on our own at 3:30 a.m. The bus got us to the wharf at five, and the boat left at six. It was a quick crossing. But we lost some time on the other side. Saolele's mother had forgotten to bring food from the village. Saolele therefore had to go back and get it.

I went immediately with Alofa to her village. The bus was jammed with jubilant Samoans. There was a kid on almost every lap. The bus bumped and jumped along the dusty, dirty road. Finally, we arrived. I was ushered into a small but comfortable fale. The matais were already assembled. We were two hours late.

Once seated in the fale, I looked about. Alofa's family had an impressive setup. In front of me stood the fono, while a number of houses stood off at the sides and the rear. Directly behind the fono, women were busy preparing food. When Saolele arrived, I was taken to another small fale where Toilolo, the high chief of Gativai, was meeting with the *faifeau* and five prominent chiefs. Saolele and nine other men were about to become *tiatias*, and I was being allowed to sit in on the negotiations. Few outsiders ever get to see what I saw.

The high chief of a village has the final say in any argument. His word is law. No one is supposed to oppose him. Looking at Toilolo as he gathered in the fine mats and the money, I could see that he was no exception. He was an imposing figure and dispatched his duties quickly and efficiently.

Everything was going smoothly until a woman stormed into the fale. She was incensed and started to argue with Toilolo. Some of the members of her family did not agree that one of the men should be given a title. The families of the village usually choose who is to become chief, and this man's name had not been mentioned during the selection process. On the day of the ceremony, however, the man had assumed he would get a title because he'd worked hard for the village. Toilolo had agreed. And since he had the power to make any man chief, he told the man to go to the fono to receive the title.

But the woman was adamant. She refused to accept Toilolo's decision. Even when he invoked his supreme power, she stood fast. This created a *fa'alavelave*. The high chief's daughter began to sob, and finally, the man was removed from the fono. It seemed the woman had won.

From the fale, we went to the fono. It was very spacious and impressive. About fifty matais were present. Each sat on the floor with his back square against one of the supporting poles. The nine new tiatias sat at the far end. Fine mats, secured by lavish sashes, were wrapped around their bodies. I could see Saolele clearly, for he sat right in the middle. He was relaxed and dignified. The kava ceremony was about to begin.

Kava is a special root. When it is dipped and squeezed in water, an alcoholic drink is made. On many of the islands, this drink is used as an intoxicant to get drunk. Not in Samoa. In Samoa, kava is used ceremonially, almost religiously. It is not an indulgence.

A *taulealea* was summoned to pull a mat in front of the matais. As the mat slid across the floor, one man rose and made an introductory speech about the kava sticks. Each matai put his kava stick on the mat. Finally, the mat was dragged before the nine new tiatias, and they placed their sticks on it. These sticks were later given to the village.

Next came the *fa'atau*. The fa'atau is an argument among the matais to see who will present the formal speech to the tiatias.

This is crucial, for the man selected is highly honored and rewarded. A man was finally chosen, and he spoke eloquently. When he finished, a talking chief released his winds of gratitude.

Then came the name-calling and the drinking of the kava. The kava was placed in the shell of a halved coconut. Whenever a man's name was called, another man scurried down the length of the fono to present the coconut cup. Even the way kava is given is important. If the man is a full chief, the cup is presented in a wide, sweeping hand motion. But if the man is a lowly talking chief, the cup is presented across the body, backhanded.

According to custom and tradition, Saolele and the other tiatias were given the kava first. Then it went to the high chief, then to the speechmaker, and finally, to the other matais. When the tiatias got the kava, each poured out a few drops, made a short speech, and drank. The speeches were rather prescriptive. All began with the words: "This is God's kava …"

After the matais had drunk the kava, an old man, representing the tiatias, rose and gave the closing speech. All the fine mats and the money were given away, including the mats worn by the tiatias. Then the feast began. Four pigs and a steer lay on the eating mats in the noonday sun. They comprised the main course. First, the food was served inside the fono, and then it went out to the rest of the village.

Bleary-eyed, I returned to the fale and ate with the women and the defrocked tiatia. He did his best to be buoyant, but his long, angular face was lined with humiliation. I took a fast nap, jumped a bus to the wharf, and caught the last boat back to Apia.

I thought I'd seen it all, but I hadn't. That night, the matais held a secret meeting. Toilolo had not forgotten the woman who had challenged his authority.

"One man still remains to be titled," he said. "I grant him his title now—*at this moment*. But as long as I live and breathe, he will be the last so honored."

And according to custom and tradition, the words of the high chief of Gativae were strictly obeyed.

Epistle Thirty-Four

July 23, 1978

Dear Mom and Dad:

Teddy White wrote a book entitled *Thunder Out of China*. If I ever get my ass in gear, I'll call mine *Silence Out of Thailand*. Not a peep. Not a whisper. Nothing from Aied for a long, long time. I feel like I've been interred in a crypt where everything is dark and dank and dead.

I'm not angry, only concerned. I've talked to a number of volunteers who have also noticed a slackening of the mail. Which leads me to speculate: Has someone either at the Peace Corps or at the post office in Apia been tampering with our mail again? I say "again," for it wouldn't be the first time. Last month, the issue came up at a meeting of the volunteer council. Many volunteers wondered aloud why they were not getting any mail from home. Joe Grossman was particularly perplexed since his parents send him a case of wine every month and the wine had stopped coming.

Of course, our country director, Dick Cahoon, denied any wrongdoing. A few weeks later, however, a Samoan woman noticed a Samoan man burning a large number of letters and parcels near her fale. Recognizing the man as the Peace Corps driver, she reported the incident. The police discovered that the driver had heisted the mail in order to get gifts and money. As a result, Dick Cahoon fired the driver. Needless to say, Joe never got his wine. Weeks ago, it had been pissed away on lava rocks.

With only four months left, I now find myself in the "PC doldrums"—that calm before the storm at the close of service.

I feel at home in the country, secure in my job, and disinterested in new sights and sounds—obvious signs that I'm getting stale and it's time for me to go.

But I still get my thrills. The other day, I received a letter from the executive director of the International Book Project. One of her volunteers had passed along some of my letters, which the director, in turn, had used to piece together an article for the IBP monthly newsletter. Moreover, the director had telephoned Peace Corps Washington and arranged that one hundred pounds of books be sent to my school every month until I leave.

Now, stop wagging your gnarled, barnacled fingers at me. I haven't become overly proud, just vindicated. The voice crying in the wilderness has been heard, and my students now have a slightly better chance. I never looked upon the Peace Corps as a two- or three-year excursion into the Valley of Riotous Romance. Life is *not* to be lived. Life is scattering bits and pieces of oneself in an effort to help others. The bits and pieces one leaves behind—the shredded fibers of the heart and mind—must be given freely, with a hopeful hopelessness. Good work is seldom recognized. Indeed, the person in search of fame and fortune is at best a fop and at worst a fool.

Yes, I've been a fop and a fool at times. Some of my idiotic acts have hurt those I love. For these acts, I'll be held accountable. Indeed, I'm already starting to pay for them. And the cost is dear. It comes when one realizes that not even gestures of the human heart can set past wrongs aright, that no amount of penance will ever pay for the pain and the broken dreams. The sands of time continue to fall, continue to mount up. And all our sins lie scattered in the vast desert of infinity and eternity.

Yet, our gestures endure. They endure with the knowledge that pain is the source of sense. Were it not, life would be meaningless. Guilt, like most demons, brings with it some good. Though infrequently used, it's the magic mirror of the soul. Last night, for instance, this magic mirror flashed before my eyes. I was over at the house of three young, sensitive volunteers. Though these men share similar goals and objectives, they wear different masks: one the active mask, another the kindhearted mask, the third the tough mask.

All three masks are effective, but the tough mask is dominant. Endowed with more strength and sting, it cuts through the other masks at will. This time, it cut through the kindhearted mask—momentarily tearing it away, leaving it bare to the bone. But in that moment, I saw myself ten years ago—sans armor, sans the numbness that comes with being pierced by many lances. For a microsecond, my mirrored-self stood exposed, humble, and vulnerable. I can't recall what I said, but it must've been the right thing, for the kindhearted mask began to laugh and the situation was saved. Still, there must've been internal bleeding. There always is with the kindhearted mask.

And so the senseless hurt continues. Did I say senseless? Poor word choice. It's not senseless at all. All of us shelter our feelings in a phony house. All of us bar the windows and bolt the doors so no one can come in and disturb the furniture. Everything would be fine if we were only satisfied with what we had, if we could sit forever in an easy chair before a roaring fire with our pipe or our knitting. But the desire to share the fire resides in every human heart. Inevitably, the bars and the bolts and the furniture become irksome, forcing us to open the door to let a stranger inside—into the core of our being.

This opening of the door does not necessarily yield a positive outcome. Often the room is thrown into disarray, with all the furniture being smashed and broken. Yet, rarely do we regret our decision, even when it ends in disaster. For behind every disaster lurks an act of courage, a noble heart that eschews hate in favor of love.

Epistle Thirty-Five

August 15, 1978

Dear Mom and Dad:

A few months ago, ACTION Director Michael Balzano published a negative article in *The Washington Star* entitled "Peace Corps—Does the World Still Want It?" Not until the *Peace Corps Times* republished this article did volunteers in the field know about this vicious attack. Incensed, I decided to write a rebuttal. Before submitting my rebuttal to the *Star*, I decided to show it to my country director, Dick Cahoon.

Dick Cahoon is a thin, laid-back, middle-aged man with wisps of gray at the temples. On the plus side, Dick is an excellent listener, always leaving his door open to volunteers. On the down side, he's low-keyed and somewhat passive. His office is located at the far right corner of the Peace Corps building. I entered the front door and walked down the hall, passed the mail rack, and turned right. Sure enough, Dick was sitting at his desk, hard at work.

"Excuse me, Dick. Could I have a word with you?"

"Of course you can, Gerry. Come in and sit down. What can I do for you?"

"Well," I said. "Have you read the article by Mike Balzano in the *Peace Corps Times*?"

"Yes," he said. "It was pretty brutal, to say the least."

"I agree. Indeed, I'm not about to take this sitting down."

"What do you plan to do about it way out here in Samoa?"

"I've written a rebuttal. I intend to send it to *The Washington Star*."

Dick frowned.

"Do you think that would be wise?"

"I don't know if it's wise or not. I only know that I can't sit idly by while lies are disseminated by a hatchet man for Tricky Dick."

"I wouldn't go that far," he said.

"I would. Balzano was made ACTION director for the distinct purpose of destroying VISTA and the Peace Corps. You know that. Any government program initiated by John Kennedy has to go."

"Hmm," he said noncommittally. "Would you mind if I read your letter?"

"Not at all," I said and handed the letter across to him. "That's why I came in. I didn't want you to be blindsided."

I watched as he read the letter. I could tell that he was not pleased with it.

"Very well written," he said after a few minutes. "Nevertheless, I'd be grateful if you did not send it."

"I'd really like to oblige," I said. "But I cannot."

"Nothing I can say will dissuade you?"

"No," I said. "I'm sorry. This is a matter of principle."

"Well," he said. "I cannot forbid you from sending it, but are you open to some editing?"

"Sure, as long as it's reasonable."

"This sentence here at the end is too inflammatory. Could you tone it down a mite?"

I looked at the sentence. Dick was right. It was over the edge.

"I agree, Dick. I went too far there. Let's delete it."

"Thanks, Gerry."

"I should thank you," I said. "The letter is better now."

I mailed the letter to *The Washington Star* that day. At best, I thought it would be printed as a letter to the editor. I couldn't have been more wrong. The letter not only appeared as a feature article entitled "The Peace Corps: Beauty and the Beast," but was also highlighted by a large photo of a handsome male volunteer standing atop a mountain in Nepal. The letter appeared almost word for word as I had written it.

Letter to the Editor

Here in Western Samoa, I have just come across your article, "Peace Corps—Does the World Still Want It?" (Jan. 26). It was very unsettling. The reasons former ACTION Director Michael Balzano gave for the dissolution of the Peace Corps are the precise reasons why it should be preserved and cherished: growing nationalism and heightened fear.

Now more than ever before, communication and cooperation are vitally needed between all nations, rich and poor. Many countries are critically behind the eight ball in the economic advancement of their societies. As the industrial countries surge forward with their newfangled contraptions and flamboyant goodies, the underdeveloped countries become more and more insecure. Nationalism and fear set in. The eyes turn to the twin sanctuaries: custom and tradition. And the desire to rush to the past, to embrace the old ways and the old beliefs, is almost irresistible.

The Peace Corps plays more of a part to reverse this rush than most people think. By sending technical personnel abroad, by sending volunteers who are both sensitive to the needs of the host country and interested in the lives of the people, the Peace Corps attempts to create material well-being through mutual cooperation and brotherly love.

We therefore have two elements at work: material objectives and spiritual objectives. Unfortunately, in recent years, I've heard nothing about the spiritual objectives. I say "unfortunately" because the Peace Corps will evaporate without the spirit of idealism and enthusiasm upon which it was founded.

As a volunteer, I've experienced my fair share of hard times. The strong legs of idealism and enthusiasm have walked me through them. Without their support, I would have stumbled and fallen long ago.

Peace Corps volunteers are more idealistic and enthusiastic than they like to admit. I've been through two PC programs—one in Thailand and the other in Western Samoa. Rarely have I heard a volunteer say he joined out of the goodness of his heart. Travel, adventure, romance—yes. But rarely altruism. Yet, as I came to know my fellow volunteers, I soon learned that they were motivated by one thing only: the willingness to help others.

This is the beauty and the beast of the Peace Corps. The beauty comes when the willingness to serve is properly transformed into actual service. The beast comes when the willingness to serve is crushed by language inability, cultural instability, training difficulty, or a lousy assignment.

The trouble with the Peace Corps is that it has never come to grips with the beast. Instead of assisting us more with our jobs, instead of supplying us with greater emotional stability, instead of giving us moral and ethical leadership, we are often left to fend for ourselves. This is a precarious position at best. The spirit of idealism and enthusiasm is very delicate, especially in the young. It is easily broken. And a volunteer with a broken spirit will invariably go home sad and embittered.

I am about to leave the Peace Corps. Saying good-bye will not be easy. The Peace Corps has been my family, my friend, my life. In leaving, I ask all those people at Peace Corps—staff as well as volunteers—not to forget "the original bloom," which Dr. Balzano claims is long gone.

It's not long gone. It's still with us. It has always been with us. It is the immortal flower that goes back farther than 1961. It goes back to the man who said: "You are to love one another." I believe he was talking to a bigger audience than us.

Gerry Christmas
Apia, Western Samoa

Shortly after the letter appeared in the *Peace Corps Times*, Dick Cahoon called me into his office.

"I have an apology to make," he said. "You were right and I was wrong."

"Never mind," I said. "Your job is different than mine. I put you in an uncomfortable position."

"But, Gerry, you don't understand. Your letter really had a positive effect. I've even received a letter from Peace Corps Washington thanking you for it. Balzano's article not only had a negative impact on the public but depressed the PC staff in Washington as well. Your letter did much to perk things up, to turn things around."

"That's nice to know." I said. "I guess the good guys won for a change."

Dick laughed.

"Yes," he said. "This time, we did."

Aied duking it out with her niece
outside her house in Samut Prakarn (1979)
With Khun Boontan caring for three grandchildren,
the situation at the time was chaotic.

Epistle Thirty-Six

September 23, 1978

Dear Margi:

My fingers drip with guilt. I've had this letter bouncing around in my bean for a good month, but circumstances have kept me away from the keys. First I had exams, then I had my markings, and finally, I had to make four chairs for my headmaster. The chairs gobbled up my two-week vacation. I'd initially planned to do them in one week. Materials, however, are hard to come by here. For the first week, I insanely scurried about town getting glue, dowels, screws, plastic wood, and stain. Since I only had a screwdriver, saw, and hammer, I had to go a-begging for a drill.

I finally hit the big time when some friends lent me their Black and Decker Wood Destroyer. Still, I was working with secondhand wood that Captain Hook would've been hard-pressed to use to dispatch Wendy to the eager jaws of a hungry crocodile. Adding to my woes was the fact that I'd never made a chair in my life, though I'd patched aplenty. Miraculously, two of the four came out well. The other two are prime candidates for the John Wayne bar scene in *The Spoilers*. Nonetheless, it was good therapy. The Japanese beat up on dummies; I beat up on furniture.

Two weeks ago, I received your June shipment. What a treat! All useable and droolable books, Margi. Rest assured, you scraped off another barnacle-encrusted layer of this mean, old heart. But it was your last letter that really touched me. The newspaper article had a delectable effect, especially on Ioana, whose growing pains of late have momentarily put her schoolwork into a nosedive. I had a good talk with her father, and that, combined with seeing her letter in print, got her back on track.

Interestingly, the isolation of island life affects the academic students more than the others. They appear to be more sensitive and vulnerable to the crunch of Western civilization. As a result, their moments of insecurity are severe and intense. Believe me, your books did much to retrieve at least one Samoan girl's pride and self-respect. God moves in mysterious ways.

I expect your July shipment to arrive this month. Your "terrible thought" about sending my kids English books is totally unfounded. Some of my students are beginning to read, so your books are a veritable godsend.

Having a classroom set of readers will both stimulate and facilitate my teaching. Thus far, I've had to scatter numerous titles about the room, and this has caused some confusion. As you know, children are notoriously paranoid about getting the short end of the stick; thus, giving them the same thing alleviates this problem. So don't ruffle your angel feathers. The Margi Stevens Educational Midas Touch has struck again.

Your duplicated tests have left my headmaster salivating. And that ain't easy. What with the bumps and bruises that Lafi has suffered from the educational establishment in this country, it's a wonder he can still crack a smile. All that drives him, all that pushes him forward, is the hope that he's not alone in caring for his flock. Thanks to IBP, much of that hope has been rekindled and the future doesn't look as bleak as it once did.

Yipes! I almost forgot. In my mad search for readers, I finally discovered the captivating books of Bertha and Ernest Cobb. Saisirita and Ioana read *Arlo* last week and are now reading *Andre*. Some of the other kids are reading these books too. The plots are good, and the vocabulary is perfect. If you can't locate any, would you mind asking Harriet for some?

Yes, I know. This is damn brazen of me, but now with the fish in the net, why let them escape? The other books in the series are: *Clematis, Anita, Pathways, Allspice, Dan's Boy, Pennie, Who Knows, Robin, Renard Ruse,* and *Busy Builder's Book*. If these books are half as good as *Arlo* and *Andre*, the children of Faleata don't have a chance: they'll be hooked on books for the rest of their lives.

Business aside, the time has come to give you the perils and palpitations of Gerry Christmas. Still not a peep out of Aied, I'm afraid. But I'm not worried. I love her and I need her and I believe the idea is slowly seeping into that pert little bean. Were she an American girl, I'd have kissed the cloud good-bye long ago.

But I know what's going on: *I must prove myself.* That sounds trite, but it's the truth. Men have hit on Aied for years, hence her defensive attitude. When I first met her, when I first looked into those large, liquid-brown eyes, hot arrows shot through my body. Love and hope bloomed simultaneously. And they have never wilted.

Though stubborn and strong-minded, Aied has a warm and true heart. My instincts tell me that. My instincts also tell me that she loves me too. I therefore must wait and be courageous in my waiting.

When I said that things would be different with an American girl, I didn't mean to imply that American girls aren't worth waiting and fighting for. I simply meant that our culture resolves romantic entanglements more rapidly. My mother and father didn't understand this until I explained it to them. One cannot compare today's American woman with today's Thai woman. The barriers that have collapsed in the past forty years in the United States have created a completely new set of rules, rules that are just beginning to be felt in Asia. One would be more on target to compare yesteryear's Victorian woman with today's Thai woman.

My mother is sixty-five years old. She's changed greatly since my father courted her. But her concept of a "lady" hasn't. Nor has it changed in any of her friends. Before living in Thailand, I believed that this concept came with age, for it was nonexistent with women of my generation.

But it didn't come with age. It came with youth. It was taught and drilled into Aied, just as it is taught and drilled into most Thai women. It's a flair, a style, a wile, which is both enchanting and oddly old-school. And being deeply ingrained in Thai culture, in the upbringing of Thai girls from an early age, it's not about to go away any time soon. As a result, a young Thai woman does not readily acquiesce to a marriage proposal. She isn't looking for a man in a hurry. Instead, she admires strength and caution, loyalty and a sincere heart.

Water on stone, water on stone … drip, drip, drip. Three more months in Samoa and then back to Aied. The time should be right to state my case and for her to state hers. This I know, since she was on the brink of stating it when I saw her last.

But then the full force of her culture will come crashing down on her. Her parents will oppose my suit. They'll tell her that she'll miss her country and her friends. They'll tell her that I'll grow tired of her. They may even tell her I'll cheat on her. I can only lay my love and devotion and sincerity at her feet. And hope for the best.

If she says no, I'll probably never marry. I don't want to marry anyone but her. This one's been burning inside me for four years, and it's still a lusty blaze.

There's only one present I want this Christmas, Margi. A nice, big, fat *yes!*

Epistle Thirty-Seven

October 15, 1978

Dear Mom and Dad:

The check will easily cover the cost of the phone call. I had to count the zeroes three times to believe my myopic eyes. Five years as a volunteer have conditioned me: any check in excess of $150 sets off the Incredulity Bomb. I don't know where parents like you come from. Displaced persons from Oz, perhaps?

I didn't tell you everything over the phone. But, judging from the size of the check, you've made some keen deductions. So let me fill you in on the details. As I told you, my close-of-service is December 17. Dick Cahoon has given me the go-ahead to depart early. I'd hoped to leave on December 2. But that would be right in the middle of exam week, so I'd have to dump my exams and grading on another teacher. I've therefore decided to stay until December 9.

Now for the confession: I want to make a quick trip through Thailand. Sitting atop this volcanic rock for two years, I've come to certain conclusions: first, I'm not a monk; and second, I love Aied with all my heart. When I met her in Thailand last year, all those weird and wonderful feelings came surging back. I can't rationalize how I feel, what that woman does to me. I only know I've felt that way for five years.

My chances are about as good as those of a mosquito caught in a spiderweb. But I must go back and ask her the big question. Letters, though permanent, are far from complete. I must see her eyes when she answers me. For then, I will know the truth.

Should her eyes say no, I'll travel on. The fissure of the heart will be substantial, but the salve of time heals all.

If the impossible happens and she says yes, I'll marry her straight off. I fear only one scenario: that her lips will say no while her eyes will say yes. In that case, I'll have to plead my case and hope for the best. I know I can make Aied happy if she gives me the chance.

I telephoned Aied last week. My letters have gone unanswered for a long time, so telephoning was the only way to find out if she was all right. Hearing her voice, I went all mushy inside. It wasn't what she said. It was how she said it. I've often wondered about Aied's witchery, about the source of her power over me. Was it something simple and fundamental, such as her voice? For, in truth, I could listen to the cadences of her rich, husky, feminine vocal cords for hours and never be bored. They've a tone and a texture the likes of which I've never heard.

"How are you?" I asked.

"Not too well," she said. "My family has many, many problems."

"I'm sorry. Did you get my letters?"

"No," she said and paused. "I thought you'd forgotten me. I thought you'd found a beautiful Samoan lady."

"Do you want to see me again?" I said bluntly.

She could've said no—but she didn't.

"I'm sorry I haven't written you," she said. "I'll write you now and explain everything."

"What do you mean by 'everything?' You're not married, are you?"

That was dumb, downright stupid of me.

"No, I'm not," she said. "I've never lied to you, Gerry. Everything I've ever said to you was the truth."

I knew what she meant, and she knew that I knew. Exploitation of women, both within her family and within her culture, had made her wary. She could wrap her feelings into a tight cocoon faster than I could eat a caterpillar. And that's precisely what she did now.

"A man's love is all sex," she said vehemently. "Electric sex!"

Had the repair work been insurmountable, I'd have given up right then and there. But hers is a kind and true heart. Besides, I love her. I love her without reservation.

"Listen, Aied. I know how suspicious you are of men. You've seen too much betrayal, so I don't expect you to trust me. Not now, anyway. But one day you might."

"I hope so, Gerry," she said gently. "I hope so with all my heart."

And with that, our conversation came to an end.

So please forgive me. My trip to Thailand will delay my return a month. But I wouldn't be much good to either you or myself if I came back directly. I'm going to be traveling with my friend Conrad Wesselhoeft as far as Manila. There, we'll part company. Conrad is young and adventuresome, so he's ripe for new sights and sounds. Me? I've my friends and my past to keep me occupied. Newness doesn't stimulate anymore. Like an old ship, I seek tranquil bays and safe havens over tempests and open seas.

Epistle Thirty-Eight

October 22, 1978

Dear Mom and Dad:

At best, this term has been drab. A serious bout of lethargy has hit both the staff and the students. I'm not about to fight it. The islands are imbued with a laxity that one learns not to resist. Anyway, I've pushed my class hard all year. As a result, I'm not exactly suffering from guilt.

For two terms, my students fought me. But now they've mellowed out, and I'm satisfied with their behavior and study habits. A few weeks ago, I realized that most of the students sincerely liked me. That is reward enough in itself, since I've frequently told them I wasn't out to win their hearts. *I was after their minds.* If they hated me, if they thought I was overly strict, I didn't care. As long as they learned to think, as long as they worked and had faith in their work, I'd be happy. Liking me was residual, totally unnecessary. Still, it's nice knowing that I'm genuinely respected, even loved by a few.

During the term break, Lafi took me to his aiga in Aliepata. Aliepata is known for its silver sands and meticulously kept villages. This, I knew in advance. Nevertheless, Lafi's house bowled me over. His family has four fales by the sea. Huge palms stretch out over the beach to the turquoise lagoon. The reef is a long way from the shore, and this has a calming effect upon the waves. The swimming is therefore ideal.

One day, Lafi and I went out in the lagoon for a dip. Lafi is a huge beast but possesses a Jackie Gleason-like agility. Still, when he challenged me to a swimming race, I was sure I could beat him since the distance he proposed was long enough to make his formidable size a real liability.

I took off like a shot. Lafi was on my blind side, but I could see his outstretched arms a good stroke ahead of me.

My God, he's fast, I thought, burying my head in the water and rotating my arms into paddlewheels. Then I saw it. He wasn't swimming. He was using the lagoon floor as a springboard. I leaped forward and grabbed him by the shoulder.

"You tricky bastard," I said.

That made him howl.

"I almost fooled you," he said gleefully. "Hey, do you see the point at the far end of the beach, the one with the piece of sand at the end?"

"Yes," I said, squinting. "Just barely."

"There's a Samoan myth about that point that you won't find in history books. Once, in Aliepata, we had this *manuia*, the most handsome man in the village. But this guy was different. When his body stopped growing, his penis did not. It grew and grew and grew. Finally, his penis was so long that the manuia did not have to go out and look for women. He just sat in his fale and sent out his worm to do its work."

His eyes danced devilishly.

"Lucky fellow, eh?"

It was my turn to howl.

That evening, I met a beautiful Samoan girl with a great sense of humor. We went for a walk on the beach together. In near-perfect English, she told me all about herself. She'd finished Form 5 and had placed high in her class. Unfortunately, she'd failed the government examination, so she was now living near Apia. Every week, she went into town looking for a job. She'd been at it for a whole year, but there weren't any openings. At sunset, we returned to the village, since it was *sa* to walk with a single girl after dark.

As I was getting ready for bed that night, Lafi's niece Leone brought the same girl to my fale. Both girls had a bad case of the giggles.

"What's so funny?" I said.

"Are you going to bed alone?" Leone asked.

"Yes," I said. "I'm very tired. It's been a long day."

Both girls began to giggle again. A middle-aged Samoan woman, seemingly unaware of our existence, sat nearby weaving a basket. Suddenly, I noticed a twinkle in her eye and felt embarrassed.

"Excuse me," I said, tightening my lavalava. "I really must get to bed."

But Leone was not about to give up. Walking away from the fale, she said, "Are you *sure* you want to sleep alone?"

I crawled under the mosquito net and said nothing.

The next morning, I told Lafi what had happened.

"Oh, I know all about that," he said. "Indeed, it was my idea. To be honest, I thought you'd sleep with her."

"What would have happened if I had?"

"I'd have married the two of you right here on the sands of Aliepata," he said. "My matai status gives me that authority."

I stood there, speechless.

"It's too bad," he said. "You'd have been a great addition to the family, a real asset to the aiga."

Epistle Thirty-Nine

December 1, 1978

Dear Mom and Dad:

Last night, I didn't have much to do, so I decided to go to the Manuia Club. Seeing few people there, I took a seat at the bar and ordered a Coke. A middle-aged Samoan woman two seats to my right turned and looked at me.

"Aren't you Gerry Christmas?" she asked.

"Yes," I said. "Excuse me, but I've forgotten your name."

The woman laughed.

"We've never met," she said. "But I've seen you over at the house many times. I'm Samaria's aunt."

"Oh," I said. "Nice to meet you. How's Samaria?"

"Not so good. A few weeks back, she gave birth to a baby boy. You knew, of course, that she was pregnant?"

"Yes. I've been meaning to stop by and see Samaria but wasn't sure if she wanted to see me or not."

The woman was quiet for a minute. I could see that she was thinking how best to continue the conversation. I didn't say a word. I wanted her to make the right choice.

"Samaria misses you very much," she said finally. "You're one of the few men who have treated her like a lady."

"I haven't been much of a friend lately," I said.

"Don't say that. Samaria's the one who made a mistake, not you. No man wants to have anything to do with her now, especially since—"

"Since what?"

"You know."

"No, I don't know. Please tell me."

"The baby ... the baby is *ugly*."

"I still don't understand. What do you mean, ugly?"

"It has dark skin," she said flatly.

"Oh," I said. "The father's Melanesian?"

"I wish he were," she said. "Then it wouldn't be too bad. But the baby's not brown. It's black."

"What? There are only two black men on Upolo. I hope the father steps forward and helps Samaria out."

The aunt raised her eyebrows and got up to leave.

"Excuse me," she said. "I have to go now. Please stop by and visit Samaria. She'd like to see you."

The next day I stopped by Samaria's house. I bought a bottle of Dewar's, her favorite whiskey. It wasn't a sensible gift, but I knew it was what she wanted. Samaria met me at the door, babe in arms.

"I've come to say good-bye," I said. "My tour of service is finished next week. I wanted you to know that I really value your friendship."

Samaria looked at me with weary, flat eyes. Her once superb, erect body was slightly stooped, and her large, firm breasts sagged under the weight of the milk. Her dress, normally a tight fit, hung from her shoulders in a loose, messy manner.

"May I come in?" I said.

"Yes, please do."

We sat in the living room on the sofa where we had had so many fine talks. But now the words were hard to find."

"That's a cute child," I said lamely.

"No, it isn't," she said with finality. "It's black and ugly."

There it was again, the two words: *black* and *ugly*. Why was black skin universally despised, even here in the middle of the Pacific Ocean? One couldn't blame this on the white man.

No, this came directly from the Samoan culture. But what was the cause? Was it some errant, worldwide gene? Or was it a weird, mental color preference with white standing atop the pyramid? Or was it a sick, subconscious aversion to the gibbon, the chimpanzee, the orangutan, and the gorilla? Damned if I knew.

"Try not to hate your child, Samaria."

"I don't hate it," she said. "I hate what life has done to me."

I gazed at her face. The eyes hadn't changed. They were still weary and flat. The spark, the life, was totally gone, completely extinguished. Would it ever come back? The chances were slim. I wanted with all my heart to help her. No, it was more than that. I wanted to *save* her. But that was impossible. Some people get dealt a shitty hand in life, and Samaria—beautiful, exquisite Samaria—was one of them. We talked for another ten minutes or so; then I took my leave.

At the doorstep, I took her hand in mine. It felt like a limp, wet towel.

"You've meant more to me than any other Samoan," I said in all honesty.

Samaria looked at me without expression or emotion. Involuntarily, I took her in my arms and kissed her on the forehead. It was like kissing a Barbie doll.

I turned and walked away. Glancing back, I saw her standing in the doorway, motionless. I wanted to cry but could not. Instead, I just bit my lip and walked on.

Epistle Forty

February 16, 1979

Dearest Aied:

I was foolish the night I said good-bye. I was worried about you and didn't want to go. I could sense that you did not trust me and felt frustrated. I wanted your mind to be at peace. Instead, I left you upset with me and upset with your feelings. That was wrong, very wrong.

During my visit to Thailand, I was happy whenever I was with you. I'm always happy when I'm with you. You know that. But one thing bothered me: your fear of being alone with me. I like your friends very much, but sometimes I need to be alone with you. The few times we were alone, you opened up your heart. That helped me to understand and appreciate you more.

I can understand your fear of walking with me in public. I know how dirty some people's minds are, and I know how much their stupid words and evil looks hurt you. Still, there must've been a few places where we could've met and talked intimately.

But you didn't give me a chance. Perhaps you don't trust me yet. You did in the past, but you don't now. This confuses me, since I've never tried to force myself upon you in any way. Nor do I ever plan to. I don't believe in force, especially with a woman. Nothing comes of it but pain and sorrow.

Remember what I said to you in the taxi, that your feelings for me are the same as my feelings for you? I'm a patient man. If you need time to figure out your life and your problems, I'll wait. Time will ultimately tell you the truth about me.

Terry Fredrickson with his Suan Dusit college students (1979)

Epistle Forty-One

February 17, 1979

Dear Terry:

I finally arrived home a week ago. I'd a great time in Japan. I stayed with a Japanese family for three days and was treated like a *shogun*. The head of the family wouldn't let me pay for a thing. This was fortunate, since I didn't have the means to live up to my surname. I wasn't even allowed to make a down payment on a Japanese communal bath, which left me with boiled balls and a diminished sperm count.

Mt. Fuji was stupendous. The bright sun set off the snowcapped peak like a diamond. Small wonder the Japanese refer to it as a person, calling it "Fuji-san."

But my real jollies came with the strawberries. Shizuoka Prefecture is noted for its terraced strawberry gardens. The terraces are covered with plastic, creating a greenhouse effect. My Japanese host paid a fee and we gorged ourselves on huge, juicy, fresh berries straight off the vine.

I traveled back to the States laden with gifts and souvenirs. I didn't know whether I should go directly to Phoenix to see my parents in their new home or shoot up to San Francisco to see Carlton Lowenberg at the Asia Foundation. I was dog-tired when the plane touched down in Los Angeles. There were no flights to Phoenix till the following day. That cinched it. I flew to San Francisco and went to the Asia Foundation the following morning.

Mr. Lowenberg was out of town. His assistants, however, were most helpful and obliging. They explained the problems with sending books abroad and gave me additional addresses

Gerry Christmas

for book donors. I checked out the warehouse and found what I expected: a sterling stock of university books for native speakers. Still, it was a valuable experience, well worth my while.

The next day, I flew to Phoenix. On arrival, I had to shove my personal interests aside. My mother was all doped up with painkillers, and my father was going crazy unpacking household belongings. During the past week, my father and I have been busy creating order out of chaos. This has left me with little time to work on the book project. Still, I've made some progress. Yesterday, I telephoned Harriet Van Meter and Margi Stevens of the International Book Project. Both want to meet me personally. I will therefore fly to Kentucky and Indiana next month.

I'll also go to Pittsburg to meet Luke Hinson, the director of the Brother's Brother Foundation. I got Hingson's name from the gang in San Francisco. His organization is brand-new, so I don't know much about it. Nobody does. Judging by the name, I presume it's run by a religious order. If that's the case, I might've stumbled upon something solid. Let's hope I don't stub my toe.

My mother's condition is worse than I thought. She had her right breast completely removed, and the aftereffects of the surgery have been debilitating. The chances of the cancer spreading are high. The doctors found traces in the lymph nodes, which means that the damn disease will probably reoccur in a couple of years.

My parents' relationship is sweet and tender. Their love is at a level that only they understand. The past comes up whenever I've either of them alone, but not in the negative sense. They're taking stock of their lives in preparation for death. This might be the last time I see them as a single unit. With this in mind, I'm trying to make every minute count. The other night, for instance, I sat down with my mother to play cards.

"Would you like to learn the national card game of Samoa?" I asked. "Literally every Samoa family plays it. The game is called Sweepie."

"I'd love to," she said. "It has always amazed me how many games the human race has dreamt up with a deck of cards."

Explaining the rules to my mother, I noticed that her smile had left her face. In its place was a look of confusion, one of deep perplexity.

"What's wrong, Mom?"

"I don't know, but this game looks oddly familiar."

That made me angry. My mother's a sweet, sensitive soul, so this attitude seemed out of character. Who was she to question the supreme Samoan divertissement?

"Oh, come on, Mom. Don't be ridiculous. How can you possibly know the rules to a Polynesian card game?"

"I don't know," she said.

My father then entered the room.

"What's going on, Gerry? I heard you raise your voice. Is there anything wrong?"

"Well," I said. "I was teaching Mom how to play Sweepie, the most popular card game in Samoa. She claims that it looks familiar. But that's impossible."

"Would you mind telling me the rules to the game?" he said.

"Not at all."

I then proceeded to explain the game to my father. I'd only explained three or four rules when he gave me a wry smile.

"What is it?" I asked.

"That's not a Samoan card game," he said. "It's a famous English card game. I used to play it with my father when I was a kid. The Samoans must've picked it up from the missionaries or the traders. The only difference in the game is the name. In the West, it's not called Sweepie. It's called Casino."

Needless to say, the laugh was on me. Still, I find it amazing that no one in Peace Corps Samoa seems to have picked up on this fact. In the two years I was there, every volunteer called Sweepie "the national card game of Samoa."

I've told my parents about Aied. Oh, have I told them about Aied! I've talked and talked and talked till I thought their ears would fall off. In spite of my delusional, romantic fantasies, I've tried to be as honest and objective as I could about her. Both my mother and father want me to marry her, despite her poor health and family problems. I came across one of her letters the other day and showed it to my mother. She wilted like a flower.

"Now I understand why you love her," my mother said. "I didn't know Aied was like this. There's a lot more to her than I'd first supposed."

Yes, I'm afraid there is. I guess I'll continue to butt my head against the wall till my brains spill out or she tells me to go to hell. The wall might give way. But I'm not expecting it to. Sometimes I think I'd have a better chance against the Great Wall of China.

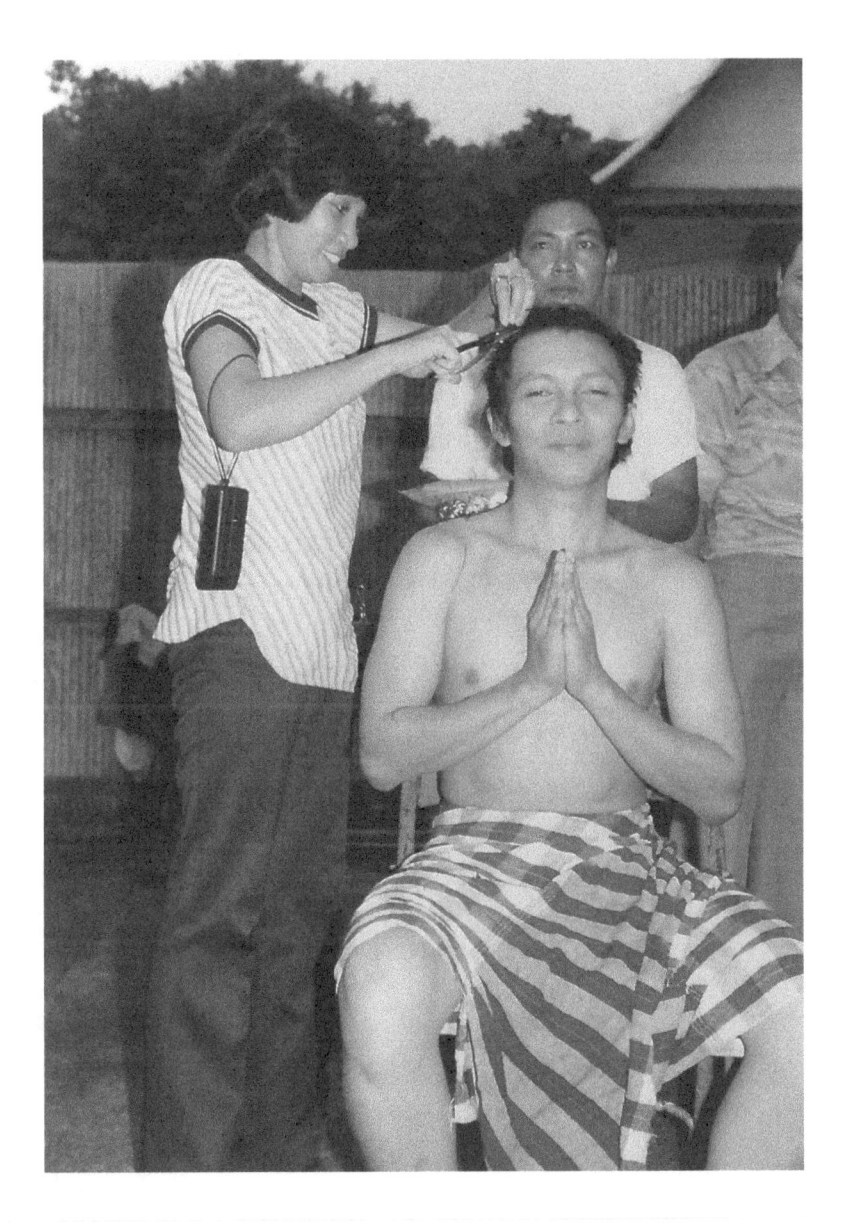

Aied cutting a lock of her brother's hair
on the morning he became a monk

Epistle Forty-Two

February 20, 1979

Dear Mr. Lowenburg:

Two weeks ago, I visited Books for Asia in an effort to get information about sending books to Thailand. Unfortunately, you were out of town, but your two assistants, Ruth Griffin and Sergio Randel, were very helpful and took me on a tour of the warehouse. They patiently answered my questions and pointed out a number of pitfalls that I might encounter. I'm indebted to them.

I plan to return to Thailand in June to teach English at Chan Kasem Teachers Training College. Before returning, however, I'd like to start a steady flow of simplified books coming in from the United States to Thailand. These books must not exceed a vocabulary level of three thousand words, since TTC students have a limited grasp of the English language.

This low reading level is social and economic in nature. In Thailand, it is important to differentiate between the reading ability of TTC students and that of university students. Most university students come from affluent families. They are therefore exposed to English at an early age. Indeed, many are even sent abroad to England and America to hone their language skills. This is not the case with the majority of the TTC students. They usually come from middle-class and poor families; hence, their only exposure to English is through schools and libraries.

Unfortunately, the Royal Thai Ministry of Education has been unable to supply the teacher training colleges with basic reading materials. For the most part, the books at these institutions are old and difficult to read. Some are even too difficult for Thai teachers. As a result, students rarely advance beyond the TTC level. In fact, they're lucky if they get that far.

I'd like to do something to alleviate this situation, to give a broader number of students a chance to advance career-wise. At the teacher training colleges, the only way to do this is to upgrade the reading materials. The students must be supplied with practical, modern books that will stimulate their interest and encourage them to learn.

I gravitated to your organization because you seem to be one of the few organizations that effectively help Thailand with books. I fully understand that your budget forces you to concentrate on universities. Still, you might be able to help me. I don't expect you to send any books overseas to me. That would be unfair. But if good, simplified books come your way, I'd be grateful if you notified me before you discarded them.

At the present time, I've neither the ways nor the means to send books to Thailand. I should be able to do so, however, in a few months. I've talked to Harriet Van Meter, the director of the International Book Project, and she's agreed to meet with me next month. I'll also meet with Luke Hingson of the Brother's Brother Foundation in Pittsburg. Mrs. Griffin suggested that I tap the school systems for used textbooks. This was an excellent idea, and I plan to meet local high school principals here in Phoenix this week.

Being new to Phoenix, I've few personal contacts. I believe, however, that my idea is sound, so I should be able to sell it. My main problem is lack of experience. I'm entering a complicated field and must learn as I go along. Nevertheless, the work needs to be done, and my position as a teacher should be of great help.

I would appreciate any recommendations or suggestions you might have. Obviously, you know more about this business than I do.

Epistle Forty-Three

March 8, 1979

Dear Aied:

My life has been going well. My mother is getting stronger each day, and this is a great help to my father and me. My mother still has to spend much of the day in bed because the operation had taken away most of her strength. We try to take her out for a walk or a ride in the car whenever possible.

My mother talks about you almost as much as I do. She respects the love you have for your mother, that special love that only a good daughter can give. My mother has been a lucky woman but has missed having a daughter. Your mother, though unlucky in many ways, has had you and your sisters for solace during her times of hardship and pain.

I'm now writing a short story about Thailand. I got the idea for the story while staying with Terry Fredrickson in Bangkok. I saw a crippled man in Terry's *soi,* and suddenly, the story began to take shape in my mind. Unlike my other short stories, I could visualize the ending first. I wrote the ending before returning to the United States. Now I'm trying to work from the beginning to the middle of the story.

The beginning was very difficult because I wrote it through the eyes of a crippled boy who wants to be a woodcarver. Of course, the boy loves the most beautiful girl in the village, but he knows that his love is hopeless due to his twisted, deformed body. He therefore dedicates his life to becoming the finest woodcarver in Thailand. And this dedication, this drive to develop his talent, gives him strength not only as a woodcarver but also as a man not afraid of life.

As time passes, the boy develops great wisdom. Still, he cannot forget his high-spirited and strong-willed dream girl, his one true love. The girl likes the woodcarver but cannot let her feelings turn to love. Her family and friends *expect* her to love a strong and handsome man. And, sure enough, she does. Only her lover is spiritually weak, a coward. She discovers this when her boyfriend loses his leg in a motorcycle accident. He can't face life. The woodcarver makes a wood statue of him in an attempt to show that life can be good even when the physical body has been permanently damaged.

The boyfriend takes the statue the wrong way. Frustrated and angry, he smashes it against the concrete wall of his house. His girlfriend is horrified. Being sensitive and intelligent, she not only understands the beauty and the meaning of the statue but also the thought and sensitivity of the man who carved it. You can guess the rest of the story, so I won't bore you with it. My mother likes what I've written thus far, but I can't take her criticism seriously. Being my mother, she likes everything I write.

I hope to return to Thailand in June. I've been working with many organizations trying to get books for the teacher training colleges. Thus far, I've been lucky. Many people have shown interest in helping me. Next week, I'll leave for Canada and the East Coast to meet with the heads of three charitable organizations. Wish me luck, bright eyes!

Epistle Forty-Four

April 14, 1979

My dear Aied:

Now don't bite your lower lip and fret, my lovely. Sure, you look cute when you're angry, but it's not good for the blood vessels. Anyway, you didn't give me a choice, did you? You told me over the phone that you were moving this month, so I was reluctant to write directly to your home. Now, don't ask, "Why didn't Gerry wait for me to write?" Had I done that, my hair would've turned white and my beard would be down to the floor.

I made Terry Fredrickson into my messenger boy because I needed someone trustworthy to get this letter to you. Now Terry isn't just another guy. He's a legendary Peace Corps Volunteer. And I'm not using the word *legendary* lightly. Being a Peace Corps trainer is one animal, but being a guest speaker is a real beast. Terry was the latter, not the former. So please use all your feminine wiles with him. He's doing me a huge favor.

Admittedly, I was stupid to send you all those cosmetics. I should've known that the Thai customs officials would charge you a huge import tax. So I'm sending you a check for one hundred dollars (two thousand baht) to make up for the money you lost. In the future, I'll send you money instead of gifts. Sure, shopping for you is a blast, but it's not much fun when you get gouged at your end. I want to help you, not bankrupt you.

I'm also sending you a picture of a girl from my past. Does she look familiar? She's lovelier now than when this picture was taken. Or, at least, *I* think so. I met her six years ago.

Seeing her the first time, my heart went haywire. The world didn't stand still. It hallucinated.

"You must be crazy," I said to myself. "You haven't even met her yet. Sure, she's gorgeous, bright, and vivacious. But you don't even know if she can speak English. Forget her."

Then fate stepped in. Not two hours later, we met face-to-face in a twilight English class. She not only could understand English but also had a gift for languages. In a flash, my hallucination became a reality.

"She may never love you," I mused. "I must learn to live with that thought."

We didn't date for at least a year. And it wasn't always smooth sailing. One day, we had a falling out.

"What do you want of me?" I asked bluntly.

"I want you to do your duty," she said.

"My duty? What do you mean by that?"

"You're a man. You must do your duty as a man."

Talk about a cultural curveball. Did she want me to take her by force? No, she wasn't that stupid. So I had to guess her meaning. My duty was to her, to be her friend. I must not expect anything in return. I must accept and respect her feelings, without a thought of hope. Hope and love make for a bad mix. Indeed, hope is often love's silent killer. Hope makes a person wish for a love that can never be.

But I like to wish. I like to hope. The world would be a nasty place if people stopped caring for others, if people stopped feeling deeply for those near and dear to them. Yes, hope brings pain, but pain teaches us about life. And life, in turn, teaches us forgiveness and understanding. My picture-girl forgives me. My picture-girl understands me. She knows my feelings are not born in the mind, but in the soul. That makes them pure and everlasting.

Terry can tell you about the work I'm doing in the United States. My letter explained it to him in detail. If the Thai government looks favorably on my efforts, I'll be returning in June or July. With all my heart, I want to see you again. With all my heart, I want to laugh and smile with you again. But don't make me your toy. Toys have a habit of breaking. And no one likes a broken toy, not even a child.

Epistle Forty-Five

June 29, 1979

Dear Steve and Margi:

Below, you'll find a copy of an article based on my recent visit. I'd like to submit it to *Family Circle,* if you have no objections. I realize that I took some liberties with the order of events. And please forgive me if I misrepresented you in any way. I tried to remain as accurate as possible while still achieving a coherent whole. I don't know if I was successful or not.

Please excuse the brevity of this note, but I told Margi most of the news last night and I'm fighting against the clock to get a number of packages to the post office before it closes.

Take care. I'll write a longer letter as soon as time permits.

"Spirit on a String"

"Please Do Not Smoke in Our House." I must've read the sign seven times before I rapped on the door. I knew very well what it meant. But no amount of knowledge could ease the tragedy, could ease the pain. "Don't let her see how you feel," I told myself. "Make this a time for fun."

I'd never met Margi Stevens, but I sure knew her. As a Peace Corps volunteer in Western Samoa, I'd sent the following SOS to the International Book Project in Lexington, Kentucky: "Academically speaking, I'm in Paradise Lost. I teach English, math, and science at a high school with three hundred students, 150 desks, and zero books. I've been told your books have rescued a number of people from the 'Educational Twilight Zone.' I was wondering: Could you do the same for me?"

Fairy godmothers do not die in childhood. I found that out in a hurry. Posters, stencils, flash cards, and textbooks poured into the school. Mostly from Margi. From the first, her letters were bright and bouncy: "I read your letter in the IBP bulletin and I can't wait to help you! I'm a sixty-year-old woman married to a seventy-three-year-old genius. We paint pictures and produce puppet shows. My hobby is the book project because I'm an avid reader and cannot bear to see good books destroyed, when they are cherished in other countries."

But even fairy godmothers have black cats. Margi never mentioned hers by name. It just crept into her letters from time to time: "I can only wrap about three packages a day. When you don't get enough oxygen in your blood, you can't do much. But I sure won't complain. I'd rather creep around and rest a lot than be bedridden or in a wheelchair!"

Margi sent school materials until I completed my tour of service. Upon my return to the United States, I went on a business trip to solicit aid for needy schools overseas. Fortunately, Margi and her husband Steve lay in my path. I phoned and asked them if I could play George Washington for a night or two. "General," said Steve, "for you, we have free straw."

That invitation had brought me to their doorstep in northern Indiana. Obeying the sign, I flicked my cigarette into the cold, night air. It fizzled and died as it hit the snow. The door opened, and a medium-sized man stood before me. His face was worn and weather-beaten. Still, he looked young and vital, especially about the mouth and eyes. The hair on his head had seen better harvests, but the growth at the sides and the rear would see him through the winter.

"Mr. Stevens, I'm—"

"Gerry Christmas!" he boomed, gathering me in like a long-lost son. "Come in before you turn into an icicle."

Steve led me through the kitchen and into the living room. There, huddled in a Morris chair, sat Margi. A small breathing machine stood on the table beside her. It had a couple of dials and a long hose that made it look like a portable Electrolux.

"Margi Stevens," I said. "Husband or no husband, I'm going to kiss you."

"I should hope so," she said. "I didn't send those books for nothing."

The woman affected me greatly. Some people live on spirit and very little else. Margi was a case in point. Her physical shell was as delicate as crystal. But it wasn't about to break. Not yet. Her soft smile and bright eyes told me that.

"Now sit down and make yourself comfortable," she said in a low, wheezy voice. "I've so many questions to ask you."

Margi looked drawn and tired, so I took my cue from Steve. Western Union couldn't have telegraphed a clearer message than the one I read in his eyes.

"Why don't we wait till tomorrow?" I said. "It's nearly midnight, and that bus ride has turned my brain to mush."

"Oh, bunk," said Margi. "If this chair can stand me for two hours, you can stand me for two minutes." She turned to her husband. "Really, honey. I'm all right. I had a tough day, but I'm much better now."

Steve melted like a bar of margarine.

"Okay," he said. "You get the KO tonight. We'll stay up and talk, but not for long. You were on the machine a lot today."

"What does the machine do?" I asked.

"It keeps me alive," said Margi. "The machine drives air into the lungs and forces me to cough. This clears my lungs of mucous and I'm able to carry on." She shook her head and smiled. "Oh, let's not talk about that. Let's sink our teeth into something juicy. Tell me, Gerry: Did the books really help you?"

"Did they ever! I don't know what I would've done without them. As far as I'm concerned, Florence Nightingale lives in Indiana."

"Hush now."

"No, I mean it. And I'm not the only one who thinks so. I've been told that you sent eight thousand free books overseas last year. Is that true?"

"That's the rumor," she said. "But Steve and I never count. Figures tend to mess up the fun."

"Steve helps you a lot, doesn't he?"

"He sure does. He wraps and I tie. It's a lot of work, but it's worthwhile. One man over in Africa has been getting books for years. His wife is about to have their firstborn. He wrote and told me that he's going to name the baby after me. I only hope it's a girl."

"How did you get involved with the books in the first place?"

"Margi has a lot in common with Willie Sutton," said Steve. "Only with Sutton, it wasn't books. It was other people's money. When the cops finally nabbed him, someone asked: 'What makes you crack safes?' Willie replied: 'Ya gotta love it.' That best explains Margi. She loves it. Why, look at this place!" He threw up his hands in mock despair. "This used to be an art studio, a sanctuary for creative endeavor. Then Margi went on her book binge. Now it's a warehouse."

Steve was right. The room looked like a mad bibliophile's haunt. Packed and unpacked books were strewn everywhere. And yet the place was not messy. Messiness has a self-seeking aspect, an unhealthy disorder that makes one squirm. Here, no such feeling existed. I felt very much at home.

"Margi, how did you meet Steve?"

"I was doing puppets myself, and his name was flying about like a comet. So I got on a train and went down to see the great man. I fell in love the moment I saw him."

"What about Steve?"

"I told her to get lost," he said gruffly.

My eye spotted a picture on the wall. It was a sleek black-and-white job, the kind used to promote shows. It was about twenty years old, and the girl in the picture was gorgeous. Her face was milky-white, and her eyes were soft and luminous. A black satin dress made her face shine like a solitary star in the sky.

"You told *that* to get lost?" I said incredulously. "Wow!"

Margi giggled.

"I had to," said Steve. "I was about to give a performance and had no time for distractions. But I can sympathize with you. Once, I sent a copy of that picture to a fellow puppeteer. His reply was highly professional. He wanted to play puppets with the babe in the picture. I shot back a short note that said: 'Sorry, my friend. She's all booked up. She's working with me, and she's my wife.' I never heard from the guy again."

"Did you have a wild and woolly romance?"

"Did we ever," said Steve. "One day, I got off the train, and forty minutes later, we were married."

"What happened during those forty minutes?"

"You'll never guess, and I'm not going to tell you."

"Did you give her an ultimatum?"

"Hah! That would've been mild compared to what really happened."

"She gave you an ultimatum."

"Keep trying," he said. "It's good for the imagination. But you'll never know, and we'll never tell. Will we, dear?"

Margi smiled and Steve squeezed her hand. A little later, we went to bed. Steve took me out back to the trailer. I was free to smoke there. Somehow, I didn't feel like lighting up.

I was up bright and early the next morning. Still, Steve beat me to the coffee kettle. The bacon and eggs hit the pan as soon as I entered the kitchen.

"Grab a chair," he said. "I'll have you fixed up in a jiffy."

I sat down at the dinette.

"What time does Margi get up?" I asked.

"She should be up soon, although I hope she stays in bed a bit. She had a rough time last night. Hardly slept at all."

"Is that unusual?"

"I wish it were," he said gloomily. "But that infernal disease never sleeps. It's at her all the time. The last few days have been particularly vicious. Don't be alarmed if we have to make a trip to the hospital today."

"How does she stand it?"

"Damned if I know. I only married the woman."

Steve put the breakfast on the table and sat down.

"I don't understand how you stand it," I said. "I know I couldn't."

"Don't underestimate yourself. Circumstances often simplify the rules of the game. One time, I heard this Zen master. Now, Zen can be heady stuff, especially if you haven't studied it. But this fellow was good. He took a stick and balanced it on the tip of his finger. Pointing from the fulcrum to one end of the stick, he said: 'This is your past, and there's nothing you can *do* about it.' Then he ran his finger from the fulcrum to the other end of the stick and said: 'This is your future, and there's nothing you can know about it. But here'—Steve pointed to the fulcrum—'is now. Not only for you but for everyone. It's the only reality you have. And it's more than enough to keep you occupied.' Believe me, Margi and I are occupied. People in love usually are."

"You and Margi are lucky."

"Luck's got nothing to do with it. You find in people what you want to find. Forty years ago, I was told that this puppeteer wasn't liked by anyone in the business. I had to meet him, and I decided, hot damn, I was going to like him. He was a tough little shit from New York, but there was something about him I liked. Indeed, he's the best friend I've got. One night, we were on top of a skyscraper overlooking Broadway. The city looked like a sea of phosphorescent plankton. My friend turned to me and said, 'Steve, there's too much out there. We can't learn it all. We must trust our hearts and be content with the lives we have.'"

His eyes grew large and theatrical.

"Now tell me," he said. "Does that sound like a man I shouldn't like?"

I laughed.

"You've made your point," I said.

"I hope so," said Steve. "People have a bad habit of backsliding, of forgetting how unique and wonderful they are." He reached across the table and grabbed my right thumb below the joint. "Don't underestimate yourself," he repeated. "See that thumbprint? It's different. There's not another one in the world like it. Something about God: he can't stand two things being the same."

"You really enjoy life, don't you?"

"You bet I do. And I don't have any sympathy for the man who doesn't. That's his fault. There's nothing in life—food and sex included—that gives a man more pleasure than worthwhile work. God made us that way. We're beasts of burden, and there's nothing we can do about it."

"Does that include puppeteers?"

"All of the good ones and some of the bad ones."

"How good is the guy who started the Muppets?"

Steve beamed.

"Henson? He's marvelous, a true joy. I met him years ago at a puppeteer convention. He was there with his wife and child. He wasn't a big name then. He was toting his baby around in a grapefruit crate."

"What makes Henson so good?"

"Technically and artistically, he's a genius. Everything he does is well thought out and superbly executed. Furthermore, he's done wonders for puppeteers in general. For years, people looked upon us as a bunch of bozos who bounced stringed dolls for children. Then Henson came along, and he was so good that everyone had to perk up and take notice. Thank God I lived to see it. You don't know how many times I've seen grown-ups stop and stare at my show, only to drop their heads and slink away."

"How come?"

"They were ashamed. The silly fools! They were ashamed someone would see that they were having a good time. People go to a lot of trouble not to have fun."

Margi entered the kitchen without saying a word. She couldn't. All her concentration—all of her energy—was focused on the chair beside me. She moved slowly and steadily toward it. I sat transfixed, terrified. She seemed half out of this world. Her gray eyes had the look of a frightened animal, and her breath was agonizingly prolonged, like someone trying to go up Mt. Everest without oxygen. Only when she finally reached the chair did her fear fall away and the smile of the previous night return.

"Please forgive me," she said. "Some days are worse than others."

The pain on Steve's face was impossible to conceal. And yet he remained silent. What was there to say? The day-to-day battle had brought about a union, a unique understanding that challenged death itself. They must've been moments of sheer terror when the ordeal began. But Margi and Steve were beyond that now.

"You know," continued Margi. "I used to smoke two packs a day. People warned me but, oh, no, I was different. Or so I thought. One day, I went to the doctor, breathless. Sure enough, he lit a match and told me to blow it out. I tried and tried. But I couldn't even make the flame quiver. That was twenty years ago."

"Twenty years is a long time," I said.

"Yes, I suppose so," she said. "Still, inevitable suffocation is not a pleasant thought. It takes getting used to."

"That's what people don't understand," said Steve. "They don't know how grim the penalties are." He paused. For the first time, there was anger in his voice. "And they're not about to find out, either. One of our sons makes short documentary films. A few years ago, he did one on Margi and her condition. He said it was the finest piece he'd ever done. But nobody would touch it. Nobody wanted to offend the big-tobacco boys. Can you believe that?"

Later that morning, Margi had to be put on the machine. She only got partial relief. Her breathing remained long and labored. Steve did everything in his power to help her. But, finally, he threw in the towel.

"We'd better get her to the hospital," he said. "She might need oxygen. God, you should've seen her before this monster got a hold of her. She had so much pep. You couldn't keep her down."

Going to the hospital was no joyride. Margi had made the trip countless times, and Steve had often returned without her. This upset her. She had nothing against the hospital. On the contrary, the doctors and the nurses were good folks, very competent and attentive. But nothing could take the place of home. Home was her art classes. Home was her books. Home was the soft rays of the sun flooding in through the studio windows. Home was waiting for a picture of her African namesake. But most of all home was Steve, wide-eyed, warmhearted Steve. Somehow, life didn't make sense without him.

Margi was with the doctors a long time. When she finally came out, she looked like she'd won the Irish Sweepstakes.

"I can go home," she beamed. "I have to go easy, but I can go home."

On the way back, Margi was on top of the world. And Steve was right there with her.

"Oh, I'm so happy," she said. "There's nothing as lonely as a hospital at night."

From the backseat, through the bucket seats, I could see Steve reach across and take her by the hand.

It was his way of saying she would never die.

Epistle Forty-Six

July 27, 1979

Dear Harriet:

While mulling over our mutual endeavors to donate books to the Thai teacher training colleges, I've come to certain conclusions that may or may not be correct. Since you'll be a huge part of the process, it's only right and proper that I share these thoughts with you. I've couched these musings in the form of a preliminary proposal. I don't pretend to know anything about proposal writing, nor is this intended to be a formal proposal, per se. I just want you to know my thoughts on the subject. I should warn you, however, that what follows is pretty dry. But without dryness, how could we appreciate a mirage or, better yet, an oasis?

Preliminary Proposal

Historically, Thailand has bent with the wind. This has served the Thais well, for no foreign country has ever colonized them. This resilience, however, has had its drawbacks. For example, whereas Japan, Malaysia, and the Philippines have used their friendship with the United States to benefit their educational institutions, Thailand has only done so on a limited basis. Just how limited can be readily seen in the *1977 Books for Asia Program Report*:

Country	Total Volume	Books	Journals
Japan	2,444,930	2,145,555	299,375
Malaysia	1,123,056	1,090,826	32,230
Philippines	6,658,172	6,098,778	559,394
Thailand	238,158	179,460	58,698

What makes matters worse is that Thailand's books go primarily to universities and technical colleges. Most students at these institutions are from affluent families, where vigorous English instruction begins at an early age. Students from middle- and low-income families usually go to the teacher training colleges if they are lucky enough to pass the entrance examination.

Thailand has thirty-five teacher training colleges. Not one of these schools has a decent supply of English textbooks. As a result, Thai students must buy books their teachers assign. Since many students are poor, the teachers tend to assign inexpensive books, usually Longman simplified readers. In recent years, however, even these books have become too expensive. Most Longman readers run to one hundred pages and cost upwards of thirty-five baht ($1.75 USD). By US standards, this seems reasonable. But it isn't in Thailand, where a worker is lucky to make one hundred baht (five US dollars) *per day*.

Furthermore, Longman readers were never intended to meet the rigors of a serious English class. Unfortunately, this is precisely how they are being used in many schools. The results have been predictable: tedium one day and ennui the next. With much of the life's blood drained from the books, I'm surprised that Thai students still approach English with warmth and enthusiasm. Just think what the response would be if the books were dynamic and alive.

The teachers are not much better off than the students. Since Longman readers usually take the form of a novel, the teachers are skewered to one story line. This is not a serious problem with such winners as *Tom Sawyer* and *Treasure Island*. But these books have fascinating characters, exotic settings, and stimulating plots; hence, they hold up well in class. Other books do not. They were written for pleasure, not for classroom analysis.

Thai students respond better to short stories than novels. The salient reasons for this are:

- Short stories can be covered quickly. If the students don't like a story, the pain is transitory. A bad classroom novel, on the other hand, is like being on the rack at the Spanish Inquisition.
- Short stories are less intimidating. The students can see "the light at the end of the tunnel" after a few pages. Not so with a novel, where they are "in the dark" for one hundred pages at least.
- Short stories allow a teacher to present many different types of prose. Even

nonfiction can be incorporated to stimulate those students more practically inclined.

Once one grasps the situation in the Thai teacher training colleges, the next question is obvious: Why doesn't someone take discarded books in the United States and pump them into the Thai schools? Well, someone should. But it isn't as simple as it first appears. There are major hurdles to clear on both sides. On the Thai side the hurdles include:

- **Shyness.** Thais are not squeaky doors. As a result, they rarely get the oil. At the root of this shyness is the concept of *granjai,* for which there is no precise English word. *Consideration* and *deference* come close, but both lack the emotional and cultural punch––the deep uneasiness that all Thais feel whenever a favor is bestowed upon them.
- **Provincialism.** Thais, though open and friendly, can be insular and timid. Only in recent years have they gone abroad in large numbers. And those that have rarely return to posts at teacher colleges.
- **Communications.** Thais are not familiar with American institutions, particularly those of a philanthropic nature. Help goes unsought not through inertia but through ignorance. Most Thais do not believe that

anyone really cares. Here, I hope they are wrong and I am right.

On the American side, the hurdles include:

- **Selection.** Though books abound, not all are useful. Many individuals and groups donate books just to get rid of them. At best, this is hit-and-miss aid—mostly miss.
- **Contacts.** Usually, the donor does not know the recipient. Sure, donor and recipient may exchange letters, but more often than not, the recipient feels uncomfortable spelling out exactly what he needs. This can be both frustrating and a waste of time and money.
- **Organization.** Book donors often work in isolation. Such individualism, though laudatory, can spell disaster. The entire process, from selection to shipment, must be done with great care in order to minimize expenses and maximize safety. This takes teamwork.
- **Shipping Costs.** A donor gets more for his dollar when he sends books to a school instead of a person. But there's a catch: *the needs of a school are far greater.* Whereas five books may help a person, a good five hundred are needed to impact a school. This takes money.

Shipping costs are the greatest threat to any book project. The present international bulk surface rate is twenty-five cents per pound. Though inexpensive on a small scale, it is not so on a large scale when a donor wishes to send thousands of pounds of books.

Fundraising then becomes essential. From a donor's point of view, this seems patently unfair. Why should the donor pay postage on top of everything else? To my mind, he shouldn't. But developing nations have a show-me-I'm-from-Missouri mentality. The donor thus assumes the heavy burden of postage costs.

Admittedly, the donor is making a sucker out of himself. Still, there is a simple solution. When the recipient comes back with a second request, the donor politely tells the recipient that, going forward, only books and labor are free. Unless the recipient has an IQ twenty points lower than a eucalyptus tree, he'll cough up. A person has to be downright dense to pass up quality books at 10 percent of the cost.

My proposal is simple: I want to establish a steady stream of books to Thai teacher training colleges. Normally, I'd never attempt such a venture. But I find myself in an unusual position. As an English teacher in a Thai school, I can expedite matters at both ends.

On the Thai side, I can make sure that the books arrive safely, that they are distributed to the appropriate schools, and that they are used on a regular basis. Furthermore, I can write periodic reports, thus keeping donors up-to-date on how their aid is being used. This will enable us to make the appropriate changes as new problems arise.

I should also mention that I'm not without official support. Dr. Arun is eager to establish a model reading room at my school. Hopefully, Chan Kasem Teachers Training College will serve as a prototype for other schools throughout the country.

On the American side, I have a number of people standing by with free books and free labor. For example, Harriet Van Meter of the International Book Project in Lexington, Kentucky, has a warehouse of first-rate books, along with an army of donors scattered nationwide. Unfortunately, Harriet cannot send a large supply of books to Thailand since she's working with a limited budget. Recently, I talked with her over the telephone.

"I can pack and send the books at seventy cents per pound," she said. "If someone can help us with the postage, we can do everything else."

This offer will be hard to beat, since I've worked with Mrs. Van Meter and can attest to her dedication, ingenuity, and integrity.

The impact of good books on Thai teacher training colleges is difficult to predict. But it could be significant, perhaps startling. It would not only benefit Thai teachers and students but would also be a positive step toward mutual understanding and cooperation. Like most developing nations, Thailand is trying to break the shackles of modern-day feudalism. In doing so, the Thais are fighting a strong tradition of xenophobia. This can be seen at all levels: from the consolidation of farms to the assimilation of modern technology.

What this will do to Thailand remains to be seen. The ordeal of change is never easy. Hopefully, the fate of the country will be determined by the will of the people. And the best way to safeguard the will of the people is through the dissemination of knowledge. For only then can mutual trust be attained; only then can we touch human hearts and create a global spirit of love and caring.

Immediate Needs: 2,000 high-content books at the fifth-, sixth-, and seventh-grade reading level.
Estimated Shipping Cost: $1,000 (USD)
Book Donor: The International Book Project
　　　　　　　　Harriet Van Meter, Director
　　　　　　　　17 Mentelle Park
　　　　　　　　Lexington, Kentucky
Book Recipient: Chan Kasem Teachers College
　　　　　　　　Director General
　　　　　　　　Ministry of Education
　　　　　　　　Bangkok, Thailand

My good friend and colleague, Ajaan Linly, on the balcony
outside the English Department at
Chan Kasem Teachers College
Linly was not only a wonderful teacher
but the author of many educational books as well.

Epistle Forty-Seven

August 5, 1979

Dear Tocher:

Reentry into Thailand has been sweet but hectic. Terry picked me up at the airport. Though tired from the long flight, I was full of piss and vinegar, so Terry had to bring me back to earth.

The next day, I had a surreal lunch with Bright Eyes. She seemed happy to have me back. It's too early to tell where our relationship will lead. Smart, saucy, and sexy, she's still a fox—Thailand's answer to Bettie Page, bangs and all.

The Thai teachers at Chan Kasem greeted me with open arms, except, alas, the departmental head, Ajaan Thomark. I don't know what's eating her. I suspect she was hoping for a more erudite and proper farang. Too bad I don't fill the bill.

With the help of Ajaan Linly, I landed a neat set of digs: two bedrooms, burnished hardwood floors, a full kitchen, and a porch overlooking a fair-sized swimming pool. The place wasn't really for rent. The owner is a Thai businessman who lets it out "to friends." My incoming phone calls would make Suzie Wong blush.

I have to wait a few days for the mia noi to move out. The guy's wife found out about her and made quite a scene. So the landlady wants the mia noi out and me in. Next door, there's a real cutie, friendly with a two-year-old, snow-white kid but no sign of daddy. The Thai beat goes on.

Now flushed with bucks, I don't know how long I can stay celibate. The Peace Corps gave me the footloose and fancy-free image that keeps bachelors off the endangered-species list. Women, as you know, seek out nest-makers, whatever they might say to the contrary. But to be a proper nest-maker takes cash and practicality. Now loaded with cash, I suspect it's only a matter of time before some woman *assumes* I'm practical. What a ludicrous deduction!

My six weeks in the States were great. My mother bounced back from her operation, and my father, despite sporting three belly buttons, appears on the mend from his prostate surgery. I packed 2,737 textbooks in Phoenix and sent them to Bangkok at a postage cost of eight hundred dollars. That's what got me my job, that and Terry's recommendation. Ajaan Pintip, one of the head honchos at the Ministry of Education, even joked with me about it.

"You got us into trouble with those books," she said. "We were all set to hire another guy and then you called and told us those books had been mailed. What could we do?"

I laughed.

"It's funny now," she said. "But it wasn't funny at the time. We had to put the other guy off till next year."

A twinkle came into her brown eyes.

"We solved the problem Thai-style, didn't we?"

But I deserve the job. No one but me is pumping books into the teacher training colleges. Moreover, they're needed more now than ever. English proficiency among Thai students has gone south since you jocked the land. The Ministry of Education has saddled the schools with a curriculum glutted with gut education courses. Thanks, Uncle Sam. Instead of granting scholarships in American and English literature, many US colleges let Thais get away with Tweedledum and Tweedledee linguistics classes. Eventually, these students came home to roost, securing lucrative and influential positions in the Thai Ministry of Education.

Aied and I still resemble Werner von Braun's early attempts to launch rockets from Peenemunde. During our first date, she looked about as happy as a baby without a thumb. But it wasn't me. Mom moved into a new house in Samut Prakan; hence, Aied had to move in with her father. This not only meant a two-hour commute to work but also living with her father's self-seeking and avaricious mia noi.

To further complicate matters, Mazda is having staff problems, and this has not helped her gut. What's with her gut? I suspect a stomach ulcer aggravated by the Thai addiction to hot red peppers. Sure, I've tried to get Aied to see my American-trained doctor. But she has repeatedly refused. Yes, yes, I know. She's even more stubborn than me. .

Still, today we had a great time together shopping and eating and eating and shopping. Of course, Aied had invited her friend Noi along. But I didn't mind, since Noi was good company. With Aied looking at me wide-eyed across the table, Noi leaned forward and asked a question that had clearly perplexed her for years.

"Do you like *everything* about Aied?"

"Everything," I said seriously. "Even her crooked front tooth. That's what I spend most of my time looking at."

Aied was visibly upset, so upset she couldn't even speak. When will I ever learn to keep my big mouth shut?

Your setup in Manila sounds sweet. A bit Tai-Panish, but sweet. As for the sixteen-foot ceiling, are you trying to be oblique? Even Scottish tree trucks don't come that big!

Aied's niece leaning over a cistern used
for collecting rainwater (1980)
Most Thai children have little but always
invent simple ways to be happy.
I rarely saw a Thai child sad for any length of time.

Epistle Forty-Eight

October 2, 1979

Dear Mom and Dad:

I'd best put the poop behind me. Aied and I broke up last week. I couldn't stand the drama and the mind games any more.

One night, for instance, I took Aied and three of her friends to dinner at Thai Daimaru. Noi, Sumalee, and Lek were pleasant and fun; Aied, on the other hand, had a real burr up her ass.

"Let's have some fun," she said. "Ask the waiter if he thinks I'm a *sopanee*."

What the heck had put that idea into her bean? Had she gone stark, staring mad? Had she left her brain on the bank of a *klong*?

"Come on," she said. "I dare you."

"No," I said. "You can dare me all you want, but I'm not stupid. Now, if you want to ask him the same question, go right ahead. I'm sure your friends would like that."

After dinner, we went window-shopping in Siam Square. I did my best to be pleasant, but Aied didn't come around. Instead, she remained stuck in bitch mode. The bum's rush is much the same in any language, and she was sure giving it to me Thai style. Finally, I couldn't take it anymore.

"Listen, Aied. I don't know what's eating you, but let me be blunt: you're not much fun tonight."

Her friends could see my anger, my unease. In such situations, the Thais are marvelous. They not only hate to lose face but hate to see others lose face, too. Noi was especially nice and conciliatory. She knew Aied was way out of line and delicately told her so with furtive glances.

Noi's efforts, however, were all for naught. Inside of an hour, everyone knew the ship was sunk. Saying good-bye was never so sweet. Still, Aied had the last word.

"Better luck next time," she said, strutting away.

I said nothing. Returning to the apartment, I decided that "next time" would be on my terms. Usually, I telephone her daily. Now I was determined never to telephone her again.

Three weeks passed with no word from Aied. This did not surprise me. In Siam, single women are not supposed to call single men. It's not considered proper. I was, therefore, surprised one night when Sumalee called.

"How are you, Gerry?"

"I'm fine," I lied. "How are you?"

I was playing for time. *What the hell is going on?* I thought. *Sumalee's not the type to fiddle with social norms. She's proud, elegant, and polite to a fault. This is not like her.*

"Gerry, you're a nice man. I want you to know that I didn't like the way Aied treated you the other night."

"Thank you, Sumalee. That's very sweet of you."

"I ... I also want you to know that I'd like to be your friend ... now that Aied's gone."

For a moment, I was speechless.

"That's very kind of you," I said finally. "But I don't think I'll date for a while. I'd better concentrate on my work."

"I understand," she said. "*Sawadee*, Gerry."

"Sawadee," I said.

The next day, I called my friend Arun and told him about Sumalee's telephone call.

Arun laughed.

"That's funny," he said. "When a Thai woman likes a man, when she respects him but does not want to become too involved, she tries to get a friend to take her place."

"But that's crazy," I said.

"Not really," he said. "Aied doesn't want you to have a broken heart, so she asked Sumalee to take her place. It's the Thai way."

It was also Aied's way of ending the affair. I'm too old to wear my emotions on my sleeve, so let me just say: "You warned me, Mom." Still, I'm disappointed with Aied. She could've taken me aside and told me directly. Instead, she chose the low, furtive, slinky, indirect way, much like Ruth Morse in Jack London's *Martin Eden*.

That hurts and will continue to hurt. How we humans waste our time, waste our money, and waste our love on low-thinkers, on people who are fickle and flighty. There's something juvenile about it all. It shows a lack of judgment, a lack of class.

Two student volunteers helping sort and catalogue books for the Reading Room at Chan Kasem.

Epistle Forty-Nine

October 7, 1979

Dear Mom and Dad:

My job is an odd bucket. The biggest hole in the bucket is what I call "the model college syndrome." The idea for a model college began last year at the Ministry of Education. Bureaucrats get their jollies by tinkering from afar, and Thai bureaucrats are no exception. Word came from on high: *Chan Kasem was officially crowned the model teacher training college in the country.*

It was a bad choice. The English Department has been in the doldrums for three years. There are a number of reasons for this, the primary ones being:

- The new curriculum that stresses education methodology and linguistics rather than basic English skills.
- The inability of the staff to work together effectively.
- The lack of leadership and vision.

My arrival on the scene has caused a stir. Some Thai teachers resent that a native speaker is now in their midst. Having identified these teachers, I've eliminated them from my orbit.

The bulk of the teachers seem to like me. They are, however, at odds as to my role, as to how to use me as a resource. And therein lies the rub. Increasingly, I find petty projects gobbling up my time. Two weeks ago, I sent a report to the Ministry of Education with a copy going to the president of the college.

In essence, the report said I was being spread too thin. Why? Well, some teachers expect me to plug holes caused by a year's sloth. Above and beyond my regular classes, these teachers also want tapes for the sound lab, teaching material for new courses, original plays, and tutoring at night. The book project? Oh, that's easy. Just settle in, scribble a few notes, and the books will materialize.

That's where I drew the line. Starting next term, the book project comes first. And if the teachers don't like it, I'm gone. I've a beautiful setup here and a great group of students, but I'm not staying to do other people's work.

Luckily, there're some rainbows. The president wants a reading room, a model reading room that he can proudly parade. Thanks to you, we have a good beginning. All the books arrived safely. Chan Kasem got only eight hundred books, but I handpicked those. The rest went to the other TTCs. I didn't agree with the decision to break up the books. Some teachers at the ministry bragged about the shipment, so the pie had to be divided. Still, I ended up with the lion's share. Two enthusiastic teachers, Ajaan Linly and Ajaan Pikun, are now busy cataloguing every book. During the term break, the three of us will work on the reading room together. If all goes well, we should have a nice little library by mid-November.

The initial response to the books has been interesting. No one knows how to use them. I'm not joking. The concept of class sets is unfamiliar to Thai teachers and students. So my teaching must begin there. Unfortunately, I'm not going to teach a reading course next term. But that's not unusual. Thai teachers feel more comfortable with grammar and reading, so native speakers usually end up with the conversation and writing classes.

The reading level of the books appears to be spot-on. The students understand the stories and are reading more. Some teachers want to continue teaching such novellas as Steinbeck's *The Pearl* and Orwell's *Animal Farm*. Within reason, I'm not against that, but it tends to be overdone. The students need to get into the habit of reading. A few choice novellas may make an excellent appetizer but fail miserably as a seven-course meal.

My apartment is great. Sure, the toilet backs up every now and then, and last weekend, the bathroom flooded. Overall, however, this is a swanky pad, especially by Thai standards.

I'm slowly getting familiar with the neighborhood. At first, I searched and searched and searched for a good, cheap restaurant, one close to the apartment. I was about to give up when I stopped by a tiny eatery not a stone's throw down the road. Bull's eye! The owner's name is Dang. Dang has only four years of schooling, but can she ever cook. About three weeks ago, she decided to adopt me. Giving me a special table in the back, she cooks my meals while her son and daughter wait on me. Talk about being spoiled!

Though you're in Phoenix and I'm in Bangkok, I don't think of you as being far away. Over the years, you've burned your souls into mine; thus, I carry the scar tissue wherever I go. This scar tissue is stronger than the rest of the flesh. It can tolerate more pain, thanks to your teaching, thanks to your love.

At heart, I'm still your child, both in age and in wisdom. I still draw from you. Only now I draw more from your spirit than from your pocket. For you, this is not a lighter burden but a heavier one. This makes me sad. Yet, I know you want it this way. I can only hope that if I ever have any children, I'll be as brave and as true to them as you have been with me.

Young Thai women are geniuses at disguising their poverty.
Aied was no exception.

Epistle Fifty

December 1, 1979

Dear Mom and Dad:

Aied didn't let me off the hook that night. She called back, and we started to see each other again. But our relationship had changed. I could tell that right away. She couldn't look me in the eye, like in the old days. As a rule, women are like that: *they break sticks slowly.*

One day, I got a phone call from her at school. She wouldn't speak in English. That would've been fine, but she was talking heavy, emotional stuff, and I couldn't follow her. Suddenly, she had to relinquish the phone to an office colleague, so she asked me to call back. I did an hour later. This time, she spoke in English. In a way, I wish she hadn't because right in the middle of the conversation, she dropped a bomb.

"Gerry, you're not a man in my attitude," she said bluntly.

I'd always loved the way Aied experimented with the English language. Even her mistakes sounded quaint and cute. This one did not. It cut me to the quick. But she wasn't finished, not by a long shot.

"What do you think?" she said after a long pause.

I was speechless. I looked out at the pond in front of the school. It looked so quiet and peaceful.

"Good-bye," I said.

I then hung up the phone and walked back to my desk. I'd work to do.

The next few days were pretty hairy. A slow rage surged within me. Somehow, I felt cheated. Certainly Aied knew how I felt years ago. Why hadn't she given me the heave-ho then?

Knowing I wasn't about to get an answer from her, I telephoned Sumalee. We met at her house two nights later.

Over tea in the living room, I told Sumalee what Aied had said over the phone.

"You're lucky to be rid of her," she said.

That surprised me, considering how close they were. But I didn't ask for clarification. I'd come for the truth.

"Has Aied ever been married?" I asked.

Sumalee knitted her brows.

"Do you really want me to answer that question?"

"Yes, I do. I need to know."

"Well, Aied has never told me outright, but her name at Mazda has a *nang* before it."

"Thank you, Sumalee."

"Please don't tell Aied I told you," she said. "She'd never forgive me."

"Don't worry. I won't."

I excused myself and left. I felt like an overused toy, but at least I was still spinning my wheels.

A few days later, Terry Fredrickson came to Chan Kasem to see me.

"Aied called me last night," he said.

"Oh, really. How was she?"

"Mai sabai jai," he said. "Those were her exact words."

"Shit."

Terry laughed.

"She's paranoid about marriage, Gerry. She went on and on about culture and language and how moody a person she is."

"Boy, I've heard that before," I said. "What did you tell her?"

"I told her that she was fooling herself, that her fears were irrational and silly. The only question was whether she loved you or not. I told her this in Thai so she understood every word."

"Thanks, Terry. I apologize for making you play Dear Abby."

Still, I had to be sure. I had to see Aied once more to clear the decks. The high school, cornball crap had to come to an end before we started to hate each other, before we declared all-out war.

We met last night at a restaurant halfway between her place and mine. It's sad when you feel sorry for the woman you love. But that's how I feel about Aied now. She didn't talk about it, but she didn't have to talk about it. She couldn't look me in the eye all the time we talked. Some bastard had taken her to bed three or four years ago and she couldn't get over it.

"There's something dirty about love, Gerry. I've two other boyfriends and they love me very much, but sometimes they are very selfish …"

Her voice trailed off into an inaudible whisper. We were eating ice cream. How oddly symbolic, how fitting.

"For God's sake, Aied. Stop living in the past. Okay, you don't love me. I can accept that. But start thinking about the present and the future. Sure, you've had some bad luck, but stay strong. Be brave. Learn to live with it."

Her head fell down.

"My insides are not strong enough," she said. "I'll never be happy."

"Are we still friends?"

Her head came up, and she smiled.

"Yes, we will always be friends. You know that."

"I'd like to continue seeing your mother," I said. "Is that all right with you?"

"Don't be silly, Gerry. You know she loves you like a son."

So Aied is gone, this time for good. I feel sure of that. Still, life is a curveball. Strange how sure things sometimes don't end up being so sure.

My way is clear: *I'm going to work my ass off.* I've divided English teachers at Chan Kasem into two groups: the workers and the drones. Too bad Ajaan Thomark falls into the latter category. All she ever does is bog me down with trivia. I've been a nice guy for three months, but I'd better put my foot down. Thailand isn't the only country in the world. If the department head doesn't like me, I'd best bug off.

Still, the college president and the folks at the ministry like my work. I've recently received a set of thirty first-rate ESL books from McGraw-Hill, and Darien Book Aid Plan in Darien, Connecticut is sending technical books to the science and technology departments. In addition, Project Handclasp wants to send two thousand books from the Philippines. So I'm holding a high hand. My best bet is to work with the workers and leave the drones to their lard. Most Thai drones are easy to please: one just has to smile every now and then.

Though devoted Buddhists, Thai students
never forego a good time,
as can be seen here at the Christmas party in 1980.
Both the nativity scene and the decorations
were made from scratch.

Epistle Fifty-One

January 1, 1980

Dear Mom and Dad:

I must be getting old. I spent last night alone. At the stroke of twelve, I gazed at the clock with a vapid, vacant look. A few firecrackers popped off next door, but besides that, the neighborhood was quiescent. The action was elsewhere: at public parks and private parties, at Pat Pong, and at Buddhist pagodas.

Thanks to my students, I had a great Christmas. They put together a Christmas party that Christians would've envied. On first coming to Thailand, I could see little of the Christmas spirit. Then, seemingly overnight, the Thais realized that they were missing out on the biggest holiday in the world. In a matter of a few years, Christmas caught on, not as a celebration of Jesus Christ but as an excuse to spend money and have a good time. Bangkok merchants began stocking their stores with gifts. Winsome young Thai women, dressed as Santa's elves, hit the streets to drum up business. Fully decorated Christmas trees, replete with lights, balls, and tinsel, stood in the bigger stores. And, yes, Christmas carols could be heard everywhere.

For three days, my students labored to prepare for the festivities. They worked painting nativity scenes, constructing a mock-up chimney with huge stockings, designing an aluminum-and-cotton snowman, and setting up a fully decorated Christmas tree. The tree was the real wonder. Chop, a fine upcountry boy, went out and scaled a tall evergreen. Machete in hand, he hacked off the upper branches, tied them

Gerry Christmas

together, and stuck them into a large, earthen flowerpot. The female students made the decorations for the tree out of papier-mâché, while the male students strung long paper garlands across the ceiling. My only contribution was a short history of Christmas along with the more famous religious and secular carols. Who in the room was the better Christian?

The students and I had only an hour to practice the carols. But what we didn't know, we faked, and no one was the wiser. The president of the college couldn't come to the party, but he did send his most dapper and debonair underling, "Mr. Slick," to cut the red ribbon, *wai* to one and all, and proclaim his self-importance. Sompit, my most energetic and extroverted student, topped the festivities off with an incredible wassail that vanished inside an hour. The punch did better, but only because we had bought too much of it.

I didn't enjoy the party as much as the Thais because I was "saving face" by taking pictures. I shot two rolls of Kodak Kodachrome. The first roll, being shots of officials and dignitaries, came out horrid, whereas the second roll, being shots of the students, came out grand. I'm slowly gaining a local reputation as a good amateur photographer. Some of my early photos, especially those of Loi Krathong and our play *Orawan's Test,* were a big hit with the students. My forte appears to be people. I've a knack of capturing facial expressions in the four- to ten-foot range. Some photos have been good enough to blow up and frame. As a result, my apartment is decorated with pictures taken during the last three months.

I even took my trusty Canon Sure Shot out to Khun Boontan's house. Now, don't worry. Nothing is heating up between Aied and me. In fact, Aied doesn't even live there.

Khun Boontan just wanted to see me because she "loves me like a son."

Add was my guide. I'd a delightful time. For six hours, I did nothing but eat and talk and take pictures. Some pictures turned out clear and sharp. Two were particularly spectacular: one of the mother and the other of the daughter. Of course, I had to get them copies. Thais may forget many things, but they never forget a picture.

Add, for instance, was looking through the photos when suddenly she stopped, turned to me, and said, "Gerry, where's the picture of me on the balcony upstairs?" Out of thirty-six photos, she'd found the only one missing. So I went back and checked the negatives. Sure enough, it was there. The man at the camera shop had neglected to process it. Add's memory would've done Robert McNamara proud.

My job is taking shape. For months, I've been telling the bigwigs at the Ministry of Education that my time has been too diced up, that it's making me less effective. Slowly, they're growing ears. Gradually, they're coming to realize that I can get books that nobody else can.

Furthermore, I've recently become friends with Dr. Pikun, a stateside-trained reading specialist. She wants to start a new reading program but can't without the following: *Barnell Loft Specific Skills Series*, *Supportive Reading Skills*, *Reading Attainment System* (Kit), *Reading Development Kit* (Kits B and C), *SRA Reading Lab Kit* (2a and 2b: ten color-coded books), *Reading for Understanding* (Kit), *Specific Skills Series*, and *Gates* by someone named Pearson.

I need to know where to write to ask for these books. Dr. Pikun doesn't know the authors' names, except for the last one. Nor does she know the publishers. So would you do some investigating for me? Don't put yourselves out. Just check the *Books in Print* at one of the big bookstores or ask a resource librarian if any of these books are being used in the Phoenix area.

I hate to trouble you, but Dr. Pikun is in a real jam. If you can possibly help her, she'll be in a much better position to do the job for which she was trained. It's hell to have twentieth-century skills with feudal tools.

Khun Boontan, Aied, and Add
outside their house in Samut Prakarn (1980)

Epistle Fifty-Two

February 15, 1980

Dear Mom and Dad:

Your generous gift and kind letters arrived safely. I've refrained from writing because events have literally swirled about me. Now that some of the dust has settled, I can properly answer a number of questions that have long been a mystery.

I love Aied, and I want you to love her, too. I know this will be hard. What I've said and what she hasn't said have not given you much to cheer about. For this, Aied and I are to blame. My remarks over the past three or four years have been a defense mechanism, a way to protect myself from being emotionally bruised. This was patently unfair both to you and to the woman I love.

Aied's silence was wrong in our social context but not hers. After the big breakup, I bounced off the walls for a couple of days. Then Add took me out to see her mother. What I saw was pretty raw, even to my hardened, jaded eyes. The walls were up but unfinished. The interior, especially downstairs, looked like something out of L'il Abner: a makeshift kitchen, dirt floor, old and battered pieces of furniture.

But in the eye of the mess lay a gem: Khun Boontan. Sixty-two years old, sexually depleted from seven birthings, worn down by poverty and deprivation, physically and mentally drained from caring for three grandchildren, she stood before me, smiling. Somehow, her legs still moved and her fingers still did what her brain commanded. She bustled about frantically preparing a dinner suitable for her daughter's old teacher.

I was touched. Impulsively, I stepped across the culture barrier and gave her a big hug. Add gasped; Khun Boontan beamed. Then she went out to finish preparing lunch.

"Aied didn't want you to see all this, Gerry. We're so ashamed of the house. We don't want you to think low of us."

So that was it: *Thai face*. I gave the place a two-minute think, pulled Add aside, and asked her how much for a downstairs floor.

"About five thousand baht ($250 USD)," she said.

Well, that was cheap for playing God, so I forced the money on her with the promise not to tell Aied. Of course, I knew she would. Still, the promise would keep Aied at arms' length for a while.

The stratagem worked for two weeks. One night, I got a phone call. The husky, throaty voice was vaguely familiar.

"Can we have dinner together?" she said.

"Of course."

We went with some of her friends to a nice little restaurant. The food was delicious. Suddenly, Aied turned and handed me a big box.

"Merry Christmas, Happy New Year, and Happy Birthday," she said.

I didn't know what to say. I wasn't overcome by the gift but by her face. I hadn't seen it so happy since my days at Thonburi Teachers College. At that moment, I knew why I loved her and would continue to love her.

I tried to go directly to Add over the weekend, but Aied wouldn't allow it. She wanted us to go to the house together, which meant meeting her at Mazda on Saturday. Once we arrived at the house, she quickly got rid of everyone, and I soon found myself alone with her on the small balcony upstairs. She clearly wanted to unburden herself, so I let her do most of the talking.

"Gerry, these are my mother's relatives from her first marriage forty years ago. The old man down the soi is my mother's first husband. He's not dead like you thought. He left my mother for a few years, and when he returned, he had a mia noi. My mother threw him out of the house. Now she feels nothing for him."

"To whom do the children belong?" I asked.

"They belong to my older sister and my younger brother. The little girl you love so much is Aum, my sister's child. The other two children belong to my younger brother. He lived with a teenage girl for two years, and they had babies back-to-back. She became bored with the kids fast but not with other men. She works on an air-conditioned bus, and her new love is the bus driver. She hasn't been back to see the children for more than a year."

"What does your father think of all this?"

"He doesn't like it, but what can he say? When I was a student at Thonburi, he took his first mia noi. She was a moody, mean-spirited woman. Finally, they broke up. My father got a new mia noi, someone who really loves him. He's much happier now. I live with him, and he gives me good advice."

I looked directly into her chestnut eyes and took the plunge.

"And what about you?"

"Do you really want to know?"

"Yes."

"Why?"

"Because it's time."

"Yes, I suppose it is. Okay, I had a husband. I didn't love him, but he seemed kind and generous. He paid my tuition when I was a student at Thonburi Teachers College."

"Do you have one now?"

"No."

"Can you tell me what happened?"

She bit her upper lip and looked down for a moment. When she raised her head again, her hazelnut eyes were soft, yet shaded with sorrow.

"I tried, but he wouldn't change," she said. "He wanted me to stay home all the time. He wanted me to talk and act like a little girl. Then there was the trouble with my parents. When we got married, my father took a second mia noi. My ... my ... what word do I use, Gerry?"

"Ex-husband. Or you can use his real name."

"No, I don't like either of those. Let's just call him 'he.' Anyway, he started to say bad things about my father. And he gave short, impolite answers to my mother. My feeling for him began to change. Finally, I couldn't stand being in the same room with him."

"So you left him? He didn't leave you?"

"Yes. He came after me twice begging me to live with him. The last time he took me to a monk. He thought the monk could solve our problems. I let the monk talk and talk and talk. But I didn't hear anything to help us. I could see the monk was getting tired, so I made my decision. I told him to leave, to get out of my life and stay out of it."

"How long were you married?"

"One or two years."

"And did you have any children?"

"What do you think?"

"I don't know, and I don't want to guess. I want you to tell me."

She smiled, and her eyes danced.

"Everybody thinks one of the children is mine. Some people even think *all three* are mine."

"That's impossible."

"Yes," she said. "But if you had to choose, which one would it be?"

"If I *had* to choose, I'd say Aum."

She laughed.

"When did I have time for the big stomach? No, I have no children."

We looked at each other. She was still very nice to look at. She wore a white blouse and a red-flowered skirt. She made me feel fresh and clean.

"Aied," I said. "What are we going to do?"

"I don't know what you mean," she said.

"Yes, you do."

Turning her head aside, she appeared to have drifted away mentally. But when she spoke, her voice was very close, very intimate.

"After my marriage, I was a bad girl. I dated many men and played with their hearts. You don't want a girl like me."

"But I do."

"Why?"

"I just do."

"I don't understand you sometimes."

"Listen," I said. "I don't care what you've done. To me, you'll always be the purest, cleanest girl in the world."

She didn't say anything, and I really didn't want her to. The light was nice and soft for pictures. When I asked to shoot her, she glowed.

"I don't have any pictures to give my friends. Go ahead, Gerry."

I never had a better subject. She did everything naturally and intuitively. She looked straight into the camera, tilted her head, and arched her eyebrows. Too bad I made a few technical mistakes.

The following week, I went out to work on the house with Add. I told her that Aied had finally "revealed her past." Add was very happy.

"Aied had a terrible time with that man," she said, shaking her head and puckering her lips as if she were sucking a lemon.

"You never liked him?"

"Never. He was so selfish. I'm glad she got rid of him."

Aied and I meet once or twice a week now. She has talked about her marriage a number of times. The guilt is heavy. That can be seen in bits and pieces of conversation.

"You don't know what marriage is like. Once you start living with someone, everything changes."

Or: "I understand you, but I don't understand myself. I get moody. If we get married, I'd get angry with you sometimes. What would you do then?"

Or: "I don't want a lover."

Or: "What would you do if I started to throw things at you?"

I had a fast answer for the last one.

"I'd try to catch them," I said.

I don't know if Aied loves me. I only know she cares for me. I found that out yesterday when I delivered her Valentine. It was a handmade job, a gigantic piece that took me two nights. Seventy odd lines of doggerel scribbled on yellow cardboard with a red border. Down the road from my apartment, I found some small hearts to stick in the open spots at the edges. And in a yarn shop nearby, I found some lace that made a cute trim.

Wrapped the whole mess up with yellow ribbon. Even put an artificial rose under the bow to give it a touch of class.

She loved it. She was going to open it up and let her friends read it, but I stopped her. An over-the-top Valentine like that is not for public display. I'd planned to deliver the card and then scram. But Aied would have none of that. Her friends were going dancing, and I was invited, too.

"Okay," I said. "Let's go."

"Not now," she said. "Sit down. I'm tired and want to talk with you."

So we talked, and she gave me a Valentine she had made: a keychain with bells and a little sign saying "Special for You" on one side and "Remember Me" on the other.

"I knew you would come," she said.

"I could see that when I came in the door. I'm getting too predictable."

"You came," she said. "Someone else did not. That tells me something."

We went dancing with a large group: six men and six women. Thai women like it this way, for they can lose themselves in the group. The gossipmongers have a hard time telling which girl goes with which boy. Unfortunately for Aied, her friends made it obvious whom she was with. Seats were arranged and rearranged until we were sitting close together.

I've danced with Aied before, but only to fast music. We've never made contact until last night. When the slow music began, I took a good hard look at the couples on the floor and, damn it, I thought we should be up there too.

"Let's dance," I said.

"No."

"Why not?"

"It's dirty to dance like that," she said, pointing to a couple that was all but fornicating on the floor.

"I'm not going to hold you like that," I said. "Come on. Let's go."

"No."

"You're afraid."

"No, I'm not."

"Oh, yes, you are."

I looked away. The colors danced before my eyes. But there was nothing unusual about them. Discos are the McDonald's of the night scene.

A finger poked my leg, and I turned around. Aied was looking straight at me. She looked like she was about to make a down payment on a house.

"Let's go," she said.

"Where?"

"Let's go," she repeated, ignoring my stupidity.

I can't remember going onto the dance floor. I can only remember my hand going to the small of her back and her hand resting on my shoulder. Neither of us danced very well. But there were other things going on that were a whole lot more important.

The vivacious Sompit carrying donated
books to the Reading Room
A few months after this picture was taken, tragedy struck.
The victim of an auto wreck, Sompit
had to have her arm amputated.
At the hospital she was oblivious to
pain and danger to her life.
"Ajaan Gerry," she said sorrowfully. "No
one will want to marry me now."

Epistle Fifty-Three

March 9, 1980

Dear Mom and Dad:

The hot, sticky, grungy weather came a few days ago. It came late, after a prolonged cool season that made everyone think that summer would never come. At first, I thought I was sick. Walking down the stairwell, I ran into my landlady, Lek. She was wan and suffering from a *boat hua*.

"I got my *men* too," she said.

Somehow, she forced a smile, something I never could've done if our roles had been reversed. Going upstairs, I couldn't believe how much better I felt.

Yesterday, I received a letter from Addison-Wesley Publishing Company, which read: "We are sending you the Reading Development Kits A, B, and C via printed matter, with our compliments."

The kits are worth a good two hundred US dollars, so thanks for the addresses. Even if the others bomb, the effort has already paid off.

Indeed, I'm riding a ridiculous string of successes that must come to an end soon. I had my students write letters to Darien Book Aid Plan and was notified last week that eight Jiffy Bags were on the way. Since Darien usually sends only two bags, the letters must've been a hit.

The spectacular donation from Books for Asia has greatly enhanced the Reading Room. Yet another donation from McGraw-Hill followed two days later. I've now exhausted most of my donors unless, of course, Commander Sherman of the

United States in Manila comes through with the two thousand volumes from Project Handclasp.

That's the good news. Nonetheless, I see storm clouds on the horizon. My friend Chuck Rice has been negligent in kissing the right bureaucratic butts. As a result, the powers-that-be at the ministry gave him the axe. Terry and I were put in a most uncomfortable position when word leaked out that Chuck's head was on the block. Sworn to secrecy, we decided not to warn Chuck hoping against hope that the ministry would have a change of heart.

It never happened. As soon as the axe fell, I went over to see him. Chuck didn't look good. His eyes had a harried, wash-and-tumble-dry look. I could well understand his consternation. Chuck has been waiting to marry a Thai teacher for six years. Finding her name unpronounceable, I started to call her Gumdrop. The name stuck.

Yes, Gumdrop has told Chuck that she loves him and will one day marry him. But, like Aied, she comes with baggage. Two months ago, for instance, she married her cousin in order to transfer jobs. Just how such a bizarre act works is beyond me. Still, she hasn't "set up house" with the cousin, so it appears to be a classic case of Thai panic. Luckily, a Thai divorce is a much easier procedure than in the West. All it takes is the signatures of both parties.

"Keep the books coming, Christmas," Chuck said ominously. "You might be next."

I couldn't help thinking how lucky I was to have gone to Samoa. Had I waited in Bangkok for Aied like Chuck had waited for Gumdrop, I would've made this place the only place and, by extension, Aied the only option. When a man does that, he loses something intangible. He becomes captive to his dreams, and all alternatives vanish. Chuck is one of the brightest men I've ever met. Still, there he sat with bloodshot eyes and quivering hands over the possible loss of a six-hundred-dollar-a-month teaching job. A witchy Thai woman can sure play havoc with the mind of a Western man.

Chuck's prediction has partially come to pass. The ministry has refused my request for a two-year extension. There's even talk about all contracts being cut at the end of next year. OPEC has arrived. The Thai government is making cuts, and it makes more sense to cut white skin than brown. Still, my new contract will take me through July 1981. Much can happen between now and then. These recent events, however, have forced me to put my long-range book plans on the back burner unless I get some reassurances in writing.

Add and I around the time we were
working on the tiled floor
Add, along with her siblings, needed
mentoring to escape poverty.
But they were never that lucky.
The amount of human talent squandered
in the world is horrific.

Epistle Fifty-Four

March 14, 1980

Dear Mom and Dad:

Aied and I had yet another major blowout, especially by Thai standards. Our date had started out fine with a good movie at the Scala but then disintegrated at the restaurant at Thai Daimaru.

"Can you help me out, Gerry? I'm having trouble paying my bills."

"I'd love to, but I can't now," I said. "All my disposable income is being spent fixing your mother's house. You wouldn't want me to stop that, would you?"

She gave me an odd, suspicious look.

"Why are you looking at me that way?" I said.

"I know why you're helping my mother," she said darkly.

"What do you mean by that?"

"You know."

"No, I don't know," I said. "I'm an English teacher, not a mind reader."

That was a silly thing to say, not because it was wrong but because it made the conversation slide into the muck and the guck.

"You're not helping my mother because you love her. I know your game. You're trying to buy me."

That stopped me in my tracks. It was true and yet it wasn't true. But how could I make her see that? I was now in a deep, deep hole, and Aied was not about to throw me a rope. Instead, she gazed fixedly at me.

"That's a bit too blunt," I said. "Of course, I probably would not be helping your mother if I didn't love you. But that doesn't mean that I'm trying to buy your affections. You're a free woman, not a slave being sold to the highest bidder."

I couldn't tell if Aied believed me or not. And she wasn't about to tell me, either. Instead, she changed the subject.

"I don't like butterflies," she said.

"Why not? They're very beautiful."

"I'm not talking about that kind of butterfly, Gerry. I'm talking about the two-legged kind."

"Now what's wrong?"

"You've been spending a lot of time working on the house with Add."

"So?"

"My sister is a very charming and beautiful woman."

"So?"

"I don't blame you for falling in love with her."

"I'm not in love with Add," I said.

"Are you sure?" she said, tilting her head to the right. "Are you *really* sure?"

"Yes," I said. "I love you and only you. So that's the end of that."

"Can you love me when I don't love you?"

"Of course. That happens to men and women all the time. It's the hell of life. Only the lucky ones are immune to it."

"I want you to love me with a sad and lonely heart."

This was becoming overly melodramatic, even by Thai standards. I therefore decided to steer the conversation into a more cerebral realm. That is never a good idea.

"Isn't that a bit cruel and selfish?" I asked.

"I can see where it's selfish," she said. "I cannot see where it's cruel."

"Eventually, such a love will die. If that's not cruel, I don't know what is."

I honestly thought that that was the end of it. I honestly thought we'd taken the subject about as low as it could go. How wrong I was. How terribly wrong I was.

"I don't mind seeing you, Gerry. You're always polite and honest and kind to me. But I want to date other men. As long as I'm honest and tell you about them, I don't see anything wrong with that. Do you?"

"Of course, there's something wrong with that. I've shared my hopes and dreams with you. I've told you that I want you to marry me. I've told you that I want to spend the rest of my life with you. And what do I get in return? You accuse me of trying to buy you, of falling in love with your sister, of being a butterfly, of *not* letting you date other men. That might be the Thai way, but it's not my way."

I could see that she was visibly shaken, that she was madder than hell. She was still angry when I saw her off at the bus stop. She stomped aboard the number-two bus as if she wanted to drive her heels through the floorboards.

I telephoned her a few days later from work. She was still fuming.

"Take it easy," I said. "*Jai yen yen*."

"I'm angry with you," she said.

"Call me in an hour at the apartment. It's easier to talk with you there."

She did, and we had a nice talk.

"I'm tired of these silly boy-girl games," I said. "Okay, go ahead and date other men, but leave me out of it. I know my place. From now on, I'm just a family friend."

That's where things stand now. I'm not sure if Aied likes it or not. I don't really care. My job and my apartment are a blast. Having Aied mad at me is just icing on the cake.

Sompit and Pirom (both standing) with
two of their friends in the cafeteria
Though Sompit and Pirom came from different backgrounds,
I never had trouble with status or class.
Both had been blessed with modesty, charm, and intelligence.

Epistle Fifty-Five

March 29, 1980

Dear Mom and Dad:

The school year ended two weeks ago. Last week, four Thai teachers and I took fourteen students to Phetchaburi. The students were not supposed to speak Thai for three days. Of course, none of us expected the experiment to work. Gregarious and fun-loving, Thai students usually revert to Thai whenever their English teacher's head is turned.

But on this trip, most of the students were good—excellent, in fact. Boarding the train, they dropped Thai and went into English. One girl in particular surprised me. Watcharatip is one of my shyest students and for two terms had hardly opened her mouth in class. But she changed on the train. She asked me question after question after question until I stopped her and said, "Watcharatip, I'm really proud of you." She smiled and asked me another question.

At Phetchaburi, we went immediately to the dormitory at the local teacher training college. I'd expected to sleep in separate quarters from the girls. But there were no separate quarters. Only a wall—a tissue-thin wall—kept us apart. Moreover, we had to share the same bathroom, which was located below us downstairs.

This living situation was a remarkable stroke of luck, for I came face-to-face with Thai fears I'd only heard about. The funniest was the fear of ghosts. On the first night, I'd just finished my shower and was returning to walk up the stairs when I met three of my students. They held their bathroom kits and towels in their hands, but I could tell by their faces that they weren't going anywhere.

"Would you girls like me to walk you down the hall?" I asked.

Their faces beamed.

"Oh, thank you, thank you, Ajaan Gerry. You don't know how long we've been trying to get the courage to go by ourselves!"

The next day, we hiked up a mountain to see a famous retreat of an early Thai monarch. Twenty or thirty monkeys lined the walkway, so we bought some bananas for them.

"Feed the monkeys quickly," I said. "Then walk away. Don't wait for the monkeys to bunch up. Like humans, they can be dangerous when they band together."

Most of the students listened to me, but a few did not. Two or three students stopped and meandered back to where a group of monkeys had congregated.

"Oh, look," said a student. "Aren't they cute?"

Suddenly, five large males went on the attack—jumping, biting, and clawing. The students got the message and broke into a run. We were lucky that no one got hurt. One of the biggest monkeys chased the girls fifty meters before deciding to give up and return to his family.

Overall, however, the trip was a success. The students' language skills improved markedly. More importantly, the students now feel more at ease with me. I therefore expect that next year, they'll come to see me more readily.

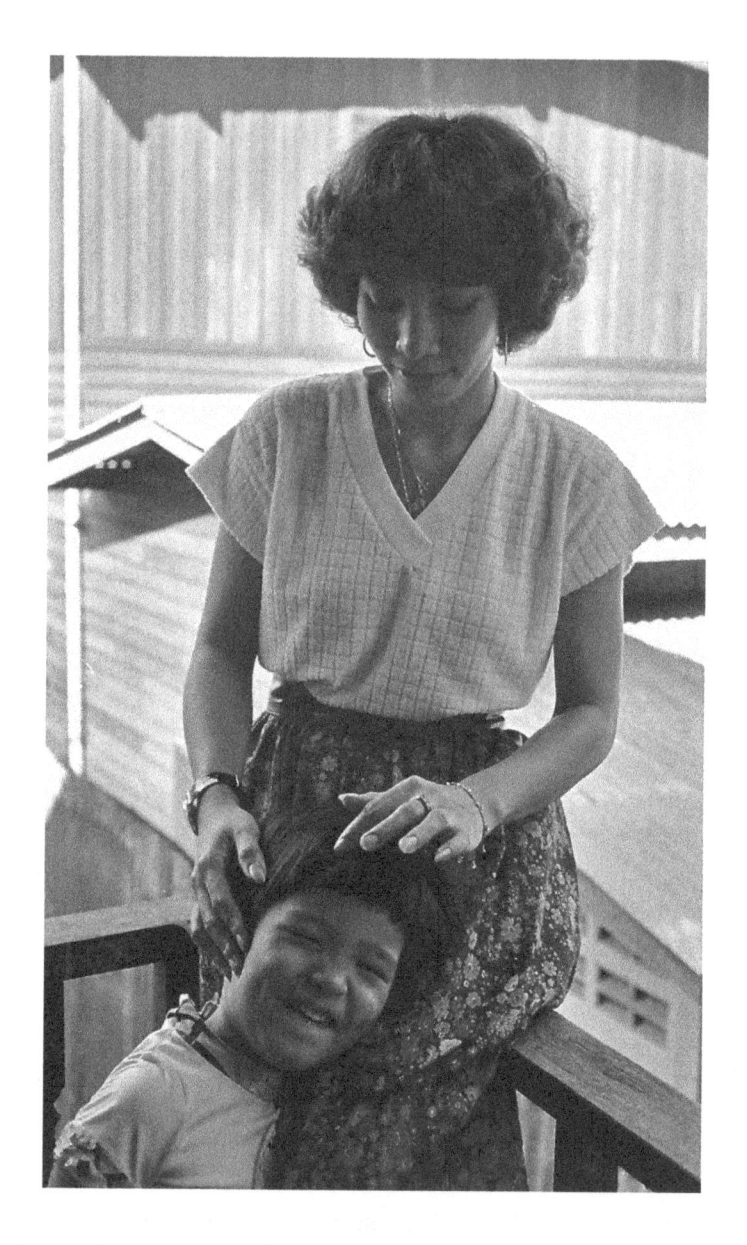

A tender moment between Aied and her niece Aum on the balcony of their house in Samut Prakarn

Epistle Fifty-Six

May 15, 1980

Dear Mom and Dad:

My correspondence has been about as constant as Moll Flanders. But I haven't written anyone in two months, so don't feel left out, just equally neglected.

I've always made it a practice *not* to write about the weather, but times change the man, not the other way around. Recent Bangkok "highs" have made memories of the Phoenix sun seem like Kool-Aid. Not that we reached such scorchers as 118 degrees. No, we only got up to 106. Still, Mr. Humidity stayed in the seventies and eighties, thus doing everybody in. The nights were especially ghastly, with most people awaking each morn in a puddle of sweat.

My fate was particularly hairy due to a protracted illness. First I contracted some horrendous, low-grade virus from Terry Fredrickson. This Louis Pasteur delight kept me bedridden for three weeks. Two days after recovering, Add, bless her heart, passed on her cold to me. I was down and out for two weeks, only this time with bouts of depression.

Between the heat and the incessant drain on my body, I became alarmed at my inability to sleep. Having gone ten years without a grand mal seizure, I didn't long for the good ole days, so one frightfully sticky night, I hailed a taxi and went to a medical clinic where Dr. Prem, the Peace Corps physician, shot me into Nirvana.

Returning home the following day, I had my fill of acting like a Joseph Conrad protagonist. I gave my aged air-conditioner a quick inspection, crossed my fingers, and threw the switch.

The decrepit machine sputtered and spurted but finally kicked in. I don't relish my electric bill this month, but I'm back to normal.

The Thais didn't escape from the ravages of the heat either. Everybody has been reeling as though bonked over the head with a crowbar. Though sick, I did manage to crawl to school and teach a special summer class twice a week. The sessions were four hours long, and at the end of hour two, the students' faces had a queer, dazed look like a walleyed bass out of water.

Still, between our efforts and mutual misery, an intimate bond was formed. Given the conditions, the students worked as hard as humanly possible. And I guess my appreciation showed. The students not only asked many questions but also begged me to teach next term. The latter request was particularly touching since these are older students (teachers, in fact) who look on time and tuition with a more critical eye than my regular students.

I appreciate your remarks regarding Add and Aied—accurate and to the point, but perhaps you should flip the names around. Sure, Aied is still a gorgeous creature, but the years and a bum marriage have dimmed that special spark, that sauciness, I found so captivating, so adorable. Moreover, she's acted very foolishly with me, especially with those teenybopper temper tantrums.

An icicle has entered my heart, and Aied knows it. On our last date, she gave me the queerest look, much like a magician stripped of his high hat, silk scarf, and bunny rabbit. I found myself oddly detached, not caring too much. For don't you see? The mystery is solved; the trick has been revealed; the mask has been stripped away. And with the unmasking went much of the tender and beautiful insanity that went with it.

What have I learned from all this? What have I learned from this long-running soap opera? Well, to be blunt, I've come to the conclusion that most Thai women are cowards. A farang has a much better chance with a poor, simple, earthy, upcountry gal. Educated Thai women, the ones with the good jobs and the long names, are for Thai men. It doesn't matter that many Thai men are loose, immoral, and irresponsible. These "nice Thai women" have been indoctrinated in race, religion, culture, and language to the point they can't think straight.

Is this nothing but bitter bile? Is this nothing but venting my spleen? Not at all. When I left the kingdom three years ago, a few Thai couples could be seen walking arm-in-arm about the city. Now it's an epidemic. But the rules haven't changed for me and other farangs. Any Thai woman seen in public with me is a whore, plain and simple. Thai men and occasionally Thai women tell her she's a whore. Tell her with their looks and their leers. Tell her with a short remark and muffled giggles.

So I can't blame Aied for running about witless. I can only blame myself for being bullheaded. Aied's world begins and ends with Thailand—no matter how it hurts, no matter how deeply it cuts. Thais are, first and foremost, social animals, and Aied is no exception. All her actions, all her behavior, are funneled toward acceptance, not happiness. It's a terrible waste of a wonderful human being. But that doesn't make Aied an outlier. Indeed, she's the norm.

A second truth needs to be thrown into the mix, namely the Thai concept of beauty. The word *sway* reigns supreme in the Thai mind. Indeed, it's used much more in everyday speech than its English equivalent: *beautiful*. Many Thai women have told me that Thai men lose interest in their wives after the first year of marriage, usually when pregnancy kicks in. Among the lower class, the philandering often comes at a high price: the loss of the male member to a kitchen knife or a razor blade. As a result, Thai doctors have become most adept at stitching penises back in place. Sadly, this cannot always be accomplished. Traditional Thai houses stand on stilts; hence, a dog or a duck often gobbles up the bloody member.

An educated Thai woman tends to eschew such a barbaric practice. Instead, she takes a more civilized approach. After a time, she gives up on her husband and aligns the children against the father. The wife also takes out her frustration socially. Rarely have I attended a Thai party in which the hostess failed to mention her husband's mia noi. But perhaps my good friend Sudaporn said it best: "Gerry, we just don't raise our men properly."

I felt embarrassed. I was sitting right in front of her husband, and to the best of my knowledge, he was a faithful spouse. The innocent suffer with the guilty.

What does all this mean? Well, I suppose I'm not as enamored with Thailand as I once was. This is good, not bad. My interests have become less personal and more professional. My time is spent more with the mind instead of the emotions. I only spend time with people who honor my friendship. With these people, I'm extremely honest and forthright, especially regarding their country. Of course, I've hurt a few people's feelings, but you'd be surprised at the slack jaws and nods of agreement that have come my way.

I am, however, somewhat cautious with Add. She's four years younger than Aied, but everyone thinks she's older. Not because of her looks but because she lacks Aied's juvenile petulance. I find myself talking turkey with her. And if it weren't for Aied's "ghost," I'd probably be a serious suitor. For Add understands me. Whereas Aied is suspicious, forever probing for the motive behind my actions, Add takes me at face value. As a result, I have a friendship with Add that was never possible with her sister. In fact, Aied once told Add that she envied our relationship.

Add is the exception to my rule that nice Thai women lack courage. She's extremely brave, downright fearless. She's been through crowds during Songkran (the Thai water festival) with me. She's ridden on the back of a bicycle with me. She's been to dinner and the movies with me. She's walked down city streets with her head held high with me. But her courage will eventually hurt her if we persist in spitting in society's face. This is not the United States with its vaunted democracy, with its enlightened ideas and ideals, with its faith in freedom and free markets. No, this is Thailand, still stuck with neo-feudalism, with its rice-paddy serfs, with its lords and ladies living off the hard labor of those beneath them.

Epistle Fifty-Seven

May 22, 1980

Dear Mom and Dad:

Yesterday, I returned from a two-day holiday to Pattaya. The place, with its Las Vegas glitter and insane divertissements, attracts a weird assortment of assholes: from Kraut mechanics to Raghead camel-beaters, from Limey jingoists to Jap bozos, from Frog fart-blasters to Yanqui yo-yos. A wide variety of suicidal amusements abound, all at exorbitant prices. Sky-riding behind errant and erratic speedboats. Zinging over the water in an odd machine that looks like an aquaplane but sounds like a motorcycle. Windsurfing through an obstacle course of tour boats, barges, swimmers, and other windsurfers.

I really didn't want to go. I wasn't up for the seashore suicide by day and the boardwalk depravity at night. But charity is a dangerous thing. Two months ago, Aied and Add had hatched the idea as a way of "paying Gerry back." I'd tried to wriggle free by pleading bankruptcy when Terry Fredrickson applied more pressure.

"Come on, Gerry," he said. "I don't want to go down there alone with Jaam. We'll bore each other to death. I need a guy to bounce guy ideas off of."

Finally, when Add said that her cousin Sudarat had gotten us a bungalow at an incredibly cheap price, I threw in the towel.

"There's only one catch," said Add. "Sudarat and her friend Nan want to come with us."

This seemed reasonable since Thais, like wolves, prefer to run in a pack.

The Sudarat-Nan twosome also told me that Aied was making herself scarce. Aied didn't like her cousin, especially after Sudarat put the moves on her one night.

Terry and Jaam went down to Pattaya three days before we did. Before they left, I made arrangements to rendezvous with them at the bus station. The only problem would be one of punctuality. If we failed to link up in Pattaya, Terry and Jaam would be forced to take a hotel room. So you can imagine my delight when I reached the Bangkok terminal and found Add and Sudarat feverishly telephoning Nan's house.

"Nan can't come unless we go and get her," Add said. "Her mother and father are very strict."

I felt like I was in Ding Dong School.

"How long will it take you to get her?" I asked.

"An hour," said Add.

"You'd better scat," I said. "Otherwise, we won't get to Pattaya in time."

I then sat down on our luggage and did a *Bangkok Post* crossword puzzle.

A Thai hour is equal to an hour and a half on any reliable timepiece. When the girls returned, one look at Nan told me what she was and how she thought. Nan was the squirrelly, squirmy type so common to Thailand, a true believer of all the nonsensical dos and don'ts of a class-conscious culture.

The nonsense began on the bus trip down the coast. And Nan wasn't the only guilty party. Sitting across the aisle in the window seat was a fashionable but forgettable hooker. I didn't even notice her till Add nudged me in the ribs.

"Look, Gerry," she said. "That woman isn't wearing a bra."

Sitting in the seat in front of us, Sudarat and Nan were ogling and goggling like two mindless cretins. I began to wonder how they'd take to Jaam.

Stop being stupid, I said to myself. *Everyone likes Jaam. She runs a beauty salon and takes excellent care of Terry. You've seen her after being attacked by thieves. You've seen her after a serious car accident. You've seen her in all kinds of predicaments and she never loses her cool. All smiles. Never a sign of self-pity. They'll like her, especially Add.*

The bus pulled into Pattaya at two o'clock in the afternoon. Terry came out grinning; Jaam came out with knit brows. The bile between the girls was instantaneous, permanent. Exactly who started it, I don't know. I've heard both sides, and I'm not satisfied with either argument. But my instincts side with Jaam, since she was the outsider and it was the other girls' duty to make her feel at home.

What I failed to realize, what even Terry didn't know after thirteen years in Thailand, was that censure and cruelty are the moving social forces among Thai women, that even the biggest smiles drop away under certain situations.

By the time we got to the bungalow, permafrost had set in. Add was still trying to be a lady, but Jaam had been labeled Terry's whore and she knew it. I decided to get a game of cards going since Sudarat and Nan had deserted us without a peep. Add came over and sat down beside me. I could tell she was upset about the card playing. But what else could I do? We were temporarily locked out of our rooms, and Sudarat and Nan were acting like real bitches. Finally, Add went away to see her sister without saying a word.

Jaam could restrain herself no longer. In a spiel that would've done Sarah Bernhardt proud, she lambasted everyone and everything. I didn't understand every word, but I didn't need to.

"Take your things and go," I said. "You don't have any other choice."

Terry winced.

"But what will you say to Add?" he said.

I gave the standard white lie.

"She'll understand," I said.

As luck will have it, we met Add at the front gate. We said our good-byes as politely as possible. I saw Terry and Jaam off alone. Back at the bungalow, Add turned on me with full fury.

"And you call *that* a nice girl?" she said.

For the first time in my life, I decided to drive some Christianity down a Buddhist's throat.

"Jaam's my friend," I said. "I try not to judge people."

Add took it but didn't like it.

My troubles were over, but Add's were just beginning. The next day, Sudarat and Nan almost left for Bangkok.

"Good God," I said. "What happened now?"

Add shook her head.

"You don't know what an awful night I had with Nan," she said. "All she could talk about was her parents."

I didn't much care anymore. The only one I cared about was Add. She'd done most of the work and had tried her best to please everyone. Finally, Nan decided to stay.

That night, I took Add out to dinner. I invited Sudarat and Nan too, but they mysteriously declined. Add was furious. And I didn't know why until we returned and found Sudarat and Nan drunk.

The irony was delicious.

Jaam didn't drink.

Epistle Fifty-Eight

May 24, 1980

Dear Tocher:

I'm about as close to marriage as Lancelot was to the Holy Grail after hosing Guinevere. If one can be psychologically kneed in the nads, Aied has bulls-eyed my jewels. Sour grapes? Not really. I'm pissed at myself for wasting some damn good years on a woman whose universe begins with her hang-ups and ends with her dark suspicions. That she's willingly swallowed all the garbage on race, nation, language, and culture scares the shit out of me. For when a man falls in love, he's essentially telling the world that he's found the embodiment of his hopes and dreams. Judging from Aied, my hopes and dreams appear to be a mad mix of selfishness, suspicions, sporadic moodiness, and spiteful rage. What an ass I am!

I wouldn't be bitching so much if Terry Fredrickson hadn't taken me to his favorite haunt, the Crystal Palace, the other night. The place is a two-room affair with deep-scarlet walls and small but tasteful chandeliers. Two go-go girls gyrate interminably: one in the far room and the other at the end of the bar.

Plopping my butt into the nearest barstool, I saw *her* smiling benignantly over the till with that huge, elastic mouth and those dimples that drove half the men in America nuts twenty years ago.

"You're ... you're Mary Tyler Moore!" I bellowed.

The nubile, young lovely looked at me, stunned, and shot a quizzical glance at Terry.

"My God," I whispered, "even her hair is the same."

Terry prattled a near-perfect translation, and the girl beamed.

"She doesn't *tio* with guys," he said in a lame attempt to placate my gaping mouth and bulging eyes.

"Everyone in the joint has been waiting for me to ask her out," Terry continued. "But I don't think I will."

I blinked in disbelief.

"You're stark-staring mad," I said.

Terry looked mournfully into his beer.

"Listen, Gerry. I'm leaving this country next year, really leaving. I'm going to hurt one girl. Why should I make it two?"

I was listening to him, but my eyes were riveted on Miss Moore. Gee, she had lovely hair—the satin kind, all soft and silky and slightly fluffed at the forehead.

"Just another nice girl, just another memory of things past," Terry said, true to his pragmatic Swedish heritage. "She could teach me a few Thai customs but that's about all."

"She could teach me more than that," I said, continuing to ogle as the never-to-be fantasies floated in and out and up and down …

Before the Crystal Palace closed, a Thai guy selling Buddhist leis came in and gave me a nudge and a leer.

"How much?" I asked.

"Forty baht," he said.

I gagged. Then I took him by the arm and went outside. I tried to get two for fifty baht but ended up with five for one hundred baht. Walking back inside, I didn't know whom to give them to, except the first was going to Miss Moore.

My entrance brought forth a big "ah" from the girls. But it was wasted on me. For there, poised proud and erect on my stool, sat a stupendous hunk of anatomy—one that the Creator took great care in carving.

She was one of the dancers, but this was the first time I'd seen her up close. She was the classical Thai beauty—the kind rarely seen now, the kind Fu Manchu insidiously used to wreck havoc on the West: flat face with large, almond eyes; hair straight and sleek down to a huge, fulsome, wholesome ass; waist small with just enough fat to take the boniness off the pelvis; legs long and languorous, beautifully formed for those long midnight gallops into oblivion. Even her breasts were of classical design: too small for High Hefner but perfect for Humphrey Humphrey.

Of course, I just stood there and leered like a walleye out of water. Finally, Fredrickson ho-hummed me back to reality, and I passed the leis around: the first to Miss Moore and the second to Aphrodite. Taking the lei in her hands, Aphrodite *waied* and all that gorgeous hair cascaded down the sides of her face and flowed over the soft rounds of her shoulders. I caught my breath; then the lights came on like a flashcube.

Oh, shit, I thought. *Just when those jolly, primordial urges manifest themselves, I get a clean, well-lighted place.*

Happily, Aphrodite saved the situation. Flat, black eyes. Hair massed in abundance. Sensuous, wet lips—fast, on target, and gone.

Nobody saw her do it, which made it on the far side of delicious.

Despite what Thais say, certain ice cream cones must be licked in public.

Epistle Fifty-Nine

August 22, 1980

Dear Mom and Dad:

Money is always timely, but yours was especially so. My living situation for the past few months had been, at best, marginal. My flakey landlord, Khun Sombat, will only turn on the water for five hours a day. This has caused all sorts of problems. My daily routine has revolved around one big question: Will I get home in time to wash the dishes and take a bath? Needless to say, this has made me edgy and, at times, volcanic. Still, I put up with it because others put up with it. I know better. Such logic can be fatal; just ask the Jews.

One night last week, I was downstairs having dinner. I made a casual remark that I hadn't seen a tenant for quite some time. Khun Sombat, well into his cups, was within earshot and didn't take kindly to my words. Bounding out of his chair, he staggered over to my table and began to give me hell. My Thai isn't great, but it's good enough to understand racist and nationalistic epithets. I listened, got up, paid my bill, and went upstairs. After talking to Chop, I decided to look for a new apartment.

The school administrators were sympathetic and helpful. Dr. Arun suggested that I talk to a teacher who owns two houses, both close to the college. I liked what I saw, and the landlady and I agreed on a price. The next day, I learned that my neighbors were both ajaans whom I knew and liked. My landlord's drunken diatribe was therefore a blessing in disguise. Life is, indeed, ironic.

Chop and I will move out of Jatujak at the end of the month, so please mail all correspondence to my workplace at Chan Kasem until I give you my new address.

Had we moved immediately, I would've lost the deposit but saved the radio. Yesterday, I went to the closet and found the radio missing. The woman in the apartment next door had hers ripped off last month, so I was sure that I hadn't left it at Chuck or Terry's house. Nonetheless, I phoned them to make certain. No radio.

The theft smelled like an inside job. Since Lek, our cleaning lady, has a bad habit of leaving the door unlocked during the day, I asked Chop to speak with her.

"Don't make a big fuss," I said. "Tell her the radio is gone but that she's above suspicion."

"Okay, Ajaan Gerry. I'll go and tell her right now."

"Thanks, Chop."

Coming home that night, I found Chop with a long face.

"What's wrong, Chop?"

"Khun Lek has asked me tell you she's sorry."

"Sorry for what?"

"Sorry she lost a pair of my socks."

Then it hit me.

"Chop," I said. "You know what that means, don't you?"

Chop blinked.

"You were too indirect. You told her about the radio but failed to mention her innocence. You all but accused the poor woman of theft."

Chop was thunderstruck. Luckily, Lek was downstairs, and I explained everything to her.

This morning, Lek came to the apartment with some news. The Thai boys living downstairs had had their radio ripped off, too.

"Are they sure it was during the day?" I said.

Lek nodded.

"Lek also has an idea who's doing the stealing," said Chop.

"Yeah," I said. "I do, too, but let's not say anything. We don't have any proof."

The caretaker, a big, moody ex-monk, hasn't been looking us in the eye lately.

Dr. Pintip, my boss at the Ministry of Education, acting like a *ling* at a Thai beach

Epistle Sixty

November 1, 1980

Dear Mom and Dad:

The Reading Room is in temporary limbo. We've more than enough books to meet any short-term objective. To be honest, we've run out of space. Books are crammed in every nook and cranny. The large cabinets at the back of the room are not only glutted but are also weighed down with books running end-to-end. Ajaan Rachanee ordered some new bookshelves about three months ago, but still we haven't heard a peep from the Ministry of Education. But that's par for the course. Nonetheless, we cannot sort and arrange the books in any orderly and sensible way until we get the new shelves. So now's the time to sit, teach, and think.

Unfortunately, I've done little sitting, except at the desk at school. Most of my time has been gobbled up with thinking and teaching. Over the school break, I came across the best— and I mean *the best*—writing book to date: William J. Kerrigan's *Writing to the Point: Six Basic Steps*. Boy, has this book ever changed the way I teach writing! Terry Fredrickson found the book at DK Bookstore and suggested that we both teach it at our respective schools.

Many of Kerrigan's ideas are nothing new. What sets the book apart is the systematic approach: the six steps. These steps are indeed basic and ironclad. What's more, they work. Expository writing, according to Kerrigan, must be orderly and logical. The student is therefore made to write a good, strong "Sentence X" (thesis statement). Furthermore, the student is not allowed to write the essay till the teacher has checked

Sentence X. Then the student must write three sentences about Sentence X—about *all* of Sentence X, not just a part of it. Here's where the fun begins, for these three sentences are, in fact, topic sentences that will later be developed into paragraphs.

Kerrigan's point is that most students cannot make a thesis sentence followed by three topic sentences. And he's right. For example, I asked Ratana to think up a Sentence X, and she came up with this: "My boyfriend is a good man." Not a great Sentence X, since the word *good* is too broad. Still, it was a sentence we could work with.

"Okay," I said. "Now what's your first topic sentence?"

Ratana pondered for a moment; then wrote: "He is a polite man." It took me fifteen minutes, along with the help of Ajaan Usa, to convince Ratana that her logic was faulty, that she had two distinct Sentence Xs. To prove my point, I wrote: "He is kind to animals" under the first Sentence X and "He opens car doors for me" under the second. My Thai colleague was fascinated.

"Gerry," Usa said to me afterwards, "you've opened Ratana's eyes in more ways than one. In Thailand, girls are taught that politeness and goodness are the same."

Now I'm waiting for a boy's paper to read: "My girlfriend is good" followed by: "She is very beautiful."

To make the writing class more palatable for Thai students, I've simplified and condensed Kerrigan's book down to thirty pages, with supplementary exercises culled from their themes. The exercises thus far have proven most successful.

Ajaan Usa has even warned me about becoming a "super teacher." That's one of the finest compliments I've ever received. If there's a super teacher in the English department at Chan Kasem, she's it. Together, we have our energetic thumbs in a number of pies: experimental reading and writing classes, a Christmas play, poetry reading, and team-teaching.

Actually, Usa is a major reason why the English department is stronger this year. Whereas last year our staff was visibly divided, we're now united and working toward similar goals and objectives. Last week, for instance, Usa suggested a new idea, namely, a strict criteria whereby we grade our students' English-language skills. This, we feel, is absolutely vital, since some of our seniors are about to graduate with English a tad above gibberish. Fortunately, our juniors, though less vocal, are more disciplined and dedicated. We therefore have great expectations for next year.

Another close friend at school is Dr. Pintip. Indeed, she's the one who turned my job from a nightmare into a dream. Pintip is directly in charge of the Language Center at Chan Kasem. Though pint-sized, she more than makes up for it in cranial capacity. Upon meeting her, I was a bit put off. She seemed aloof and straitlaced, a Thai-style Empress Dowager with every hair in place and every fingernail chiseled to perfection.

Still, whenever I wanted something done and done correctly, Pintip was my go-to gal. Who backed me with getting books to other schools? Pintip. Who asked for addresses for thank-you notes? Pintip. Who got me funds to run an experiment with Harriet Van Meter at the International Book Project? Pintip. And, finally, who saved the huge shipment of books that had to be dumped on Pattaya Beach? You guessed it: Pintip.

Project Handclasp did send us the six thousand books. I won't go into detail about what we had to do to sort and use these books. That would take two pages, single-spaced. How do I know? That was the length of my report to Commander Tevelson in San Diego. And I was being concise! Nevertheless, the biggest problem concerned the five hundred secretarial books that stood idle in storage long after the other books had found a home.

Good grief, I said to myself. *What are you going to do with these? Open a Kelly Girl School?*

I finally decided to cry on Pintip's shoulder.

"I'm really at a loss on what to do," I said. "If the books stay there much longer, the termites will get them."

"What do they cover?" she asked.

"Almost the entire spectrum. Typing, shorthand, transcription, even some filing."

"Um. Let me talk to some people at the Ministry."

A few days later, she came bounding back, ecstatic.

"The timing couldn't be better," she said. "The Director-General wants to get a secretarial course started, and he needs books desperately."

"How many?"

"How many did you say you have?"

"More than five hundred."

"We'll take them all."

"You got to be joking."

"I'm dead serious. The DG wants them all. And he wants you to pass along a message to Handclasp."

"Yes?"

"We're grateful, very grateful."

"Will do," I said. "I'm sure he'll be happy that his books are being used. He wasn't too happy when the Thai authorities would not let his men come ashore at Pattaya. Maybe this will make up for it."

Aied and I sitting on the new floor at her mother's house
Notice how limber her legs are compared to mine.
I never did master the lotus position.

Epistle Sixty-One

December 6, 1980

Dear Mom and Dad:

I just got off the phone with Aied. The dialogue had its predictable twists and turns.

"Hello, Aied, were you sick last Saturday?"

"Yes, I had a stomachache and a headache. I drank a little Mekong (cheap Thai whiskey) and ate too much spicy food."

"Did you call Dr. Pranee?"

"No. I'm bored with doctors. I don't want the hospital. I want the temple."

"That bad, huh?"

"There's too much wrong with me. Doctors can't solve my problems. I'm... I'm a bad girl. I've told you that many times."

"What do you mean 'bad'?"

"I hurt people. I make some of them cry, even."

"Oh, yeah, who? Men or women?"

"Men. Both times, it was a man. First two years ago and then again last year."

"Why did you do it?"

"I started out being friendly. I just wanted to be friends with both of them. But they wanted more. They wanted to marry me. So I hurt them to get rid of them. That was bad of me."

"Did you love either one?"

"No."

"Then what you did wasn't bad. Some men force women to be cruel."

"But I don't want to do it anymore."

"You sound as if you have someone who is serious about you."

"I do. Only it's not one. It's *three*!"

"Well, do you love any of them?"

"Um. The first three-fourths, the second one-half, and the third a quarter."

"Makes sense. Makes typical Aied sense."

"Don't make fun of me, Gerry. I like all three, but I don't want to get married. Not ever."

"Hah. You'll get married again. You'll find a good man, and everything will be fine."

"No, it won't. We'll end up throwing things. It always ends that way. Oh, let's change the subject."

"Gladly. I've something to tell you."

"Yes?"

"I've been alone too long, Aied. I'm tired of it. I want you to know I'm going to date other girls."

(Unintelligible Thai)

"There's one thing I want you to do for me. When you get up tomorrow and look at yourself in the mirror, when you look at those big brown—"

"Ugly eyes."

"Have it your way. When you look at those big, brown, *ugly* eyes, I want you to say: 'Aied, you're a good girl.' Promise me you'll do that."

"Um."

"Come on. Promise me."

"Okay, Gerry. I promise."

"Good-bye, Aied."

"Good-bye, Gerry.

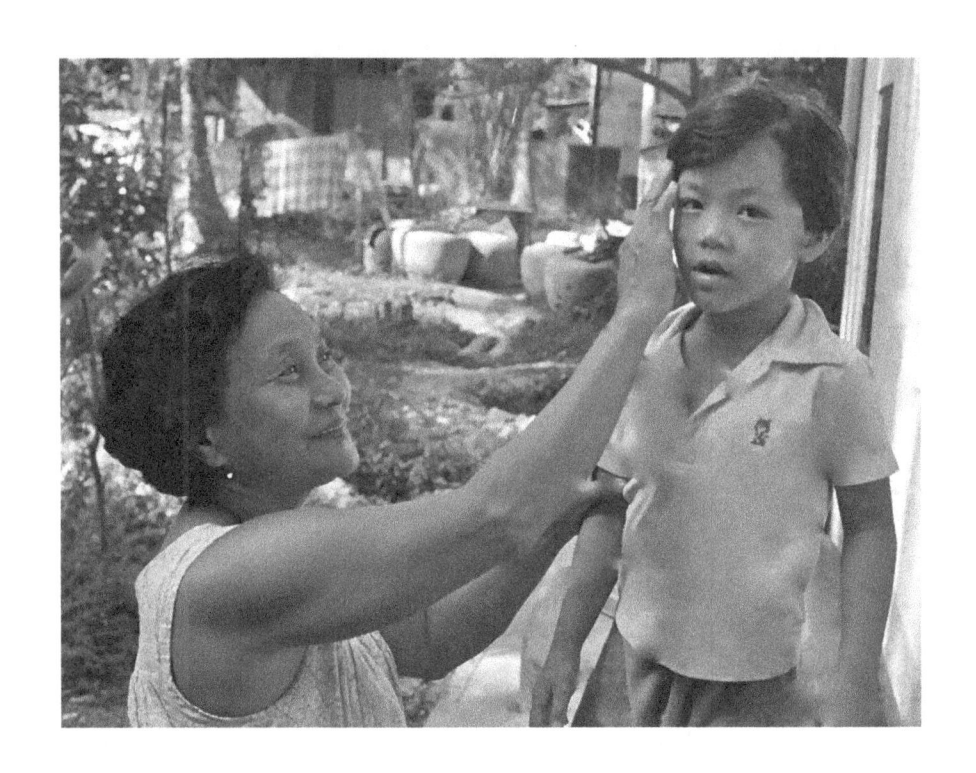

Khun Boontan with her grandson in Samut Prakarn
Children gave her great happiness, as can be seen
with her gentle touch and elastic smile.

Epistle Sixty-Two

January 10, 1981

Dear Mom and Dad:

My frenetic phone calls deserve a detailed explanation, so here goes.

Life with Aied has ceased being the yo-yo game of yore. Indeed, in the midst of our move from Jatujak, I'd pretty much written her off. Still, as a final *beau geste*, I decided to telephone her. To my surprise, Aied was genuinely happy I called. Her mother had just suffered a stroke, and her uncle had died under mysterious circumstances.

"Can you come to the temple tonight?" she asked. "We're having a special ceremony to honor my uncle. He liked you."

"I'd love to come," I said. "But Chop and I are right in the middle of moving. Your place is two hours away. I don't know if I can make it on time, but I'll do my best."

"I understand," she said.

Aied did not expect me get there and, to be honest, I didn't either. But I did, a half-hour on the late side. Seeing me strolling down the soi through the evening gloom, Aied lit up like a sparkler. Why was she so happy on such a glum occasion? Then it hit me. By coming, I was showing respect to both her uncle and her religion.

As befits a proper Thai girl, she greeted me in the most formal manner, then took me to her father. The monks were in the middle of their incantations while the guests were being fed. So my timing was perfect. I was able to have a good talk with Aied's father while simultaneously being waited on by two beautiful women: Aied and Add.

"I'm glad to see you again," I said. "It's been a long time."

"More than five years, I think."

"You haven't changed," I lied, looking at the gray hairs about his temples.

"Thank you, Gerry. But I know I have."

His head dropped to his chest. He seemed to struggle momentarily before raising his head and looking me square in the eye.

"I don't know how to thank you," he said. "You've been a great help to my family."

I felt embarrassed. To have a Thai man express deep gratitude is rare, especially to a younger man. At heart, Aied's father was a good man, a fine provider. For years, he had not only supported his immediate family but slackers in his extended family as well.

"Don't mention it," I said. "Tell me. How did he die?"

"He drank himself to death."

"Aied said something over the phone about him 'seeing things.' Was that tied to the alcohol?"

"Yes. He thought he saw ghosts coming to get his daughter. Or that's the story. Add was staying with his daughter, Sudarat. During the night, he tried to get into the bedroom, but the girls kept the door bolted. Add escaped the next morning by crawling through the window. The next day, he was dead."

"I knew he'd lost his job. Was he depressed about that?"

"Yes. But the drinking began years and years ago. It really got awful when his marriage broke up. He never recovered from that."

We talked of other things, but nothing of substance. After a while, I excused myself to take some pictures, a delicate process, but I knew the family would want them. Finally, I paid my respects to the uncle. As the men carried the sarcophagus to the crypt, I took pictures of the monks. Behind me everywhere was Aied. When the coffin was placed into the vault, everyone tossed a baht on the lid for luck. Ten minutes later, Aied and Add said good-bye to their father at the bus stop.

After that, things began to roll. A couple of days later, I went to visit Khun Boontan. The floodwater forced me to take off my shoes and wade through the mud. I'd a hundred yards to go before gaining the highland in front of the house when I saw her, plowing through the knee-deep water, barefooted, with the sun in her chiseled, black-lacquered hair and a smile that stopped me dead in my tracks.

All men in love have special moments, moments when the heart lifts from the chest and flies. This was one of those moments. There, in the muck and the guck, she met me—not for society, not for family, but because she wanted to. As she took my shoes from my hand, I thanked her. Then we giggled like two children all the way to the house.

In the house, the scene was not gay. I was taken immediately upstairs to Khun Boontan's room. One look told me how serious her condition was. Her face was wan and drawn, and the sparkle that once danced in her eyes was gone. Here was one tired old lady, burned out from over a half century of skivvydom.

I sat down on the bed and took her by the hand. Unlike her husband, who speaks excellent English, Khun Boontan doesn't speak a word; hence, we had to communicate with gestures and broken Thai. The following is an English version of our conversation.

"How are you?" I asked.

"Tired," she said. "The blood broke in my brain. The headaches hurt my head. It's hard to rest."

"I'm glad the grandchildren aren't here to bother you."

"Me, too. I can't rest when they're around. Still, I worry about the house."

"Don't worry. Aied will take care of everything. You're lucky to have such a good daughter."

"It's too much work," she said. "Caring for me and three children day in and day out will wear her out."

The old lady lay back against the Dutch wife as Aied came in and sat at the foot of the bed.

"Do you want me to stay here or go downstairs?" I asked.

"Here's better," said Aied. "Mother likes people around her. It doesn't bother her at all."

"You're doing a great job," I said. "I've never heard the house this quiet. It's good you came home."

Aied paused and looked down. In her faded jeans and threadbare shirt, she looked extremely womanly.

"My life has changed a lot this past week."

She raised her eyes and looked deeply into mine. I didn't say anything. I could see something was troubling her. The last thing she needed was another mental barrier.

"I must tell you, Gerry. A man has been seeing me for six months. He seemed very polite, very nice. Then, last week, I felt something odd, like there was another woman in his life. So I forced him to tell me who the woman was. He admitted that he had a wife and three children. But he wanted to leave her. Not divorce her. Just leave her and live with me. Make me his mia noi. Suddenly, I saw how insane my life had become. Suddenly, I knew how shallow my friends were, how lightly they viewed life. Now, all I want is to stay and care for my mother. I don't want to waste my time with those crazy people. Do you understand me?"

"Yes. Very much."

Into the room scurried Aum. Aum and I have always had a special bond, so I wasn't surprised when she wrapped her arms around my legs and laughed.

"I hear she's doing well in school," I said.

"Yes. Everyone is shocked. We thought she was retarded."

"I never did."

"True. But she's always been your favorite."

"Come on. Give me some credit."

"Okay. You were right. She's not retarded, only special."

"What do you mean 'special'?"

Aied bent close to me, as if she were going to reveal the identity of Deep Throat.

"Top secret," she said. "Promise you won't tell anyone."

"I promise."

"Well, you know all the problems my older sister had with her husband?"

I nodded.

"During the second month of her pregnancy, she tried to get an abortion. Somehow, by some miracle, Aum survived. Most of us thought that she would be retarded when she was born. Luckily, she seems all right."

"God, your sister must feel awful."

"She doesn't talk about it much. None of us do."

"And to think I used to think Aum was yours."

"That would be more difficult than you know, Gerry. Haven't I told you many times that my body is full of diseases?"

"Yes, but I've never quite been able to figure out exactly what you meant."

Aied turned red.

"After my mother gets better," she said, "I'm going to the hospital and have an operation. I want to be a complete woman."

"What do you mean by that?"

"I ... I can't tell you. It's not something a nice Thai girl talks about with a man."

"Oh, I think I know."

That made her brain shift gears. The shyness fell away before the possibility that I might have guessed her problem. I could see that she wanted to hear more, so I went ahead, with deliberation.

"Tell me if I'm right or wrong," I said. "Does it have anything to do with the fallopian tubes?"

I used the medical term on purpose. No matter how serious the conversation, Aied is always thirsty for new words.

"Fallopian tubes?" she said, taking the bait. "What are they?"

"The fallopian tubes carry the egg down every month, Aied. Some women have trouble with them and can't have babies. Is that your problem?"

She smiled.

"Perhaps," she said. "But I really have two problems. The other one has given me trouble for a long time."

"Especially when you were married?"

"Yes, and before that, too. When I was twelve, to be exact. There, you know too much. Let's stop."

"Only when I know how you're going to pay for this."

"I'm going to borrow the money."

"How much?"

"Six thousand baht (three hundred US dollars)."

"But you'll be forever paying that back. Let me help you."

"No," she said adamantly. "You've helped us too much already. If I keep taking your money, you'll be a poor man."

"Some things are worth being poor for," I said. "Your health is one of them. Listen, Aied. If we were talking about the house, I could see cutting corners, saving money. But this is your body. You can't take the chance."

"Poor people have to take chances with their bodies. That's what makes us different from rich people."

"Not you. Not while I'm around. Please let me do this for you. Then, when you get all fixed up, I'll blast off for the moon and leave you alone."

She laughed.

"Okay," she said. "I'll let you help me again. You always seem to be helping me *again*."

Thus began the search for the right clinic to do the operation. I talked to Aied on a daily basis. I soon learned that she was *still* cutting corners. A good operation would run not six thousand baht but ten thousand baht. The first figure I could handle, but the second prompted my call to you. I know you must think I'm stark-staring mad, but the thought of an incompetent butcher tinkering with Aied's reproductive organs was too much for my feeble fuses. Now at least she has a good chance with a reputable physician.

And she deserves a good chance. After all the emotional knocks and the downright bad luck of the past five years, she's trying to piece her life together. Whether or not I become a permanent fixture after the healing process is not important. What I told her about the moon is true. Some time ago, I put God first and my work second. Truly, I did. And ever since then, my life has become clearer, richer. What's more, Aied is now closer to me in a deep and profound way. No more do we hassle over trifles trying to second-guess one another. Instead, we talk, laugh, and enjoy each other's company. In short, we're dear friends.

That's putting it modestly. The truth is that on one particular night in one particular cab, I held one particular girl's hand. Now, in the States, that doesn't add up to much. But in Thailand, it does. She's told me it does, and she's told me that she's not ready yet. But that's all part of the script. If a nice Thai girl didn't say that, she wouldn't be nice and Thai. Both Aied and I know who sat conspiratorially with hands clasped. And we know that it was nice and sweet and that we got a helluva kick out of it, not to mention some profound lines.

Aied: "Gee, you've smooth hands."

Gerry: "Gosh, I could ride like this forever."

Still, I must go slowly. The idea, as I said before, is to get her in the right frame of mind to make the right decision. That means putting her first and myself second, something that has taken me a long time to learn. All too often, I've tried to impose my will, to push my agenda. No wonder she rebelled. This is what she has gotten all her life, what most women have had to swallow for centuries. If I've anything to give Aied, if I love her with a true and a pure heart, I must make her look at life with courage and optimism. I must make her see that life and living are, indeed, sweet.

It's a man's task, a real teaching task. Well worth a lonely trip to the moon.

Epistle Sixty-Three

February 21, 1981

Dear Mom and Dad:

I first came across Hemingway's "The Killers" in a dog-eared Pocket Book that Dad had dragged through World War II. I was sixteen at the time and can still remember reverently turning the thin, rationed pages till I came to the end and said, "Something is moving under the surface of all those simple words, but dang if I know what it is." In an attempt to find out, I read the story again. It wasn't my night, I guess. I felt like a cat that had spent two hours chasing a rat up a greased pole.

I tried to forget the story, but could not. I always went back to it, especially when I got bogged down with one of Mr. Fowler's algebra problems. Indeed, reading "The Killers" became almost a religious experience. However, unlike most religious experiences, where emotions and gut instinct are vital, I needed the opposite. I needed a neat little intellectual key to the story. But what was I getting instead? Nothing but a big, immovable door with a sign that read: "Enter if you can."

I was therefore elated when, three years later, my English professor said, "Your next assignment is 'The Killers' by Ernest Hemingway. Be here Wednesday prepared to discuss it in depth." Boy, was I ever ready! Of course, I didn't have to read the story, for by now, I knew it like my soul knew my acne. Nevertheless, read it I did, just to make sure.

I came away from the lecture with an odd mix of disappointment and satisfaction. We'd discussed a number of interpretations, including Cleaneth Brooks and Robert Penn Warren's "The Discovery of Evil: An Analysis of 'The

Killers.'" Basically, I agreed with Brooks and Warren. Yes, "Hemingway ... focused not on the gangsters but on the boys in the lunchroom." Yes, a gangster "lives ... by a code which lifts him above questions of personal likes and personal animosities." And yes, Nick discovers evil. Why, then, wasn't I satisfied? Why did the door, now apparently open, still seem to be hiding something? Indeed, hiding a whole lot.

Fast forward to yesterday. I'm teaching "The Killers" to my senior English class here at Chan Kasem. All's going according to Brooks and Warren. As in prior years, the students latch onto Max and Al. To underscore their folly, I write "THE KILLERS" in huge, block letters across the face of the board and ask dramatically, "Who are the killers?"

The question drives the students back against the rear of their chairs like a hurricane hitting a row of bamboo. I should back off, but the devil is upon me and I boom, "I repeat: who are the *real* killers?" It's an instinctual thing, one that all ESL teachers and Pentecostal ministers are guilty of. Still, it's I who am in for the real shock. Ratana, one of my braver students, leans forward and says, "Why, all of them are, teacher."

At first, I cannot believe my ears.

"What was that, Ratana?"

"All of them," she says placidly. "They all killed Ole Andreson."

In a flash, I see what she's driving at, but I want her to explain it, not me.

"Who are *they*?" I ask.

"Nick, George, and Sam," she says hesitantly. "They all had a chance to save Ole Andreson, but they didn't. In a way, they are worse than Max and Al."

"How's that?"

"Max and Al are brave. Nick, George, and Sam are not. They're cowards. I hate cowards."

"How is Sam a coward?"

"Sam minds his own business. He knows better than to get mixed up with white people. George calls him a nigger. Sam knows what can happen to a nigger in America."

"And George?"

"I hate George the most. He wants to help Ole Andreson but is afraid to. So he tells Nick to go to the boardinghouse to warn Ole."

"What about Nick? Why don't you think he's brave?"

"All young men *think* they're brave. Nick, being a young man, thinks he's brave too. But he's not. We can see that at the boardinghouse when he talks with Ole. Nick doesn't offer to stay and fight against Max and Al. Even as he leaves, we can see how nervous and frightened he is with Mrs. Bell."

"Let us get your interpretation straight, Ratana. You think the theme of the 'The Killers' is cowardice?"

"Yes, teacher."

"Actually, three types of cowardice: Sam is a coward and knows he's a coward. George is a coward but is ashamed he's a coward. And Nick is a coward who at first thinks he's brave but later discovers he isn't. Is that correct?"

"Yes, teacher."

"Okay. But a theory must be tested against contradictory elements in the story. For instance, if what you say is true, why does Nick state 'I'm going to get out of this town' toward the end of the story. Nick might be a coward, but he's not stupid. He knows Max and Al want to kill Ole, not him. Why, then, does he want to get out of Summit so fast?"

Knitting her brows and averting her eyes, Ratana appears stumped. The class goes silent, as Thai classes do when a student has been shot down. Momentarily, I feel guilty of hurting her feelings and am about to apologize when she looks back at me and says, "I–I think Nick is trying to run away from his guilty feelings, teacher. But he can't. Someday he'll have to stop running and face himself. We all have to do that or there's no meaning to life, is there?"

I'm thunderstruck. Sure, I know Ratana is smart but not smarter than Cleaneth Brooks and Robert Penn Warren. Or is she?

Then Ratana frowns.

"What's wrong?" I ask.

"Nothing, teacher. I was just wondering what kind of a coward you are."

I laugh.

"That easy," I say. "I'm a George. Say, we're running out of time. Now, here's the class assignment for next time. To further test Ratana's theory, think and decide what kind of a coward you are, and come to class prepared to defend your position. Of course, if you're not a coward, state that. You must, however, have the courage to tell us why you are brave. Class dismissed."

To be honest, I find Ratana's interpretation the only one that satisfies all aspects of the story. But so what? Why does Hemingway make us work so hard, when he could've told us straight away? Ah, that's the question. Could it be that, as an artist, Hemingway wants to go to the inner core of man's ultimate fate, namely *his fear of death?* If this is the case, "The Killers" should have someone who transcends life, someone beyond good and evil, someone who's not only willing to die but eager to embrace Death itself. And, lo and behold, we have Ole Andreson waiting placidly and stoically for Max and Al to kill him.

Courage now appears not to be an end in itself but a means to an end. But what end, exactly? There's only one answer: a separate reality, a modern-day version of Nirvana or heaven or what have you. A place where all sensation, all action, ceases to exist.

We don't usually think of Hemingway as a theological or a philosophic writer. But with "The Killers," he obviously is. Indeed, that is the key to the Hemingway enigma. Beneath the swagger and the bravado, beneath the plain language and the things left unsaid, there lurks a religious mystic in disguise.

Wisan and Namthip
(in "The Champs" T-shirt) with three friends
on the balconey at Chan Kasem.
A teacher should never have a favorite class.
So let me put it his way: this one was second to none.

Epistle Sixty-Four

March 15, 1981

Dear Mom and Dad,

I knew something was up as soon as Ajaan Thomark walked through the doors of the English Department last month. Though never disliking the woman, I'd never clicked with her either. The planets of the solar system revolve around the sun at different rates and at different distances. In this particular instance, she was Jupiter and I was Mars.

"Ajaan Gerry," she said, sitting down at her walnut desk. "May I speak with you for a minute?"

This simple request took me by surprise. Ajaan Thomark rarely initiated a discussion with me. She much preferred chitchatting in Thai with the ajaans in the English Department.

"Of course," I said, walking across the room and sitting down in the chair beside her desk. "What can I do for you?"

It was then that our eyes met, and it was then that I saw it: *fear*. I'd seen many emotions in those eyes before, but not that one.

"I've just come from a meeting at the Ministry of Education," she said with pursed lips. "All the English Department heads from the nearby teacher colleges and universities were there. A terrible decision has been made."

"Can you tell me about it?"

"AUA (American University Alumni Language Center) is hosting a poetry contest next month under the auspices of the Royal Thai Family," she said with a real edge to her voice. "Prince Prem will be giving out the awards. He's a noted Thai poet, so this is no ordinary contest. I really don't think that it's fair. Our students cannot compete with the university students. Some have spent years abroad. They speak English like you do."

"Is the contest for original poetry?"

"No," she said glumly. "The students are being asked to read their favorite American poet. But it doesn't matter. We don't have a chance against the Chula and the Thammasat students. It'd be like going up against Harvard and Yale in your country."

"It can't be that bad," I said.

"I need you to coach one of our students," she said, ignoring my words. "I know we can't win, but I don't want to lose face. Do you understand? That's all I ask: *that our school doesn't lose face.*"

"I'll get right on it tomorrow," I said. "Let's do it on a voluntary basis. We can have the teachers announce it to all the classes. Then I can interview the students and go from there."

"I don't care how you do it," she said. "Just make sure the student gives a *passable* performance."

Only five students volunteered: two seniors, two juniors, and a sophomore.

That's odd, I thought. *I don't teach sophomores. This Namthip kid must have some spunk. I'll talk with her last.*

The juniors and the seniors did well, but, to be honest, no one stood out. I was mulling over which student to choose when Namthip appeared in the doorway. She had short-cropped hair, big, bright eyes, and a killer smile, even by Thai standards. Though saucy and vivacious, she was still polite and respectful, greeting me with a formal wai some ten feet from my desk.

"Ajaan Gerry. My name is Namthip."

"How do you do, Namthip? Please, sit down."

"Thank you."

"So, you want to represent our school at the AUA poetry contest," I said. "Can you tell me why?"

"It'd be a great experience," she said. "I only use English around school. This'll give me a chance to communicate with the outside world."

I had to admit that I liked Namthip. She had a glow, an inner fire that was both becoming and infectious. So I decided to roll the dice.

"Tell me, young lady," I said. "Should you be chosen, would you be satisfied with a passable performance or would you like to win?"

"I want to win," she said flatly.

"The competition will be tough," I said. "We'll have to take some chances to beat the university students. Are you willing to do that? Are you willing to try something unusual? That's the only chance you have."

"You're my teacher," she said. "I'll do whatever you want."

"Okay," I said, making up my mind on the spot. "Here's what we're going to do. There's a famous poem called 'Mother to Son.' The poem was written by a black American writer named Langston Hughes and is told from the point of view of an African slave mother. You'll therefore have to mimic the accent of an uneducated southern black woman. But I can show you how to do that. You'll also have to act the part of an old woman beaten down by poverty. But that shouldn't be too hard either. All you'll have to do is put a shawl about your shoulders and walk with a cane. What do you think?"

"*Sanuk maak*," she said. "When do we begin practice?"

"How about tomorrow, right here, after school," I said.

"So I'm the one?"

"Yes, Namthip. You're the one."

Ajaan Thomark was a bit shaken that I'd chosen Namthip.

"Are you sure she can do it?" she asked. "She's only a sophomore."

"Yes," I said. "She has the spark. She'll represent the school well."

"I sure hope so," she said. "Remember what I said? I don't want the school to lose face."

"Don't worry," I said. "It won't."

Namthip was a natural. I'm not great with accents, but I'd lived in the Deep South for eight years. So I could do Hughes's fictional slave mother quite well. Inside of one week, Namthip could do the poem as well as I could. And a week later, she had it down pat. Indeed, the experiment had succeeded beyond my wildest dreams. I'd hoped the slave lingo would mask some of Namthip's Thai tones. I was wrong. It masked *all* of them.

During the last week, I had Namthip use two props: a cane and a shawl. She didn't miss a beat. By now, she'd memorized the poem by heart and sounded like a character from *The Sound and the Fury*. But a rehearsal is a far cry from an actual performance. So I gave her one last piece of advice.

"Listen, Namthip. I don't expect you to forget your lines, but it could happen. If your mind happens to go blank, don't panic. Try to control yourself and get back on track with whatever enters your head. Not many Thais are familiar with this poem, so there's an excellent chance that you can hide your mistake and no one will be the wiser. Do you have that?"

"Yes, Ajaan Gerry."

Finally, the big day came. Ajaan Thomark, Ajaan Wasana, and I accompanied Namthip on the school bus to AUA. In need of a support group, Namthip had invited at least ten of her friends. What a great idea! It not only kept her loose but helped loosen us up too.

Arriving at AUA, I could see immediately that this was a major event. Prince Prem greeted everyone with grace, elegance, and charm. Here was a man who truly loved poetry, who honestly was excited for the students. Looking at the program, I noticed that the Thammasat and Chula students preceded Namthip. I didn't know if that was good or bad. It just was.

The Thammasat student was the first to perform. He did a good job, but not as good as I expected. Namthip could beat him if she didn't flub up.

Three teacher college students followed. They, too, were good, but their pronunciation was off.

Next came the Chula student. She did an impeccable rendition of Robert Frost's "Stopping by Woods on a Snowy Evening." Everything was perfect: the pace, the pronunciation, even the paralinguistics. The only thing she lacked was originality. I looked at Ajaan Thomark. She didn't have to say a word. It was written all over her face: *there's the winner.*

Finally, it was Namthip's turn. Leaning forward on a cane and with a blue shawl about her shoulders, she teetered across the stage. Squinting out at the audience, she launched directly into the poem.

Namthip was doing a fabulous job. Had I closed my eyes, I would've thought I was in the bayous of Louisiana instead of the hustle and bustle of Bangkok. Then it happened. Five lines from the end, Namthip's mind went as blank as John Locke's tabula rasa. She hesitated for an instant, then jumped the line and finished the poem.

The applause was thunderous, especially from the rear, where our students were seated. Ajaan Thomark turned to me, beaming.

"Oh, my word," she said. "We might get second place. Wouldn't that be wonderful?"

The director of AUA announced the winners in descending order.

"Third place," he said, "goes to Thammasat University."

The Thammasat student walked up proudly and took his award from Prince Prem.

"Second place goes to ..."

I looked over at the Chula student. She sat straight and true, picture-positive that her school was not in the offing.

"Chulalongkorn University."

The Chula student rose from her seat in a daze and staggered forward like someone had bopped her over the head with a poleax. Finally, true to her class, she politely accepted her award. Nonetheless, she was visibly stunned.

"First place goes to ..."

Ajaan Thomark was agog like a frog on a lotus pad. One side of her was in a psychic shock, whereas the other side was aghast that her alma mater had lost.

"Chan Kasem Teachers College."

Namthip bounded from her chair. Then, seeing Prince Prem, she collected herself, waied deeply, and took her award with the grace of a born aristocrat.

Ajaan Thomark was beside herself. All I could hear her mutter was "We won, we won, we won ..."

At the reception, the Chulalongkorn student walked up to me. To my surprise, she addressed me by name.

"Congratulations, Mr. Christmas. You did a great job coaching your student. But I still think I should've won. You beat me with a trick."

"I'm sorry you lost," I said. "That was as fine a reading of Robert Frost as I've ever heard."

"Thank you," she said.

We talked for a bit. She was a brilliant linguist, fluent in three or four languages. But I didn't feel sorry for her. With her intelligence, refinement, and education, she'd go far, both inside and outside of Thai society.

Still, Chulalongkorn had the last laugh. The following year, the AUA poetry contest was terminated.

Ajaan Thomark was not the only one who hated to lose face.

Aied in her favorite casual shirt
The lettering on the back reads: "Don't Follow Me."
I didn't get the double meaning till it was too late.

Epistle Sixty-Five

June 12, 1981

Dear Mom and Dad:

I've moved yet again. Upon returning to Thailand, I found that Chop had not stayed at the house all the time I was gone. This played havoc not only with the yard (now a jungle) but also with the mail (now scattered to the four winds). I therefore decided to ask Ajaan Linly to look for a new place for me. I figured with luck, she'd find an apartment in a few weeks to a month. Instead, she found what I wanted in a day: two rooms adjacent to a nice Thai couple.

The couple has a one-year-old girl who fortuitously lost her crying cords somewhere along the way. The apartment is absolutely safe for my epilepsy. Were I to have a psychomotor seizure, I'd have to walk by Prapun, his wife Jum, and daughter on the second floor, then over the bodies of two students on the first floor, then through an iron gate with a padlock before escaping into the night. That would be quite a trick, even for a fit-meister like myself. So don't worry, Mom. I'm in good hands.

Of course, I had to extricate myself from the previous place, the house owned by the Ajaan Pochanat. By Thai standards, Ajaan Pochanat is an odd goose hovering somewhere between the neurotic and the schizophrenic. Plump and pushing forty, she recently snagged a husband, much to the amazement of students and staff. As fate would have it, I'd paid Ajaan Pochanat two months rent the same day Linly found the new place. Having made a number of improvements to the house (a nifty screen door and a stainless-steel kitchen sink, just to

Gerry Christmas

name two), I thought it only fair that Ajaan Pochanat return a portion of my June rent. I didn't know what to expect, but what I got was on the far side of the bizarre.

For a moment, Ajaan Pochanat sat motionless, like a toad on a turd. Then, with a face reminiscent of Krakatoa, she erupted.

"I ... I know you'll think I'm hard," she exploded. "But I'm going to keep all of it. Do you hear me? All of it!"

There was nothing I could do but absorb the loss. My only satisfaction came with the knowledge that in two months' time, I'd recoup my money. How? Well, I now pay Prapun $75 a month for service with a smile, whereas I used to pay Pochanat $150 for service with a scowl.

Soon after my return, I learned from Chop the whereabouts of Pirom, the student Harriet Van Meter wants to sponsor at the University of Kentucky. Pirom is blissfully teaching English to poor students at a new government school in Korat. I was therefore somewhat hesitant to approach her about leaving Thailand for Kentucky. To my astonishment, she was eager to go.

Though reluctant to abandon her charges, Pirom is not satisfied with her English oral skills. Furthermore, barring a Communist takeover, she can always teach English when she returns, whether it be in the boonies of Korat or the asphalt jungle of Bangkok. After spelling out Harriet's generous offer, I asked Pirom what she thought.

"Ajaan Gerry," she said, looking at me square in the eye, "is there any chance I can stay with Mrs. Van Meter for *more* than one year?"

Now, that sounds brazen, but *brazen* is not the right word for Pirom. Soft-spoken, gentle, understanding, and deep, she once stopped me in the hallway and said, "Ajaan Gerry, I don't understand. Why do you lose your temper with us, when we love and respect you so much?" What could I say to that? Rare is the student who is soft on the outside and hard on the inside. Pirom is one of those rarities: a perfect candidate for a scholarship abroad.

But I digress. Pirom is not only interested in going to Kentucky but has also talked to her father about it. In the final analysis, her father will determine if she can go or not. Though a Thai farmer, he doesn't have the peasant mentality. Sure, he tried to marry his daughter off a few years back, but that was more an attempt to protect her from male predators than it was to pigeonhole her. I met the man and was instantly impressed. Not many Thai farmers know how to rotate crops and use fertilizers. And even fewer let their daughters leave home to teach. Pirom's father is both a modern farmer and a modern parent.

"Don't worry, Ajaan Gerry," Pirom said as I left her house. "My father and I understand each other."

I sure hope things break her way. Pirom, Harriet, and the University of Kentucky would make a great threesome.

As promised, I had a physical shortly after returning to Thailand. Dr. Wanida did find that my heart had a slight abnormality.

"Don't worry," she said. "This is quite common for someone in your age bracket. Actually, I'm quite pleased. I can't see any signs of heart disease."

Dr. Wanida also gave me an upper GI series, which I passed with flying colors. Finally, she sent me to see a neurologist, Dr. Chandrakasem.

"I don't like the numbness in your fingers," he said. "That's probably due to the Dilantin. But let's stay with the present dosage for two months. Sometimes, the numbness goes away. Should it continue, however, I'll substitute Phenobarbital for Dilantin."

So don't fret. I'm in good hands.

In closing, Aied would like to thank you for the gifts and letters. Truly, she's overwhelmed and calls you her "American parents." Though concerned about her mother, Aied is now living with her father and his mia noi. At the urging of her father, she's become deeply involved with a radical political group. I've asked her about this group, but she remains tight-lipped.

"Aied," I said. "We shouldn't have secrets between each other."

"I'm sorry," she said. "I can't tell you a thing. I've been sworn to secrecy. I also don't want you to take any pictures of me. That'll put me in danger."

That was all I needed to know. My suspicions were confirmed. Aied is now a committed Communist.

Epistle Sixty-Six

September 4, 1981

Dear Mom and Dad:

I've been trying to get a letter off to you for two months, but events have overwhelmed me, as you will see.

First, I had to come to grips with my gastrointestinal tract. Dr. Wanida gave me enough tests to purify a toad. In the end, she had to treat the symptoms, not the cause. Fortunately, the anti-gas pills worked, and I now feel fine. Still, it was an ordeal. Being temporarily thrown off my psychological wheels, I hesitated to write until my health returned to normal.

Second, Terry Fredrickson left Thailand. This was an event comparable to Mohammed fleeing Mecca for Medina. Terry, being a wise and wily soul, hopped a 1:00 a.m. BOAC flight. Naturally, I saw him off along with Jaam and his Thai friends. On the surface, Jaam was remarkably calm, much like the Vietnam babe in Graham Greene's *The Quiet American*. Terry, on the other hand, was visibly shaken. Thirteen years in Thailand hardwires strong emotional circuits that aren't easily ripped out. Indeed, I could see that Terry was replaying a number of scenes in his mind as he went through Passport Control. Impulsively, Jaam ran to him, but it wasn't one of those cheap, hysterical moments, just a tender farewell. How do common women exude such class?

A week later, I received two letters on the same day: one from Jaam and one from Terry. Odd, huh? Terry said that he was moving through Europe sans the élan of youth. I could've told him that. The older we get, the more loneliness becomes our partner. Jaam's letter was even more predictable.

"You're the only one," she wrote, "who understands how much I love Terry. Could we talk about it someday?"

This request hit me as a bit obscure. I could only see two paths for her to follow: fly to the States and fight for him or wait in Thailand and hope for the best. The second path is the one that most Thai women take, but Jaam is far from typical. To my thinking, Terry had left a true gem behind.

Third, I'm about to move again. No, I haven't lost my screws. Here's what happened. With his departure, Terry not only left many Thais disconsolate but many of them broke, especially Khun Knee and her family. Terry paid Knee 1,200 baht a month, and with that, she supported four people. In return for the money, Knee enabled Terry to live like a king. She washed his clothes, cooked his meals, and kept the house spotless.

I came into Terry's domestic scene about three weeks before he left. Shortly thereafter, Chuck Rice telephoned me and said he was in a real bind.

"What's wrong?" I asked.

"My landlord just screwed me," he said. "He wants to renovate the apartment, so I have to get out."

"Can you stay somewhere temporarily and then move back in?"

"Yes," Chuck said. "But it would really bleed me. My rent is now 3,200 baht a month, but my landlord is going to jack that up to five thousand baht. That's too rich for me."

"As you know, Terry has just left here. I'll talk to Knee and see if she has room for you."

"Thanks, Gerry. I'd appreciate that."

Chuck was in luck.

"The landlord is moving from the small house next door," Knee said. "Your friend could rent it for 3,500 baht a month. Do you want to look at it?"

"Please," I said.

The place was a single man's dream: living room, dining room, kitchenette, bedroom, patio, and an American bathroom. Though a steal at 3,500 baht, Chuck hesitated. Being in the midst of a tempestuous romance, he had to pinch his pennies and could only offer Knee five hundred baht a month. To say the least, Knee was shaken to the core.

Enter the Yuletide Kid. After moving into the big house, the landlady found that she had an extra vacant bedroom. She offered it to me for eight hundred baht a month. The idea was a simple one: Knee would get enough from Chuck and Gerry to counterbalance the loss of Terry.

"The offer is really tempting," I said to Knee. "But I cannot abandoned the nice Thai family that I live next to."

Then it happened. Prapun and Jum had marital problems. Since something of this nature had happened to me in Samoa, I decided not to stay around and play amateur psychiatrist. I therefore bolted. Knee was ecstatic. She'd known me for three years and always wanted me to live with Terry.

Of course my colleagues think I'm nuts for moving away from Chan Kasem. They can think whatever they want. I've lived near schools for eight years, and I don't like what it's doing to me. Life has to be more than food, bed, and students. Sure, I'll have to get up fifteen minutes earlier and mount the bus each morning, but the weekends will be so much more fun, as will the weekday nights. Moreover, Chuck and I go back a long way. Now we can socialize on a daily instead of a weekly or biweekly basis, so I'm happy.

Finally, there's Aied. She telephoned a month ago to tell me that she was quitting her job with Mazda. Instead, she wants to help poor upcountry Thais. How can I begrudge her?

"When do you plan to come back?" I asked.

"My future is not clear, Gerry. Perhaps in three months."

"I wonder if this is our last good-bye."

She paused.

"Gerry?"

"Yes."

"Will you ever love another woman?"

"I don't think so," I said. "Not like I love you."

She paused again.

"I'll write my mother, my father, and you," she said softly.

"Keep it in that order," I replied. "You know what my parents said about you, Aied?"

"No, what did they say?"

"They said that you love your country more than you love any man."

She didn't laugh.

"You're parents have great wisdom," she said. "Good-bye, Gerry."

Somehow, I couldn't say good-bye too. I listened as the line went dead.

"Even spoiled children don't get all the toys they want," I said, putting the receiver back onto the cradle. "You only have ten months left on your contract, so try to have fun in this 'Through the Looking Glass' country."

Gumpol being carried from a Buddhist
temple on the shoulders of a friend
Notice that he has not yet donned the
saffron robe. That would come later.
Many Thai men become monks for
three months before marriage.

Epistle Sixty-Seven

November 17, 1981

Dear Mom and Dad:

Shortly after I returned to Thailand seven months ago, Aied started to act out of character: no time for me, no time for her mother, no time for the essentials of Thai womanhood—cosmetics, shoes, and skintight clothes. Sure, I saw her off and on. But it was more off than on, and I wasn't too pleased with what was coming from her pouty orifice: "I've wasted so much of my life;" or "My friends are so stupid and boring;" or "I might go far, far away."

Well, I have to give her credit on the last one. She did go far, far away. Three months back, she left me and Mum and job for a better life in the jungle. That's right. *The jungle.* Only in this case, it had nothing to do with the "me Tarzan, you Jane" syndrome, more like "Workers of the World Unite" standard deviation. Now Comrade Aied is in Laos "going to school." No one knows where she is or what she's doing. I only know that Daddy is behind it.

"I'd be proud if you would join your sister," he said to Add. "The country is riddled with corruption. Our only hope lies with the Thai Communist Party."

"But what if the Communists are corrupt too?" she asked. "They are human too."

This incensed Add's father.

"Don't talk nonsense," he said. "Either you're for us or against us."

But I can't lay all the blame at the father's feet. Though far from a fanatic, Aied is a true believer. She firmly believes that with the right people, a better world can be built. When first we met, she was so nice and bright and religious. Sure, she was a bit dingy with all her merit-making and her temple-trotting. But I loved her for it. Too many Western women have taken religion out of their lives. I don't want that to happen to Aied, although, right now, I don't see what I can do about it. She's going down a dark and dangerous road with power on one side and sex on the other. That doesn't leave too much room for peace and love: two things she is truly looking for.

Thank God, she still sends me letters through the Communist grapevine. Perhaps I should call them cryptic epistles. No word of where she is except to mention a plain here and a plateau there. Nevertheless, she seems happy. For once in her life, she believes in something, however harebrained. Too many people have no vision, cannot think beyond themselves to the greater good. At least I picked a girl with spunk, someone who wants to squeeze life through gray matter instead of glands. Still, trying to solve a nation's problems politically is about as practical as shoveling water with a sieve.

The last time I saw Aied was surreal. One night, she telephoned and asked me to meet her the next day at a remote bus stop outside of Bangkok.

"Would you mind seeing me off?" she said. "I don't know when I'll be seeing you again."

"I'll be there," I said.

"Please get to the bus stop before noon. That's when the bus leaves for upcountry."

The next day was stinking hot, but it didn't faze Aied. She walked beside me stiff and straight, like a Navy Seal on a top-secret mission.

GERRY CHRISTMAS

As the bus came into view, I wanted to grab her, toss her over my shoulder, and flee. But I hesitated for an instant, and in that instant, all was lost. The hydraulic door sprung opened, and Aied bolted forward.

"I love you, I love you, I love you," I screamed, half out of my mind.

Aied turned around on the steps, her black hair aglow in the morning mist.

"Will you still love me even if I'm a Communist?" she said with a twisted, wry smile.

For a moment, I was taken aback. Never before had she used that word to describe herself.

Then the door closed and the bus pulled away, leaving me in a cloud of dust.

That was three months ago.

Last week, I took Add to Dr. Wanida's clinic on Sukumvit Road. Add had been sick for more than a week, so it didn't take much arm-twisting to convince her to see my doctor. In the waiting room at the clinic, Add brought me up-to-date on Aied.

"We got a letter from her the other day," she said.

This should have made me happy, but it didn't. For once, I decided no more Mr. Nice Guy.

"What did she have to say about me?" I asked.

"She wanted to know if you were still coming over to the house."

"No letter for me, huh?"

"No."

"That's sweet of her."

I paused. Suddenly, a thought flashed across my mind. A mean, devilish thought.

"Tell me, Add. Did Aied give your mother any money before she left?"

Add beamed, then took the bait.

"Why, yes, she gave her one thousand baht (fifty US dollars)."

"That's nice. She asked me for five thousand baht ($250 USD). She said your mother was desperate for money. I thought it was odd. Never before has Aied asked me for money. Being a good Buddhist, she wouldn't. But now the Communists have changed her. The ends justify the means."

"Don't be upset, Gerry,"

"I'm not upset. Just disappointed."

Add's head dropped.

"But it's your father who baffles me," I said. "What possessed him to put Aied in harm's way? That's not a natural thing for a father to do."

Add couldn't look at me. She seemed to be tying her shoelaces with her eyes.

"You don't understand me yet," I continued. "The only one in your family who does is your mother. Do you know why I love your mother? Do you *really* know?"

"I think so," she said. "You pity her."

"No," I said. "I don't pity her. I respect her. I respect the way she works and fights for the ones she loves. She's got more guts and goodness than anyone I know. Pity? I can't pity greatness. I stand in awe of it!"

The next day, Add telephoned me and asked if I was still angry.

"Angry?" I said. "Yesterday I wasn't angry. I spoke from the heart, and what I said was true. So let's leave it at that. Agreed?"

"Agreed," she said.

Epistle Sixty-Eight

February 27, 1982

Dear Mom and Dad:

You probably got my letter about Aied a few days ago. I'd grave misgivings about slamming her on paper that way. But you've always taught me to be honest and forthright, so why make an exception with her? Now let's get down to important business: my future.

As you know, I'd planned to leave Thailand this year to pursue graduate work. I've run into a few snags, however. First, the Ministry of Education has asked me to stay at Chan Kasem for another year. Two weeks ago, I walked into the Ministry and was met by my good friend Ajaan Monipen.

"Gerry," she said blithely. "How would you like a raise next year?"

You could've knocked me over with a paperclip. The Ministry of Education never gives a raise. A teacher must put in for it.

"That would be nice," I said. "But only if I could go home for six weeks like I did last year. My parents are not getting any younger."

"That can be arranged, as long as you return in time to teach in June."

Returning to Chan Kasem, I drafted a letter to Ajaan Thomark. In the letter, I was quite blunt. Besides requesting a year's extension, I spelled out the following goals:

- Publish an ESL writing book based on Kerrigan's six steps approach.

- Organize reading lessons into a second book on comprehension.
- Develop an experimental listening and speaking program.

Ajaan Thomark didn't waste any time taking me to task.

"Your letter is not detailed enough," she said. "You need to do it over again."

"I'm sorry," I said. "But I don't understand. What exactly did you dislike about it?"

"The tone was all wrong," she said sternly. "All you said was that you wanted to stay to get a book published and make a lot of money."

I couldn't believe my ears. Ajaan Thomark never did anything that she didn't have to. Moreover, she was always the first ajaan to go home. I could never remember her staying beyond 3:30 in the afternoon.

So how dare she? How dare she insinuate that I was mercenary and greedy, when she was the biggest slug in the English department? But I bit my tongue. I'd worked around her for three years and was not about to make a fool of myself now.

"I'll take up my request with Dr. Arun," I said.

Ajaan Thomark knew Dr. Arun was a personal friend, so this did not sit well with her.

"That'll be fine," she lied. "*Sawadee.*"

"Sawadee."

Were Ajaan Thomark a major player in my life, there's no question that I'd have quit Chan Kasem years ago. But she's about as significant as a tick on a water buffalo. I know why she dislikes me. I'm popular with the students, especially the more serious ones. Ever since telling the students that I might not stay for another year, I've had student after student ask me to reconsider. Take Wasan, for instance, a wonderful young man who has transformed himself from an above-average student into one of my stars.

"Ajaan Gerry," he said. "Please don't leave us. You're my favorite teacher."

I nearly said, "Gee, Wasan, don't waste those eyes and those words on a man. Keep them for a nice, pretty, young thing and get proper favors." But now was not the time to joke. A compliment from a male student is not to be taken lightly.

"Thank you, Wasan. I want you to know that you and your friends have been a joy to teach. Indeed, I doubt if I will ever see the likes of your class again."

Then there's reason number three: *pride*. I've too much pride to let this country or any other country lick me. When I leave Thailand, I want it to be a better place. That sounds disgustingly trite. But sometimes disgustingly trite things have an air of truth to them. Aied's gone, and I accept that she's gone. But still, there are things to be done for her mother, things that only you and me and Khun Boontan understand.

Then there's the book. Yes, I want to see if it goes over. I want to be here when it flops or flourishes. Not for the money, Ajaan Thomark. Just to see if it flops or flourishes.

Finally, there're the students. Every class is special, and only a fool would compare one with another. Yet this junior class is unique. For the first time, I've a balance of boys and girls who get along with each other, who feel that they can accomplish great things. I want to be around when they do.

Still, I might make this my last year. My duty to you comes first. If you feel my presence is needed at home, if you feel six weeks is not enough, reel in the line. I won't put up a fight. On the other hand, if you see it my way, I'll come home in mid-April and return in early June. Moreover, during my home leave, I'd like to put out some feelers to graduate school. Terry has had some trouble because he came home without laying the proper groundwork. He therefore wrote to warn me not to make the same mistake.

My immediate problem is my airfare home. The ministry will pay me some money when my contract expires, but there's no way I can get my hands on it now. So please send me a check for two thousand dollars. I'll reimburse you later with either the ministry money or the money from the sale of our stamp collection. And, yes, do write soon. This letter was written in haste, so I've left many questions unanswered. I'll try to telephone you in a few weeks, so we can iron out our problems.

Epistle Sixty-Nine

April 20, 1982

Dear Mom and Dad:

I'd better come clean. My decision to return to the United States has been predicated on one thing: declining health. During the last four or five months, I've noticed an alarming trend. About every three or four weeks, I become sick, usually with a respiratory ailment. At first, I paid it no mind. But it persisted, so I went to see Dr. Wanida. She was furious with me.

"How long have you had this?" she asked.

"About five weeks?"

"Why didn't you come and see me earlier?"

"I figured it was just a cold that would go away," I said. "How come? Is it something serious?"

"Yes, it is," she said. "You've a bad case of bronchitis."

"Bronchitis?" I said incredulously. "That can't be. This is Thailand. There's no bronchitis here."

"Oh, yes, there is. You're an educated man, a college ajaan. You should know that bronchitis has nothing to do with climate, with how hot or cold the weather is."

I was thunderstruck. I didn't know what to say.

"We can still knock it out," she said, seeing the concern in my eyes. "But you might have trouble later in life, so be careful. Go and see a doctor whenever you have respiratory trouble."

Since that time, I've been going to see Dr. Wanida practically every month. Not only is it draining me physically but financially as well. As a Peace Corps volunteer, I made less money but received free medical. Now I'm finding being sick on a monthly basis is killing me financially. So I took the matter up with Dr. Wanida.

"I don't know why you are chronically sick," she said. "I suspect that the air and noise pollution have much to do with it. How long have you lived in Bangkok?"

"For the last four years," I said. "Seven years all told."

"Hmm ... I don't like to lose you as a patient, but for your health's sake, you might want to go back to the United States, where the air is cleaner. Tell me. Are you tied to Thailand emotionally?"

"I love my job," I said. "My students are swell."

"I didn't mean that," she said. "Do you have someone special here?"

"I did," I said hesitantly. "But not anymore. She's moved away. Far, far away."

"I'm sorry," she said. "I didn't mean to pry. But if that's the case, then you'd better think about going home. That way, you'd give your body a better chance to recover."

The decision to return home has not been an easy one. I really love my students, and they love me too. Still, the constant battle to stay well has taken its toll. I've therefore decided to return home.

Last week, I decided to visit Khun Boontan one last time. I tried to control my emotions, but it wasn't any good.

I was still torn up inside about Aied. As a result, I took all my pictures of Aied and her family and gave them to Khun Boontan. There was a pained look in her eyes as she took the albums from me.

"I'm sorry," I said to her in Thai. "But I've waited for Aied for more than six years, and I cannot wait any longer. I must go back to the United States."

I could feel the tears well up in my eyes but was able to beat them back.

Khun Boontan looked at me blankly. I'd meant for the pictures to be a going-away gift. Suddenly, I knew they were just the opposite: a knife to the heart. But it was too late. I couldn't take them back now. The damage had been done. My insides felt like crystal breaking into a thousand pieces. I couldn't stand it anymore, so I turned and walked away.

I went home, my mind in a muddle. I lie down on my bed and reread Aied's letters. One in particular touched my heart. I've typed it out pretty much as she wrote it: ellipses, parentheses, underlines, and all. That way, you can hear her voice.

> Dear Gerry,
> After you read this letter, burn it. <u>Please</u>.
> I read your letter a few days later. Oh, poor Gerry. I know you may have no money but you still try to give me. It's the wage for reading your letter, isn't it?
> I know you wonder about my work. So I will tell you <u>as I can</u> ... First I must go to the town that is very far from Bangkok. I worked at the stronghold for one month until the end of September. After that I prepared to go to the town (plain and plateau) for three months. I mean I will stay at the town to do my duty until it finish. I can't go to Bangkok or anywhere. And I can do the things I want after that. But something changed. I waited and waited for my "guarantor" who will protect me from the danger road. My

boss told me at last. The messenger said, "He's dead (was killed)."

So my boss will choose the new person. He wanted me to live and wait in the town that is very far from Bangkok but I didn't agree. I think of my mother, brothers and sisters. I want to talk with my father. I came back when I had the time and went to that province to do my duty. I "go to and fro" to do my work. I asked everyone in the house don't talk about me to another persons. I'm tired but I hope.

You wonder where my house is. I rent a room in the house, the police family, for a few months. Oh, really near the muzzle. I can't stay at my mother and father's house because I want to escape secretly from my friends, my relatives, kith and kin.

Nowadays I have my odd life. You read and you maybe understand. So I write this letter to say "thank you" to you that helped me. If you want to advise me or talk with me, you can give your letter to Gumpol. He will keep it and take to Phrapadang's house. I will take it after that. But if it makes you perplexing or difficult, you don't write to me. I can understand. I'll not hate you. I know it is unjust for you.

Now I have the half-life. I dare not to say anything too much. Just tell you about my work and why I "go to and fro."

Thank you about everything ...

Thank you a son of my mother ...

You helped her when I unemployed no salary.
Thank you – bye bye my God.
Aied (not Eat)
Please, burn this letter. Thanks a lot.

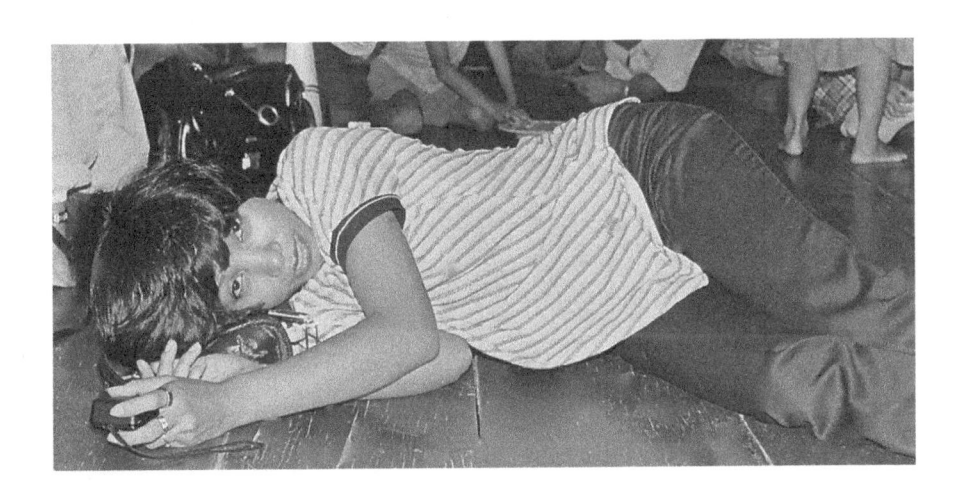

Aied shortly before she left Bangkok "to do my duty"
She has that "bye-bye, baby" look in her eyes, doesn't she?

Epilogue

Thus my career as a Peace Corps volunteer and contract teacher for the Thai Ministry of Education came to an abrupt end. Returning home, I assumed that Aied was out of my life, that she was nothing but a fading memory. But it wasn't that easy. What the head forgets, the heart remembers. Decades would pass before events would conspire to bring us together again. Once reunited, I'd learn the brutal truth: that she had never lied to me, that she had never deceived me, that she had always loved me.

In going over these letters, in reliving the past, I've come to realize that my story is not melodramatic and sad but rather a comedy of errors with a happy ending. I can only hope that you are as fortunate with your life as I've been with mine.

Samoan Glossary

aiga. Extended family.
aitu. Ghost; spirit.
alaisa fa'apopo. Samoan-style coconut rice.
fa'alavelave. Great trouble.
fa'a samoa. Samoan way of life.
fa'atau. Argument among the village chiefs.
faifeau. Religious minister.
fale. House.
fale palagi. Foreign-style house.
faleuila. Toilet; bathroom.
fiafia. Party.
fono. Village meeting house.
kava. Samoan ceremonial drink made from the kava root.
keke pua'a. Samoan-style bao (pork buns).
laki. Lucky.
lavalava. A colorful cloth worn around the waist.
manaia. The most handsome man in the village; titled leader of untitled men.
matai. Village high chief.
moetotolo. Nightcrawler; rapist.
oka l'a. Fish salad.
palagi. Foreigner.
palusami. Corn-beef and coconut milk wrapped in taro leaves.
paifala. Samoan half-moon pies.
sa. Taboo.
susu. Breasts.
tala. Samoan monetary unit.
taulealea. Untitled man.

taupou. Village maiden with high status, usually the daughter of the matai.
tiatia. Untitled man.

Thai Glossary

ajaan. Teacher.
baak wan. Sweet mouth; too complimentary.
baht. Thai monetary unit.
boat hua. Headache.
farang. Foreigner.
granjai. Consideration; deference.
hong naam. Toilet; bathroom.
jai dee. Kind-hearted.
jai yen yen. Calm down; stay cool.
khun. A polite form of address used for both men and women.
klong. Canal.
krathong. Lotus-shaped floating lantern used on Loy Krathong.
Loy Krathong. Religious holiday held in the twelfth lunar month.
mai pen lai. Never mind.
mai sabaay jai. Unhappy.
mia noi. Minor wife; mistress.
men. Menstruation.
pakama. A checkered cloth worn by men around the waist.
sanuk maak. Very happy; great fun.
sawadee. Thai for hello or good-bye.
soi. Lane; side street.
Songkran. Water festival to celebrate the Thai New Year.
sopanee. Prostitute.
sway. Beautiful.
tio. Go out for fun (can have good or bad connotations).
wai. Thai greeting with hands brought together at the bridge of the nose.
wat. Buddhist temple.

The Face Behind the Typeface

Claude Garamond (a.k.a. Claude Garmont) was born in Paris in 1499. After working for printer Antoine Augereau and type-founder Geoffroy Tory, Garamond struck out on his own and soon became a master punch-cutter and font designer. Commissioned by King François I to come up with a Greek typeface, he produced the *"Grecs du Rois"* for the publishing house of Robert Estienne. Garamond's true genius, however, would not emerge till 1531 when he began designing his famed Roman fonts based on metal types rather than handwriting. Noted for their clarity and effortless readability, these fonts quickly swept through Western Europe. Sadly, Garamond's acumen as a businessman did not match that of a font designer. When his publishing house failed, Garamond was left destitute and died a pauper in 1561. Still, his noble fonts have lasted for more than 450 years and show no signs of fatigue or diminished popularity.